Learning from Life

All of life can be a resource for our learning. In his fourth and most personal book, Patrick Casement attempts to understand what he has learned from life, sharing a wide range of those experiences that have helped shape the analyst he has become.

Patrick Casement shares various incidents in his life to demonstrate how these helped lay a foundation for his subsequent understanding of psychoanalysis. These examples from his life and work are powerful and at times very moving, but always filled with hope and compassion.

This unique book gives a fascinating insight into fundamental questions concerning the acquisition of analytic wisdom and how personal experiences shape the analyst's approach to clinical work. It will be of great interest to all psychoanalysts and psychoanalytic psychotherapists.

Patrick Casement has been a psychoanalyst and therapist in full-time private practice for many years, having previously been a social worker. He is the author of *On Learning from the Patient* and *Further Learning from the Patient*. His last book, *Learning from our Mistakes*, received a Gradiva award for its contribution to psychoanalysis.

A moving and compelling story, beautifully and evocatively told, and impressive in its unsparing honesty, this book gives us rare insight not only into the making and creative thinking of a brilliant and compassionate psychoanalyst, but also into those qualities of heart and mind needed to overcome pain and adversity in childhood and to transform a life in the remarkable way that Patrick Casement has. There are invaluable lessons here for all of us.

Ted Jacobs, MD

This book is full of psychoanalytic wisdom about how to be with a traumatised patient, how to think about a patient who does not attend, how to make trial identifications with patients to support and inform internal supervision, and much more. I recommend *Learning from Life* to anyone who values the link between the exploration of themselves and their work with patients and clients.

Donald Campbell, British Psychoanalytical Society

In *Learning from Life* Patrick Casement engages with his readers even more personally than in his previous writings. The thoughtfulness, wit and expressive talent for which he is noted are particularly evident in this book, an account of the private experiences behind the public, professional voice. As always, Casement's words resonate with the timbre of emotional truth. For therapists interested in improving their work, for students of personality and professional development, and for all of us who appreciate the inside story of how one wise human being attained his wisdom, this account of personal maturation as a psychotherapist will strike many responsive chords.

Nancy McWilliams, Graduate School of Applied & Professional Psychology, Rutgers University

In this fascinating account of the creation of a psychoanalytic self, we are privileged with an inside view of the complex forces that shaped Casement's identity. Through all of this, we are gifted with a sensitive and intelligent guide to a sophisticated practitioner's personal dilemmas about self-disclosure, about living and working in uncertainty, and about the abiding mysteries of our field.

Estelle Shane, PhD

Part reflective autobiography, part clinical and theoretical exploration, and part philosophical meditation on the profession of psychoanalysis, Casement continues to surprise, challenge and move us with his insight and his refusal to be claimed by any one psychoanalytic orthodoxy or school. This is a truly 'independent' thinker and practitioner at work. Like all his earlier books, *Learning from Life* has much to offer the social worker, counsellor, mental health nurse, indeed anyone who works with mental pain in a professional capacity. It is a beautifully accessible, brave and quietly iconoclastic work.

Andrew Cooper, Professor of Social Work at the Tavistock Clinic and the University of East London

Learning from Life

Becoming a psychoanalyst

Patrick Casement

To Jenny

With best wishes

Patrick Casement

Nov 06

Routledge
Taylor & Francis Group

LONDON AND NEW YORK

First published 2006
by Routledge
27 Church Road, Hove, East Sussex BN3 2FA

Simultaneously published in the USA and Canada
by Routledge
270 Madison Avenue, New York NY 10016

Routledge is an imprint of the Taylor & Francis Group, an informa business

Typeset in Times by Garfield Morgan, Mumbles, Swansea, West
Glamorgan
Printed and bound in Great Britain by TJ International Ltd, Padstow,
Cornwall
Paperback cover design by Sandra Heath

This publication has been produced with paper manufactured to strict
environmental standards and with pulp derived from sustainable forests.

British Library Cataloguing in Publication Data
A catalogue record for this book is available from the British Library

Library of Congress Cataloging-in-Publication Data
Casement, Patrick.
        Learning from life : becoming a psychoanalyst / Patrick Casement.
        p. cm.
        Includes bibliographical references and index.
        ISBN13: 978-0-415-40314-6 (hbk)
        ISBN10: 0-415-40314-6 (hbk)
        ISBN13: 978-0-415-39931-9 (pbk)
        ISBN10: 0-415-39931-9 (pbk)
        1. Psychoanalysis. 2. Psychotherapist and patient. 3. Casement,
Patrick. I. Title.
        [DNLM: 1. Psychoanalysis. 2. Physician–Patient Relations.
        3. Personal Narratives. WM 460 C3375L 2006]
        RC506.C319 2006
        616.89'17092–dc22

                                                                2006008735

ISBN13: 978-0-415-40314-6 (hbk)
ISBN13: 978-0-415-39931-9 (pbk)

ISBN10: 0-415-40314-6 (hbk)
ISBN10: 0-415-39931-9 (pbk)

To Barney

Contents

Foreword by Professor Paul Williams   ix
Acknowledgements   xi

Introduction   1

PART I
Development   5

1 Learning from life   7

2 An emerging sense of direction   22

3 Finding a place for theory   46

4 Learning to say 'No'   72

5 Hate and containment   86

6 Samuel Beckett's relationship to his mother
   tongue   100

7 Mourning and failure to mourn   120

8 Internal supervision in process: a case
   presentation   132

9 Developing clinical antennae   151

PART 2
Reflections   165

10 Some things difficult to explain   167

11 Certainty and non-certainty   183

12 Looking back   196

   Bibliography   203
   Index   207

Foreword

Patrick Casement has written an unusual book. Those who are familiar with his body of work will recognize the theme 'learning from . . .' which characterizes his papers and books, his attitude to patients and his approach to the discipline of psychoanalysis. In this book, he takes the theme much further by talking openly about ways in which he has learned from life, and in particular from his own life experiences. The experiences he selects are wide-ranging and include reflections on his family background where he was considered to be a 'difficult' child, conflictual experiences with family members, moments of revelation and painful discontinuity, and certain pivotal changes deriving from his analysis – not least his decision to pursue a training in psychoanalysis.

To write in this way is a bold move, some would say foolhardy, as a certain type of received wisdom decrees that revelations about the analyst's life are by definition intrusive. Casement is aware of this dilemma but tackles it with a combination of frankness and careful consideration for the reader. The frankness is assisted, I suspect, by a sense of new-found freedom in having retired from full-time private practice. The consideration for the reader lies in giving only enough detailed information to further the book's theme of learning from life. There is nothing confessional or indulgent about the way Casement talks about himself. What characterises his personal disclosures is their heart-warming ordinariness. We recognize in this particular human being's struggle to develop throughout a complex childhood, adolescence and early adulthood many facets of our own developmental anxieties and crises. It is to Casement's credit that he manages to reveal significant markers in his emerging personality without usurping the theme of the book or unduly perturbing the reader –

even when discussing a brief period of breakdown in his early twenties.

Casement gives the impression in this book of feeling able to engage with new and fundamental questions concerning what makes a psychoanalyst – questions he perhaps felt previously constrained from pursuing whilst still working as an analyst. The book is therefore not simply about Casement's life: it is much more an account of sources of experience that can contribute to the acquisition of analytic wisdom, as opposed to simply analytic knowledge. For example, he is preoccupied time and again with the need to identify and take profoundly seriously the pain that many of our patients live with and which they bring to the analyst.

One way of reading the book is to see it as a cautionary tale of the innumerable pitfalls that can distract us from this task. Casement discusses the need to set limits and to be able to say 'No' with conviction in the service of the analysis, the need to contain hate in the transference and countertransference, the price of the failure to mourn, the dangers of certainty and the importance of lifelong supervision. The book concludes with personal reflections on his life and experience. Having finished the book, my sense was that no one can read it without learning a great deal from it and, perhaps more importantly, without being moved by it.

Professor Paul Williams
Joint Editor-in-Chief
International Journal of Psychoanalysis
December 2005

Acknowledgements

There are more people than I can name or remember who have contributed to this book. At every stage of my life I have been affected by those around me, and the enriching influence of that is reflected throughout of this book, for all of which I shall remain eternally grateful.

In the process of writing this book, there have been many colleagues and friends who helped me with various parts of it, and encouraged me to continue writing it. My thanks to each and every one of them. I wish especially to extend my gratitude to the late Harold Stewart, my analyst, who gave his particular blessing for me to go public in the way that I do in the second chapter. To no-one am I more indebted than to my wife who encouraged me to write this book, believing that I still had a contribution to make in this series of 'Learning from'. She has therefore had to endure once again that familiar absence of a husband caught up in the process of writing. I also wish to extend once more my special thanks to Josephine Klein for her skilful editing of the manuscript, this being the fourth time she has helped me to prepare a book for publication.

As always, I am indebted to my patients and supervisees, who have continued to be a source of much learning and inspiration, and I wish to express in particular my thanks to those who gave permission to publish some extracts from my work with them.

The publishers and I wish also to acknowledge permissions received to use material that has been published before, the details of which are given in relation to the chapters or passages in question.

Introduction

All of life can prove to be a resource for our learning, presenting a challenge for us to understand the demands that life makes upon us, whether it is in what we enjoy or in the experiences which cause us conflict and pain. In this attempt to understand what I have learned from my life, I have included a wide range of those experiences that have helped to inform me as I have moved from the youth I was, with no sense of direction in life, to the analyst I later became.

I regard myself as especially fortunate that I was in no doubt that I needed psychoanalysis. I have included some detail of my breakdown during my mid-twenties, when old ways of being had to fail en route to a breakthrough which has continued to serve me well. That sequence has been a major resource in my passion for psychoanalysis.

I have made a choice in this book to use the freedom of retirement, now that I am no longer taking new patients. This allows me to take the risks of self-exposure, which is usually inappropriate while we are still engaged in analytic work. We aim to preserve an anonymity about ourselves so that patients may use us to represent the significant others in their lives, as far as possible not inhibited by knowing too much about their analyst.

I trust that my former patients will be able to cope with the self-revelations in this book. I may, however, be taking a greater risk with regard to my colleagues. Revealing things about myself may tempt some of them to speculate about me, perhaps building a case to see me in this way or in that, but I hope they will bear in mind that such speculation can only be 'wild analysis'. Making something of the personal details given here would be easy, even a fun thing to do, using analytic theory to that end. But it is always questionable how valid analytic speculation can be in the absence of the person concerned. I am taking that risk knowingly, but I do not think that I have much to fear from it. I am who I am, and my analytic work is what it has been. I stand by both.

I share various incidents in my life, some of which might not seem very significant in themselves, but I include them because they have helped to lay a foundation for my subsequent understanding of life, and in due course they have also shaped my understanding of psychoanalysis. Quite often I am laughing at myself and I invite the reader to laugh with me.

I also include examples of my early attempts at applying theory to life, in my work as a probation officer and later as a family caseworker. Some of these examples show a clumsy misapplication of theory. I believe that many of us, especially as student analysts and therapists, can slip into a similarly naive use of theory. These examples are offered here to illustrate how not to work. We may all be able to learn something from them.

My view of psychoanalysis has changed a great deal during the time of my clinical practice. One very important shift has been from my earlier belief in the value of 'corrective emotional experience'. I have come to see how this can deflect the analytic work from where it may most need to go. In the course of my exploratory journey towards psychoanalytic ways of working I had to learn the importance of setting limits, saying 'No' when that was needed, and being there for the angry testing that often comes when a client or patient is not getting what is being demanded. I then discovered the essential work that can be done in the negative transference, much of which might be circumvented when the analyst or therapist is too readily available as an obviously good and caring person. In fact, it often takes a great deal more caring to be there for a patient's anger, even rage, than to divert this inappropriately by being too obviously a 'good' person for the patient.

I have included the paper I wrote on Samuel Beckett's relationship to his mother tongue, particularly for the light it can throw upon the struggles of an authentic self seeking to emerge from beneath the constrictions of a false self. I have added here some details of how this paper came to be written, and the aftermath when Masud Khan showed interest in this. I believe the latter throws an interesting light upon that brilliant but complicated man.

I have also included a chapter on mourning, even though it has been previously published, as my work with people who have had serious losses, in their childhood as well as more recently, has been a significant part of my clinical work at different times. I have learned a lot from that.

In the course of my development as a psychoanalyst I came to discover the key importance of the analytic space, learning to monitor it with the help of *trial identification with the patient in the session*. I have often written about *internal supervision*, and in Chapter 8 I give the detail of how things went during the clinical workshops I used to run: 'Internal Supervision in Process'.

I go on to outline some ways of viewing what happens in the consulting room that have helped me to develop what I am calling *clinical antennae*. I like to shift perspective in order to remain alert to different possible meanings, monitoring the analytic space in order to recognize the implications of what may be intruding into it or affecting the analytic process.

In the later chapters of the book, I reflect on issues that I have not often seen discussed, including coincidences and what might be telepathic communication, diagnostic dreams and other matters that have fascinated me or caught my attention. I was prompted to explore these matters because it has worried me that psycho-analysts often seem to think that they know best about so much, coming up with analytic explanations about life in all its mani-festations. As a counterbalance to this I have enjoyed those times when things happen that do not so readily lend themselves to explanation.

I return to the issues of certainty and, by contrast, of non-certainty that I regard as an essential mindset for much of our work in psychoanalysis. I also revisit some issues to do with religion. Should analysts continue to dismiss the beliefs of others simply because we do not share them? Perhaps there is a place for reverence and a place for remembering that we are not necessarily able to know best about everything. Finally, I look back and try to put into context at least some of the journey of this book.

The issue of confidentiality

As always I am concerned that the privacy of patients be protected, especially when some clinical work is published for the benefit of others. I have discussed these matters quite fully elsewhere

(Casement 1985: Appendix II; Casement 1991: Appendix II), and I stand by the position outlined there.

I continue to hope that those patients and students whose work I have drawn upon will appreciate the care with which I have sought to protect their anonymity. Anyone who recognizes themselves or their supervised work amongst the vignettes presented here will, I hope, choose not to have themselves identified by anyone else.

Part 1

Development

Chapter 1

Learning from life[1]

Introduction

For many analysts, the choice of a career in psychoanalysis can be found to lie deep-rooted in our own experience. It is therefore likely that our approach to clinical work will have been influenced, sometimes quite profoundly, by our own lives. So the theoretical orientation at which we eventually arrive, the approach to clinical work and the technique we come to prefer, may well have been selected subjectively rather than chosen as objectively as we might wish to believe.

Unfortunately it is rare for the connections between life experience and clinical orientation to be openly addressed, probably because most analysts choose to keep their personal details out of the public arena, and with good reason. Such self-disclosure is almost bound to contaminate the transference, interfering with the clinical work that lies at the centre of their professional endeavour.

I have often been asked how I came to be a psychoanalyst. This is a question I have not usually felt free to answer, at least not in any detail and not in print, because of how that might affect my work with patients. But now that I am no longer taking on new patients I am under no such constraint. I trust that any past patients who might read what follows in this book will be able to take what I reveal here without too much difficulty or disturbance. I hope their transferences to me will have been sufficiently worked

---

1 An earlier version (Casement 2002a) was published in *Psychoanalytic Inquiry*, 22, 4: 519–533.

through to be able to bear facing realities that do not lend themselves to any continued idealization.

In what follows there will be vignettes from my own life and experience, with comments on what I have since come to recognize in these examples. When appropriate, I shall say something of the ways in which these experiences have contributed to how I have since come to regard the clinical endeavour. Even though some of these vignettes may not seem to be particularly important, for me they have come to stand for something of much greater significance than was present in the events themselves at the time.

Turkish delight

When the Second World War had just ended, my family began to have new kinds of food that we children had not heard of before. One such special treat was the first box of Turkish delight to come into our home. It was a large box with many wonderful cubes of this special new sweet, all embedded in icing sugar. Being such a treat, we were each allowed 'just one piece' after lunch. That was the rule, watchfully supervised by an adult at the time the box was being passed round.

To my shame, which I laughingly recall even now, when no one was looking I made some useful discoveries about these pieces of Turkish delight. They were not all the same size. Therefore, if one of the bigger ones was cut in half, the giveaway face (where the cut had been) could easily be concealed by dabbing it in the sugar. It then looked just like all the other pieces. Or, to be more precise, it looked just like the other smaller pieces. I was then free to help myself to more than my daily ration without it being all that obvious. However, having got into the way of helping myself by stealth, and it was so easy, I continued doing this. As a result, all the pieces got smaller and smaller, but nobody seemed to notice.

Though I kept on getting away with my 'crime', it was not without guilt. Years later, when reading Winnicott on the *antisocial tendency* (1956), I came to understand this particular experience quite differently. I had been repeating my crime with the *unconscious hope* that I might be caught. But as my delinquency remained undiscovered, there had been little or no reason for me to give this up. I had needed someone to notice what was going on in order to help me to stop. In the absence of discovery, I had been left with the hollow victory of repeatedly getting away with what I was doing. My deeper hope, I now realize, had not been met by the parental action that was unconsciously being looked for. Instead of the relief of being helped to stop this 'stealing', I was left with a guilt that stayed with me for years.

This experience served me well in my clinical work. From my early work as a probation officer, through to my work as a psychoanalyst, I could recognize when there had been that unconscious hope that Winnicott wrote of when he was describing the 'antisocial tendency'. I have since come to paraphrase Winnicott in writing:

> [Winnicott] observed that when a child has been deprived of something essential to security and growth, and has been deprived of this for too long, the child may go in search of this symbolically, through stealing, *when hopeful*. Who other than Winnicott would have been able to recognize that thrust of unconscious hope, even in stealing?
>
> (Casement 2002c: xxii)

It was Winnicott's genius that he could see this, and I have been struck by how frequently his observation has been true of those who have later become delinquents, whose unconscious hope had not been met.[2]

Now say 'sorry'

From all accounts, in my family I was seen as a particularly difficult and tiresome child. So it is not surprising that I had often to be called to account for my bad behaviour. One time, when I was about ten, I had been sent to my room 'to cool off'. I vividly remember the quite new awareness that came to me on that occasion. I had spontaneously come to realize, for the first time ever, that I had really hurt my father. Also, for the first time that I know of, I had felt real concern. This I think was a moment when I began to discover a *capacity for concern*, of which Winnicott (1963) also writes.

---

2 I return to this in Chapter 3.

However, all did not continue well. I remember going downstairs with what felt like a precious gift. I was feeling sorry *of my own accord*, and I went to say 'sorry' to my father for hurting him, to say this and really to mean it. Of course my parents could not have known the transformation that had occurred within me while I was left alone in my room. Instead, as usually happened at such times, I was greeted by my mother saying to me, 'Now, say "sorry" to your father.'[3] I can remember feeling completely devastated. The gift I had found in my heart to say felt entirely ruined. I could not say the 'sorry' being demanded of me as it was not at all the same thing as the apology that I had in my mind. So, to comply with that parental demand (understandable though it was) would, it seemed, have been to betray the gift I had come to offer. I know that my gift was not given, at least not then.

In later life I came to see that the crisis for me at that moment had to do with finding a level of *true self*, which was of a quite different order to anything that went with compliance or with good behaviour that was not necessarily felt.

I think that my subsequent sense of this vital difference, between compliant behaviour and that which flows from the inner/true/ core self, originated from this moment in my life. It is also the essence of what we encounter in our clinical work, and this is so much more real to the patient than any surface adaptation or compliance would be. Some patients need us to be acutely aware of this, not only in their own lives but also within the analytic relationship.

Even though it felt devastating to me that the gift of my first true 'sorry' had not been communicated or recognized, that moment has continued to serve me well over the years. Some of my patients may indirectly have come to benefit from it also. I have since come to realize how natural it is that I have so often been helped by Winnicott's writing. I repeatedly felt a relief in finding someone who had been where I had been, who also offered an understanding that was experience-near and so often relevant to key experiences of my own.

---

3 I have no doubt that children need to be taught to say 'sorry'. Parents, hopefully, will find some way to allow for the key difference between just saying it and feeling it. For instance, they may sometimes leave an older child to say 'sorry' when he/she *feels* sorry.

Being believed in

Having been a difficult child at home, it was not surprising that I was also difficult when I went to a boarding school. Towards the end of my time there (aged 13) I was summoned, as so often before, to the headmaster's study. He was a most unusual man, combining a firm discipline with an unmistakable affection for the boys, and they loved him in return. But, despite my love and respect for this headmaster, I had remained incorrigible. So once again I was expecting more 'telling off' or more punishment for whatever my latest misdeeds had been. Instead, the headmaster gave me a short lecture. He said to me:

> I have news for you. All the staff have now given up on you. Everything has been tried and nothing has worked. At least, everything has been tried except for one thing. No one has thought to put you in a position of responsibility because no one has seen you as capable of being responsible. So I am going to take a risk with you. I am going to give you the responsibility of being a school prefect. Please don't let me down.

I remember being totally amazed. No one had ever seen me as having even the least potential for being responsible. I had been seen as 'difficult' or 'bad', a reputation I had evidently deserved, and I had continued to live up to that view of me. But now, for the first time, someone was seeing me as capable of being different. I then determined I would do whatever I could to live up to the headmaster's trust in me.

Here was a profoundly new experience. Here was an acknowledgement of my potential to be different, and the affirmation that went with this had always been lacking until then. It was also very different from what I had experienced from others. So it is not surprising that I later came to be drawn towards Alexander's notion of *corrective emotional experience*.[4] That headmaster's trust in me had clearly been 'corrective'. It had also been a key emotional experience. Maybe, I thought, *this* was what helped to bring about change in people.

4 Alexander (1954); Alexander *et al.* (1946).

For a while I began to believe that it was through caring for and believing in people, such as clients on probation and patients in psychotherapy, that they could begin to experience themselves differently and so begin to live their lives differently. However true that may be, it took me a long time before I came to realize that there was something very important missing in this view.

An experience of discontinuity and the deep unconscious

One particular experience stands out as having given me a striking awareness of the unconscious at work. From that time I have remained most impressed by this deep part of the mind, which can operate so immediately and yet so entirely beyond our ken.

When I was first beginning to be interested in psychoanalysis, I had gone to a concert given by Rostropovich, at which he was playing the Dvorak cello concerto. When I got to my seat I found I was sitting in the second row from the front and immediately opposite the soloist. There was almost no one else between the soloist and me, allowing me to feel as if the concerto was being played just for me.

I don't remember having heard this concerto before. Then, in this most intimate setting (being oblivious of anyone else), I felt lifted to a new level of existence. Not knowing the concerto, the last movement came as a total surprise. Just when it seemed to be coming to an end, the cello was joined by a solo violin and together the two instruments began to soar into yet a further realm of the music. It was a completely unique experience for me. I was also especially glad I had gone alone to this concert, as I felt I could not have borne the shock of having to talk afterwards. I needed to remain undisturbed in this newly revealed world that lay so far beyond words.

I really needed to go for a long walk by myself after that concert, to take in the experience and to savour it, and to come down to earth very slowly. Unfortunately, I had promised I would go on to a party. There I came down to earth with a bump, with Bob Dylan music being played so loudly that no one could communicate with anyone. It was a shocking anticlimax.

It was not until a few weeks later that I had occasion to realize some of what that break in continuity had meant to me. I had been watching the television by myself, a programme about childcare in what was then Yugoslavia. We were being shown how mothers in that country were encouraged to go out to work while their babies or young children were looked after in nurseries. It was said to be more efficient than having only one or two children being looked after by each mother. With this regime there could be quite a number of children looked after by a single nurse, and the mothers released to go out to work. We were then shown a scene in which a one-year-old child, who had become attached to the first-year nurse, was being handed over to a new nurse who would look after the child for the following year. The child was turning back to the nurse who was known to him, still trying to cling to her.

At this moment some background music was introduced. I heard only the first four notes and suddenly I found myself in tears and crying more profoundly than I could ever remember. This crying seemed to come from a place so deep inside myself that the whole of me was wracked with pain. I thought I was going mad. Then, very gradually, I began to notice the music again. It was a cello playing with an orchestra, and it was a slow movement that seemed familiar, but I could not place it. Then it dawned on me that it might be from the Dvorak cello concerto. I had just bought a record of this but I had not yet played it. So when I felt sufficiently recovered I put on the slow movement and there were the four notes that I had heard immediately before my crying, the first notes of the slow movement.

For some years I regarded this as an extraordinary example of the timelessness of the unconscious and the immediacy with which the unconscious can remember and make connections. Only four notes had connected me with the concert in which I had felt so uplifted; notes I had heard played only once before. I thought my crying had to do with the disruption of that experience being so suddenly broken into by such different music at the party.

Years later, when I was eventually in analysis, I began to see this sequence differently. My analyst had simply asked me: 'What was the programme about?' I had then told him that it had been about childcare arrangements, and I described what I have given above about that television programme. He simply picked out one detail from this: 'So it was about a child being handed over to a new carer.' He didn't have to say any more, as I immediately realized the obvious connection with my own early experience. It is interesting that I had not allowed myself to see such an obvious connection until then. I too had been transferred from one nanny to another during my first years. The family memory of this had been that I used to be so difficult with each of them that no nanny would stay for more than about a year, or less. So my experience of attachment had been frequently disrupted. No wonder I had found myself crying when I had been reminded of this, together with the emotional experience of the concert being so harshly interrupted.

On later reflection, I noted it was only when I was in a strong relationship (i.e. in my analysis – once I felt sufficiently secure in this) that I could allow myself to begin to recognize a meaning here that went beyond the music. However, some years later still, I came to realize an even deeper level of my crying, which had come from before any of those nannies. My first attachment had naturally been to my mother, whom I had seemed to lose so abruptly when I had been handed over to that series of nannies. It was probably during that earliest time with my own mother that there had seemed to be music just for me, which I had then seemed to lose, suddenly and traumatically, as if for ever. So the crying, at its deepest, had come from a time that was completely beyond any conscious memory.

Agreeing to train as a psychotherapist: affirmation or compliance?

I had begun my first therapy in a state of crisis. I was seriously depressed and not seeing any sense or purpose in my life – a despair that had continued for some years into that therapy. It had therefore seemed to be extremely important to me when my therapist of that time had cut across yet another stream of my self-attacking by saying that I seemed to be unaware of my gifts. 'Like what?' I had retorted. She had then tried to persuade me that, in her opinion, I could become what she called 'a gifted therapist' if I allowed myself to train. Naturally I felt flattered and I eventually thought: 'Why *not* do the training?' It was better than having no purpose in life at all.

So I did the psychotherapy training, but I delayed in taking my first training case until I had completed all three years of theoretical training. No one understood why I delayed, and neither did I. My explanation at the time was that I hadn't got a consulting room. But I was also in no hurry to find one, or to fix up a room for myself to use as a consulting room.

After that long delay I did eventually start taking patients. Over time, they all seemed to be getting better. But I had an uneasy sense of being a fraud, a feeling that became even more serious when I noticed, in clinical seminars, that other therapists spoke of 'working with the negative transference' whereas my patients seemed only to experience me positively.

I now began to sense that my patients were getting better to please me. Then it occurred to me that they might be responding, in their therapy with me, in much the same way as I had responded to my therapist. I had done the training to please her, as the decision for me to train had not really come from within myself. So, what had first seemed to be my response to an affirmation of my potential, as with that headmaster, might have been a compliance with someone's flattering view of me. Retrospectively, my therapy seemed to have been not much more than a 'false-self analysis'. It had not radically attended to what remained unacknowledged and unattended to within my core self or in my self-attacking.

The way on became clear to me in a most dramatic way. I had been taking part in a gestalt weekend along with a number of colleagues. Among these was my former therapist, who at one point chose to work on her relationship with another colleague (Dr X) who was also present. As part of the gestalt procedure, Dr X was invited to answer for herself to what had been said to her in the 'empty chair' of the gestalt therapy. Then, during the course of the heated exchanges that followed, my former therapist collapsed in tears, admitting that she could not cope with any open anger or aggression.

I happened to meet my former therapist on the way out from the last gestalt session, so I said to her: 'I found what happened in there, between you and Dr X, very disturbing. But it has also been very useful. It has helped me to understand why I could never get angry with you.' To this she replied: 'Was there so much to be angry about?'

That answer sent me into analysis. It showed me, in a way I could not fail to see, that throughout my quite long therapy I had never felt free to get into any negative transference with my therapist. Any anger addressed towards her, even when it may have been transferred anger, seemed always to have been taken personally and as something she could not tolerate. My therapist had always deflected this away from herself onto someone outside the consulting room. The result had been that the view I had of my own anger, as too much for anyone, seemed to have been regularly confirmed. No wonder I had not been able to accept anger from my patients, even as transference. No wonder too that my patients had only been able to appear to get better, to please me.

I was now faced with a fresh crisis. I could see there were very good reasons why I had come to feel fraudulent as a therapist. Perhaps I should stop being a therapist. I therefore sought out the best analyst I could find, either to help me stop working as a therapist, hopefully without too much further harm to my patients, or to help me make good the deficiencies of my earlier therapy so that I might be able to work with patients more genuinely.

Out of that renewed analytic work grew my eventual decision to train as a psychoanalyst; a decision, this time, arrived at truly from within myself. The analysis felt so very different from my previous therapy. In particular, I was given a real opportunity to be as I felt, as I was fortunate to find I was with someone who was able to take whatever I 'threw' at him in the process. There was indeed much angry relating within my internal world, and my analyst was prepared to be used to represent whomever I felt most angry with at any given time. He was able to take this, as often as necessary, without becoming defensive. He could even take my anger as if it were only for him, without deflecting it. Only gradually was the transference dimension brought in as also relevant. In that sense my anger was being taken as something to be survived, directly in relation to himself, rather than being too quickly treated as if it were only transference or as something that could not be borne (as with my previous therapist).

None of my more important clinical work would have been possible if I had not had the benefit of this very different experience. Here I had begun to discover how inadequate is the notion of 'corrective emotional experience'.

The person who offers himself or herself as 'better than' someone else, who had been experienced as 'bad' in a patient's past, does not change anything of that earlier experience. Instead, that so-called corrective experience is likely to confirm an inner sense of the feelings that belonged to early bad experience as being too much for anyone. So, however important some affirmation may be in its rightful place, and there may be a place for it in analysis too, I became aware of its dangerous tendency to deflect what ought to be addressed. The ongoing effects of bad experience really need to be allowed into the analytic relationship and not kept outside it.

This later experience, in my analysis, also highlighted how important it was to revisit the difficult behaviour that I had chosen to suppress in order to live up to my headmaster's trust in me. It was necessary for that behaviour to be engaged with and to be understood. It is not enough, then, just to be persuaded out of this as by my headmaster, or manoeuvred out of it as with my first therapist. There is often some essential communication in the behaviour of 'being difficult' that has been missed before.

Being a 'better' mother

There is another way in which being 'better than' can be damaging. When my wife and I had our first child I was keen to be involved and to help in any way I could. But I had a lot to learn here, in particular about what helped and what did not help. On one occasion, which I remember still with sadness, our baby was crying to be fed. Usually we were prepared for this, with a bottle warmed and ready for when she was likely to wake. But on this occasion my wife had been exhausted from her day, while I had been away at work, and the bottle was still in the fridge needing to be warmed. I remember being unfairly critical of my wife about this, and her responding understandably with annoyance: 'If you think you are such a good mother then *you* go and do it.'

To begin with I did just that, warming the bottle and picking up the now very distressed baby to feed her. I remember my wife then commenting: 'Why don't you just take over and do it all?' I immediately realized that I had done something terrible. I had come between our baby daughter and her mother, as I had been offering myself as the 'better' mother. I saw in a flash how destructive this could be. The only way I could see to re-establish things between the baby and her real mother was to step back from any notion of being the better mother. I remember putting our baby back in her cot and putting the bottle back on the table beside it. I then withdrew, leaving the baby to protest in her own way, which of course she did. My wife picked her up, comforted her and fed her, while having plenty to say to me: 'How could you do that? How could you just *leave* her like that?'

Our daughter definitely had a bad experience with her father putting her down and leaving her to cry. However, there could also be an important shift here, from my presenting myself as the better mother to my being available as the bad one who had left her to cry. My wife was then able to be the one who could rescue the baby from (at that moment) her neglectful father, rather than my wife still being allocated a neglectful role by me. It could also be the beginning of a better balance between us in our shared caring for our daughter.

In addition, this experience brought to my notice how damaging it can be, in different settings, when there is a rivalry over who is the better caregiver, whether this is between parents over their child or between any other kind of caregiver and whoever is there to support that person. This insight has subsequently led me to lay emphasis upon Winnicott's notion of the *nursing triad*,[5] whereby a mother needs to be supported *as mother to her baby*. Instead, too often we find that a mother is being undermined by people telling her that she has been doing things wrong and showing how much better they could do things.

In the training of analysts and therapists too we discover how important it is for there to be a *supervisory triad*, with a supervisor supporting the therapist *as therapist to his or her patient*. Instead, we can sometimes find a supervisor who undermines the supervisee, even seeming to take over the treatment of the patient in such a way that the supervisee feels reduced to a virtual messenger between the patient and the supervisor.

Learning from clinical practice

There is so much more in analysis than the giving of insight; there is also the patient's experience of the relationship. This can be misunderstood, however, and often the implications of this are missed as well. Moving away from what Alexander advocated, I have come to feel dubious about any deliberately corrective use of the analytic relationship. That use is almost bound to be manipulative, with any apparent gain likely to be short-lived, as with charismatic cure. But we do not have to go to the other extreme of remaining, or thinking that we can remain, poker-faced analysts who eschew any sign of being emotionally affected by the patient.

Unconscious responsiveness

What has frequently struck me in my clinical practice is how we, as analysts, are often drawn into ways of relating to a particular

5 I have not been able to find a reference to this in Winnicott's writings, but I am not going to take credit for this concept as I am sure I learned it from him.

patient that can have much to do with the patient's own history and the unfinished business from the past. If, for instance, we allow for the *free floating responsiveness* that Sandler (1976) wrote of, rather than struggling to prevent this out of some misplaced concern for technical correctness, we will sometimes find we begin to relate to a patient in ways that can feel quite alien to us, in ways that may not only puzzle us but may on occasion leave us feeling concerned or even alarmed that we have slipped up in such a serious way.

Of course, we try not to let our patients down. When it seems that we have, we try to examine ourselves for any *personal countertransference* that may have contributed to this. But beyond that we can sometimes find we have been drawn into *unconscious role-responsiveness*, such as Sandler describes in the same paper. We may then find we seem to have 'become' some version of a key object relationship in the patient's inner world, wherein the patient may then begin to work with us on aspects of that relationship which have remained disturbing or in some way unresolved.

Similarly, we can be drawn into relating to a patient in ways that resemble those Alexander wrote of, when something emerges in the analytic relationship that may in itself have directly therapeutic implications for the patient.

But a key difference here is how we get to this. Sometimes we get to it in a way that is more determined by the patient's own unconscious, and our own often unconscious response to it, rather than by any deliberate choice of our own. Not infrequently, we may also find ourselves beginning to behave like some version of a bad object in the patient's inner world.

At other times, we might find we are drawn into relating to a patient in ways that are quite new to the patient. But when there has been serious deprivation, even privation, we may find that a patient's response to this new behaviour is by no means always appreciative. For instance, a patient may be responding badly to something that might have seemed to have been a good experience with the analyst. I have come to think of this as being a response to *the pain of contrast*.[6] It may come about through a patient's beginning to realize some of what has been seriously missing in his or her past, and maybe seeing this more clearly than ever before. It

---

6 I give an example of this elsewhere (Casement 1990: 106–107, 1991: 288–289), the occasion when the *pain of contrast* first occurred to me as a useful concept.

is not, I think, always due to envy that a patient can spoil a good experience with an analyst. It may also be a way of unconsciously seeking to reduce this pain of contrast by lessening the difference, thereby seeking to dull the realization of what had been painfully missing for the patient.

In being drawn into relating to our patients in these ways, it can also happen that we find ourselves beginning to behave similarly to some aspect of what had been most traumatic in a patient's past. When this happens, we may well find that we are used by the patient to represent some key person who was experienced as having failed them, as at a time of trauma. What can then be most surprising is that patients can, in due course, find release from their intense feelings and phantasies, which had formerly gripped them in relation to such trauma, by working them through in relation to the analyst – that is, if the analyst is adequately able to manage the ensuing experience.

We often find that the key figure(s) of a patient's past have been, in some way, unable to be truly 'there' for the feelings that were being experienced by the patient at times of trauma. It is not only by finding insight into those occasions that a patient can begin to find release; it may also be that a patient needs to be held in a relationship that can bear to be used in this way, with the analyst being able to see it through.

At times such as these we encounter much that goes beyond the giving of insight, and I don't think there is any way to prepare for this other than finding our way through it with a patient, helped by such insight as we find from psychoanalytic understanding. But here, at these crucial times, I think the function of insight is initially to hold the analyst through the experience, while the analyst holds the patient through it.

One further area of particular discovery I have noted in my work with patients is that it is also very important to some patients that we allow *them* to interpret to *us*. Patients quite often have had their own insights that have not been adequately valued by others, and this is most especially true of patients who were perceptive children. It quite often happens that parents and others have felt threatened by a child's uncanny perception of truth which these adults would have preferred to go unrecognized or unknown, even by themselves. These patients may need an analyst who is not just an insightful analyst but also able to bear their perceptive insights about him or her.

Finally, it was almost by chance that I came upon the theme of my first book *Learning from the Patient*. But once this phrase had come to my mind it would not leave me alone, even though I had no book in mind to write at the time.[7] As I reflected upon it, I came to realize that it described much of the previous 20 years of my professional life, during which I had been learning so much from my patients.

But what is more important I have also come to realize that the very nature of the analytic relationship we find emerging with each patient grows out of this *learning from*, which closely parallels how a mother learns to become the particular mother her infant needs her to be, at each stage of infancy and in later childhood, and with each child. I believe that we too can let ourselves learn from our patients in this dynamic way, whereby we can more nearly become the analyst our patients need us to be, at the various stages of any analysis. This may be significantly different with each patient and it may also be different from our colleagues. But that, I believe, is the very essence of the analytic venture.

7 I return to this in Chapter 11.

Chapter 2

An emerging sense of direction

Two roads diverged in a wood, and I –
I took the one less traveled by,
And that has made all the difference.
(Robert Frost 1920)

Introduction

Some further vignettes from my childhood and early life help to
illustrate the strange progression that led me eventually into the
world of psychoanalysis. They not only show how a sense of
direction can emerge even out of the tangled web of a life, but may
also prompt others to wonder about their own roots and the ways
by which each arrived at where they are in their life's journey so far.

Family setting

I was the second of four children. My brother is two and a half years
older than me, my two sisters being seven years and nine years
younger. I was born into a family that had its own strong traditions
and family expectations. On my father's side all the males before
me, for three generations, had been in the Royal Navy. My grand-
father was an admiral, my father became a captain, his two brothers
were also senior naval officers; and then my brother joined the navy,
later becoming a commander. Although I was very different from
my father and brother there seemed to be an unspoken wish in the
family that I might eventually come round to seeing things in the
same kind of way, perhaps even to join the navy as well. In the end I
was 'the one that got away'.

There is a photograph of me with my brother, both of us in sailor suits. He was six and a half and I was about four at the time. My brother is standing very straight, giving a proud salute to our father and looking very correct. I, by contrast, can be seen saluting with the wrong hand. I have enjoyed thinking of this as a prophetic sign of my different way ahead, even though it probably only shows that I hadn't yet learned to conform.

Being difficult and/or different

Throughout my early years I was often seen as 'difficult', and I have no doubt that I was. But I have since wondered whether some of that being difficult may also have been an attempt to stand up for myself against pressures to be different from myself.

I can clearly remember a time when I was five or six years old and a war refugee who came to live with an uncle and aunt, where we were also living at the time, insisted on changing how my hair was parted. Until that day it had been parted on what used to be regarded as the girl's side. When my mother protested about this interference, the woman replied: 'You are trying to make a girl of this boy. He should not have his hair parted on that side.'[1] My mother claimed it was only because my hair grew that way, which this woman said was 'nonsense'. She then demonstrated that my hair grew naturally for a parting on the boy's side, where it has remained to this day.

Making sense of the past

Many years later, my analyst formed the impression that my mother may have had a miscarriage when I was between four and five. His reconstruction had been prompted by hearing I had an uncanny awareness of early pregnancy in those around me. Once I even sensed this in someone whose pregnancy had only just been confirmed.[2] Another element in this reconstruction was found in the fact that I had developed colitis when I was five which, interestingly, did not subside until my sister was a year old. By then I

---

1 In those days, at least in the world my parents lived in, it was assumed that boys would usually have their hair parted on the left side and girls on the right.
2 I return to this in Chapter 10.

was aged eight. So it seemed I may have experienced my earlier wish to get rid of my mother's next pregnancy as if that wish had been dangerously powerful, perhaps feeling that I had killed her baby. Therefore, when my sister was born it would have been very important for me to see that this next baby was surviving. I may then have begun to feel less of a need to be punishing myself internally, my colitis seeming to combine some pain in myself with a frequent getting rid of whatever seemed to be bad, even lethal, inside myself.

This reconstruction made sense of a lot that had otherwise been difficult to understand, and my hypersensitivity to pregnancy disappeared soon after my analyst had made sense of it in the way that he did. I became increasingly convinced by his hypothesis, to the point where I finally asked my mother straight out: 'Why did you never tell me you had a miscarriage?' She was clearly very shocked that I had heard about this, saying: 'Who told you? *Nobody in the family was ever meant to know about this.*' I proudly replied: 'My analyst told me.'

I then learned that there had been a miscarriage shortly after I was four, but what I did not like to ask was the gender of this lost baby. I suspect it may have been a baby girl. Perhaps my mother had later been trying to turn me into a kind of substitute daughter. She had also taught me, around the same age, such feminine arts as crochet and knitting. Compounded by the absence of my father during the war years, this left me to identify more readily with the women around me than with the few men in our lives at that time. This may later have helped me, in some ways, to work with patients who were reliving early times with their mothers. But it became important that I also find male role models in order to achieve a better balance in my gender identity.

Looking back to that time, my mother would have conceived just before or just after the beginning of the war, amidst all the uncertainties about the future. In addition, my father was subsequently away for long periods at a time because of the war. So I can imagine that her pregnancy just then may well have carried a huge emotional investment for the future, possibly also heightened by an anxious awareness that people in the services did sometimes get killed during a war. This pregnancy could therefore have felt like a last chance for my mother to have another baby – perhaps also carrying a hope that the baby would be a daughter as she already had two sons.

Where do babies come from?

One family memory, recounted to me by an amused aunt, comes from when I was about five. We had been sent out to a tea party on a hot summer's day. When we got back I told my mother that we had all been swimming. As I had gone out to tea without my bathing costume,[3] my mother showed some surprise at this. She enquired: 'Were you all little boys, or were you little boys and girls together?' I am told that I replied: 'I don't know. We were not wearing any clothes.' I clearly had no idea about gender, even at that age. In fact I didn't work out the gender thing until my second sister was born, by which time I was nine. Only then did I realize it hadn't been that my first sister had something wrong with her. She and my other sister were different from me because they were both girls. Well, better late than never to find out about these things. I was clearly a late developer.

My father was away for most of the war years. Although he came back from time to time, for short periods of leave, I remember him as mostly absent. In relation to that, when I was seven, I was travelling by train with my mother who was holding my baby sister. In the railway carriage we met a friendly lady who, as a way of making conversation, asked me if this was my sister. I am told I had proudly replied that she was, whereupon this lady asked (as it was wartime) if my father had seen my sister yet. My mother remembered, with embarrassment, that I replied: 'Oh, no. He's been away for years and years and years.' I had clearly not yet worked out how babies were made, or I had repressed any sense of that.

Being impossible

From the age of four my brother and I were taught at home by someone known as our 'governess'. She also found me very difficult, but stayed on for nearly seven years despite this. She was the first person who stayed. All my nannies had left after a very short time, so it was with this governess that I had my first remembered experience of someone who was prepared to 'see it through'. This

---

3 In those days a boy's bathing costume included a front, with straps, rather like an overall. It was the fashion then for males as well as females, even children, to keep their nipples always covered when in public.

she did until well after I had been sent to boarding school. I went there when I was aged eight and our governess didn't leave until almost three years later.

When this governess finally announced she was going, I remember crying myself to sleep every night for the first few weeks of that term, convinced she was leaving because I had been so bad. When my mother heard of this she quickly reassured me that it was not to do with me. It was allegedly because our governess didn't want to have to look after small babies, my second sister being then about one year old. However, years later I met this governess again and told her I had once imagined she left because I was so difficult. 'But that is exactly why I did leave,' she said. 'You were just impossible.'

Another memory of my time with that governess, also reported to me by an aunt, was that I used to infuriate her with my readiness to make a nonsense out of what she was asking me to do. For instance, she would try getting me to concentrate and would say: 'Patrick, put your mind behind it.' I am told that I would feign ignorance as to what she meant, replying: 'Put my mind behind it? Where do I put it? Do I put it here, or do I put it there?' I can readily see why she often found me impossible. That is a clear example of how infuriating I could be, but it can also be seen as an early expression of my not wanting anyone trying to control my mind, or telling me what to do with my mind. Interestingly, we can also see this as demonstrating a child's concrete thinking.

Children are often slow to understand metaphor and even more slow to understand sarcasm. I vividly recall a time when I was at boarding school, aged nine and being taught by the headmaster, when I was called up to his desk to have my Latin sentences corrected. Trying to complete just one more sentence before going up, I half stood while continuing to work out the verb to complete the sentence. He said: 'Don't hurry', so I sat down to finish it properly. He then yelled at me for being insolent. I suspect that I was often insolent but on this occasion I was simply taking him at his word.

Schools

We lived a very sheltered life, surrounded mostly by other members of the family: aunts, uncles, cousins and people who were 'out of the same drawer' as the family. I also recall being told off, as a teenager, for wearing my shirt collar outside my sweater. My mother said I must never do that as I 'might be mistaken for a grammar school boy', a degree of snobbery that appals me when I think of it.

Steps to reach out to people not like us were discouraged. I was stopped from going on cycle rides with a boy I met in our neighbourhood because he was 'a village boy'. While still at boarding school, with no one from there living anywhere near, I remember school holidays as being very isolated and lonely, especially after my brother had joined the Royal Navy when I was 15. This led to me becoming introverted and defensively self-sufficient. I also found it difficult adjusting to being back home after having been in the communal rush and tumble of school. I recall an occasion, at the beginning of one school holiday, when I was trying to get my mother's attention, as when trying to get a master's attention in class, and saying to her: 'Sir, Sir, *please* Sir,' not realizing what I was saying. My sister has also reminded me of an occasion when I had expostulated at my mother with the words 'My dear man', an expression of emphatic disagreement often used by boys at Winchester.

I have already written about how my prep school headmaster had the imaginative insight to see beyond my difficult behaviour, making me a school prefect. For the remaining time at that school I became a model of virtue, but this did not mean I had become a radically different person. Instead I had discovered how to present a compliant surface, which worked with people in authority because that was encouraged and praised. This surface way of being, even if hiding much of what I really felt, seemed to be what was most required in order to be accepted.

At my next school, Winchester College, I had no reason to play the prefect as I was years away from that possibility. So the awkward and problematic child which I naturally was surfaced again. This was largely how I came to be known until the seductive pull of authority again began to be felt, as I came to be in line for promotion to house prefect and later school prefect.

I took my 'O' levels during the first year of that changed form of examination. In those days no grades were given; they only gave a 'pass' or a 'fail.' For some reason, I was so little worried by exams that I didn't even notice that I hadn't received the results letter, which the housemaster had promised to send to each of us during the holiday. Nor did I remember to ask him about this when I returned for the next term. The exams had slipped entirely from my mind until I found other boys comparing their results. I seemed to have had very little sense of competition with others, at least in relation to the exams, with one significant exception.

In one maths class I found the work very easy and got 100 per cent for my first week's 'out of school work' (the boarding school equivalent of homework). Another boy, who has remained a lasting friend from those days, also got 100 per cent. So for every week of that term I competed with him, afraid to get anything less than full marks, which during that term I never did. I was placed top of the class for the term's work, but when I took the end of term exams I came bottom. I had become so reliant upon checking the textbooks, finding similar examples so that I could check the methods to be used, I had failed to internalize what I was meant to be learning. So the polished surface of success, with my perfect results throughout the term, had been disguising a hidden failure to learn. All my homework of that term had been based on copying the textbook methods rather than finding solutions from within myself. My failure in that exam was a most salutary experience.

Those exam results had been a much more true assessment of my ability. Regrettably, however, the school rationalized these away as some aberrant performance on my part and I was prematurely promoted to a scholarship class. There I totally failed to come up to the teacher's expectations and had to be moved down to a lower class where I still needed to learn what I had been failing to learn before.

Attachments

In my final year at school my parents were in Germany, my father being stationed there as part of the British military forces posted there after the war. During my final Easter holidays I had a chance to take part in a Royal School of Church Music course, when senior choristers from cathedral choirs throughout Britain would join together, under the auspices of the RSCM, to sing for two weeks in a selected cathedral. It was to be in Winchester Cathedral that year and I was fortunate enough to be allowed to join the RSCM choir for their fortnight of training and cathedral singing. This meant that I remained in Winchester for the beginning of my holidays, staying with the master of music and his wife, who had become substitute parents during my last years at the school while my parents were abroad.

For the remaining two weeks of that holiday I was left to fend for myself amongst my extended family, my parents having decided that 'it wasn't worth paying' for me to travel to join them for only two weeks. So, after wandering between various aunts and uncles, I ended up with my father's elderly mother. Although I was fond of her, I also found her exhausting to be with. I therefore decided to go back to my school house three days early. I excused myself from my grandmother, claiming that the holiday had ended, and made my way back to Winchester. There the house matron agreed to make up a bed for me until the term started. I was clearly showing a major attachment to my school.

Like my preparatory school, Winchester had become the most stable part of my life. My parents had lived in 17 different homes in about the same number of years. I can remember how frequently I would wake up in my bed finding that it took me quite some time before I could make out where I was. But at each of these schools the place always stayed the same, in contrast to my homes that kept on changing.

My attachment to the school itself became very evident when the time came for me to leave after my last term. In my final hours there I could see just how attached I had become to the bricks and mortar of the place. When everyone else had packed up and left, with barely a second thought about not seeing them again, I spent a long time walking round, weeping my 'Goodbye' to the buildings, the chapel, the music school where I had spent so many hours, and all the places that had been significant to me. I was showing an attachment to places rather than to people. I had too often experienced people as unreliable. They had kept on leaving and we had kept on leaving people as we moved from one home to another. The school buildings, however, remained the same.

A flirtation with certainty

During my last year I came under the influence of a group of evangelical Christians who drew me into a different kind of conforming. I think this may have appealed to me because it seemed like a kind of *non*-conforming, not going along with religion as taught at home or at school.

With a large number of other boys, I was lured to a 'holiday camp' where a group of enthusiastic evangelicals were able to find an opportunity for playing upon impressionable young minds. We were offered 'sure and certain salvation', and no stone was left unturned to convert the boys to an evangelical view of how to be a Christian. I remember (with great unease) the last few days when, during evening prayers, we were asked to 'pray for the two boys who have still not received Jesus into their hearts'.[4] I knew that I was clearly one of those.

After discovering I was in a minority of two, not having yet been through the process of being converted, I hesitantly accepted initiation from the person allocated to be my guide. He then took me through the steps of admitting my 'sinfulness' and accepting the blessings of salvation being offered. Although I had to admit (to myself) that I didn't feel any different after this than before, there was definitely something that got into me then that I was not able to outgrow until quite a few years later.

With embarrassment, I remember going home from that camp and challenging my parents to see that they had apparently not yet become true Christians. They were quietly devoted members of their local church, accepting the rituals of matins and communion without question. And there was I arrogantly demanding that they face what I had been told to regard as 'the error of their ways', in order to have them join me in the same evangelical state of mind I had been persuaded into. But for me, an adolescent who was feeling pretty much at sea and without any real sense of purpose, this new thinking seemed to provide what was lacking. It was appealingly definite. For a while I seemed to have found a sense of direction, even a mission in life.

From this grew the idea that I might have a vocation to become a priest, an idea that stayed with me – on and off – for several years. However, as could be imagined, this was not greeted with much enthusiasm in my family. 'What career prospects are there in *that?*' asked a concerned uncle, who then half answered his own question: 'I suppose you could go on to become a bishop.' But I don't imagine it would have worked very well if I had approached an ordination panel claiming that I felt called to become a bishop! I never got beyond the idea of taking the first steps of that journey.

---

4 I can respect some people who believe in this kind of Christianity, but I still have a problem about the pressure that is put on others to accept the same way of seeing things.

National service

After Winchester I went almost straight into national service, which was then still obligatory. Rather inevitably, I applied to go into the navy, having been encouraged to do so by my father. To be more precise, those of us who chose the navy were required first to join the Royal Naval Voluntary Reserve (RNVR). I had to go through a period of intake training in what was known as Victoria Barracks, in Portsmouth, an establishment which I later heard was condemned as 'unsuitable for human habitation'. My task for six weeks was to clean the toilets. I did this with great vigour, singing in my head the hymn by George Herbert with the lines:

> Teach me, my God and King,
> In all things thee to see,
> And what I do in any thing
> To do it as for thee.
> A servant with this clause
> Makes drudgery divine:
> Who sweeps a room as for Thy sake
> Makes that and the action fine.

I eventually made the toilets so pristine that I was tempted to bar the way to anyone who tried to use them.

After this my training was to prepare me for becoming a supply officer if I managed to make the grade. This took place at a naval shore establishment in Yorkshire called HMS *Ceres*. This involved doing everything at the double, when not marching on the parade ground, and generally having to demonstrate that I had what it takes to become an officer. We were meant to demonstrate what were known as 'OLQs' (officer-like qualities) or what national servicemen called 'oily qs', suggesting that we would be judged on how well we were fitting into everything expected of us.

Of course, this dovetailed all too well with that side of me which had become ready (yet again) to push aside my true feelings about life in order to win acceptance from those in authority. In due course, I was commissioned and sent off to be a midshipman in HMS *Glasgow*, the flagship of the Mediterranean fleet, under the command of Admiral of the Fleet Lord Louis Mountbatten.

Meeting real people[5]

In my next ship, HMS *Aisne*, I had an opportunity to explore Rome for three days as part of a scheme initiated by Mountbatten. He wanted sailors to have a chance to explore the sights and cities around them while they were serving in the Mediterranean. In Rome I met up with six sailors from my ship and we spent three days seeing the city together, during which I time I got to know them more closely than I had yet been able to know any people like sailors. This opportunity was only possible because we were all in plain clothes.

I was later required to write up an account of those three days. In my summary of that experience I said that, as well as the obvious benefits of having had the opportunity to see around Rome, one of the most significant gains for me had been the chance this had provided me for getting to know the sailors. Through being with them in this full-time way I had come to realize that, when not separated by our different uniforms, we could be joined by having much in common. Out of uniform we were all ordinary men.

I was reprimanded for this report, being told I had clearly misunderstood the reason why I had been given permission to go to Rome on this excursion. I should either have seen the city on my own, away from the sailors, or I should have taken charge of them and, as it were, marched them round Rome – with them following my orders. I was told that I could have had a valuable experience of leading the men. Instead, I had 'shown a disrespect for the uniform' and I might even have to be disciplined for this.

My report was duly submitted to the fleet officer responsible for overseeing such excursions, who then forwarded it to Mountbatten. When it was returned to me I found that my summarizing paragraph had been marked with approval in the margin. It had been selected by Mountbatten himself to be quoted in the fleet report as an example of what could be achieved by those who took advantage of the scheme he had initiated.

---

5 Members of my family, in their own ways, were real too – but when I was growing up I experienced them as representing a pressure on me to conform to their values and expectations. By contrast, I began to find my own sense of self more clearly when I was with others who were different from them.

This experience became a kind of beacon for later on. I had met real people, seemingly for the first time in my life, meeting them without the protection of uniform or status. I had begun to meet life beyond the cloistered world of my family or boarding school, and most recently in the wardroom on board ship. It was partly because of those memorable three days that I would continue to seek chances to be with real people, for that is how I came to think of those who, unlike me, seemed to have escaped the pressures to conform to the expectations of others.

University

I had applied to Trinity College, Cambridge, while I was still at Winchester. It seems strange, looking back, to realize that I had been accepted simply on the basis of an interview. It was taken for granted that I would pass my 'A' levels, no grades being given at that time. I had chosen physics, which was a natural choice as I had won a school prize in that subject. My father later found out that I could have all my university fees paid for by the Royal Navy if I joined to become an 'electrical officer'. I would also be paid a salary throughout my time at Cambridge. It seemed as if I had laid myself open to the danger of being drawn into the 'family business' after all, in spite of myself. I could not bear the thought of this, so I wrote to Trinity withdrawing my choice of physics and suggesting economics. I have no idea why I chose that, as I soon discovered that I would probably never understand any of it.

Nevertheless, I left it on record that I was going to read economics until I arrived for my first week in Cambridge. There I met my tutor who said that I could change again if I insisted, but to what? I admitted I didn't know so he went through the list of possibilities. At the end he was puzzled as I had given him reasons why I could not imagine studying *any* of the subjects from the list, and there were no others. He therefore offered me a suggestion. 'The weakest excuse you have given me was with regard to Anthropology. You said you didn't know what that is. It might be useful if you attend lectures at the Faculty for Anthropology for two weeks and come back to see me.' I immediately made further enquiries into the meaning of Anthropology, and discovered it had been defined as 'a study of Man – embracing women'. That sounded promising!

After the recommended fortnight I was completely sold on the idea of Anthropology and, in many ways, I regret not staying with it for the full three years. During that first year's study I came to learn about the essential discipline of maintaining an open mind, especially when trying to understand how others live their lives and how societies different from our own are structured and maintained. I had never had to engage with such an idea. It inspired me to learn more of this open-minded approach and what we could then learn about 'the otherness of others'. This was to become a central issue in my approach to psychoanalysis.

During that first year I had settled into a decision to read Part II Theology for the remaining two years. This was to test out my earlier notion that I might become a priest, but it was also in order to have a chance to be taught by Harry Williams,[6] who was then Dean of Chapel in my college. He was one of the most inspiring minds around in Cambridge at the time.

One of the things I learned from Harry was his notion of breakdown as breakthrough, he having had his own quite serious breakdown, for which he had received some years of psychotherapy. He saw this as having provided him with an opportunity to break free of old ideas, old ways of being, old dogma and ideas of certainty, to find beyond these a chance to discover life afresh and a new meaning in life. This fired my imagination, but I never realized how it might eventually come to be my own experience.

While at Cambridge I came to realize how our assumptions about people can profoundly affect how we relate to them. I had been attending sermons preached by Mervyn Stockwood (later to become Bishop of Southwark) in the university church of St Mary's, which he used to fill to 'standing room only' when he was preaching. I was very impressed by his sermons but I hated the way he delivered them.

Whenever Mervyn Stockwood was addressing the congregation he used to speak out of the side of his mouth and I quickly developed an intense dislike of him because of this, as I was assuming this to be an affectation. Why, I thought, did he have to spoil such excellent sermons with this most unattractive manner of delivery? However, I later learned that he had suffered a serious stroke. Since then he had only been able to continue preaching by taking no notice of what he might look like. He could only make himself heard if he worked the muscles on one side of his face to

6 The late Revd H.A. Williams.

compensate for the other side where he had lost all movement. I was shocked. I had totally misjudged this man through seeing him only in terms of my assumptions about him. It was a most useful lesson. It was the first time I had come to realize that we all relate to others in terms of the image we have of them in our own minds. Only later did I learn that this is what psychoanalysts mean by 'object relationships'.

What to do?

I left Cambridge with my degree but with no plans. I only knew that I probably would not become a priest. Having no idea what to do with my life I was looking for some way to spend a year out. I was then fortunate to hear of a training programme in Sheffield which had been set up specifically for ordinands, those in the process of training to become priests, allowing them a chance to work and study in the context of an industrial community before taking their final steps towards being ordained. There I joined several others, all of whom were halfway through their theological college training before offering themselves for ordination. Although I was not so clear about my own future I had a link with them through my degree in theology.

During my year in Sheffield I spent the first six months working in a factory that made steel and steel magnets. I was employed as a bricklayer's mate which involved me in hod-carrying, when that was required, and just about every other rough task that was needed when not actually working with the bricklayer. I had to muck in with what was known as 'the building gang' in this factory. They were building onto the premises, so there was plenty to do: digging foundations, digging a tunnel for a new weighbridge, shovelling wet concrete into a chain of barrows (at the rate of five tons per hour for each man with a shovel, and I was one of them), and learning to throw bricks up 30 feet (without them spinning) where they would be caught and stacked on the scaffolding for the bricklayer to use.

When underground, digging the weighbridge tunnel, I was working closely with an Irishman who liked to call me Pat (which I tolerated even though I usually don't like to be called that). He once looked up from our tunnelling, both of us on our stomachs, black in the face from dirt, and said to me: 'Your father should see you now, Pat!' It would certainly have been a shock for him to see his son alongside this hard-drinking Irishman, down a hole and shovelling earth back along the tunnel using his hands like a mole.

The second six months in Sheffield was spent 'in community' with five ordinands and the charismatic Canon Roland Walls as our spiritual leader and pastor. During this time I became somewhat clearer that I would not become a priest. Instead, I applied for an interview with ICI for training in personnel management, mis-spelling 'personnel' in my letter of application. I was not accepted. Later I applied to the Home Office for training as a probation officer. I then had to acquire a diploma in social studies, for which I studied at Barnet House, Oxford.

Breakdown

While doing the Barnet House course my life began to fall apart and I became almost unable to sleep. (When first writing this, I had not intended to give details here but I have since been persuaded that some explanation might help to limit speculation.) Two things had thrown me. The person around whom I had been building my life, and whom I had set my heart on marrying, had contracted an illness from which she would die. Some time later she had decided to marry a friend of mine. Not only had I lost her, but I felt I had also lost the only way I could imagine for coping with her dying: being with her to the end.

That was why I could not sleep. After a week of this I sought help from my GP who referred me to the local mental hospital where, he said, they could offer me assisted sleep. I had ten days in which to find my feet again before going to my first fieldwork placement in a probation office. The medical director of the hospital offered me a week in a private ward where I could be given all the sleep I needed and this should be sufficient to set me back on my feet. It seemed an ideal solution.

I arrived as arranged on the Friday evening to find that no one was expecting me. The medical director who had told me to arrive then was away for the weekend. I was at my last gasp, still having had next to no sleep. I felt hugely let down and was in no state to cope with this new crisis when I was already feeling so close to collapse. For want of any other option I agreed to be admitted, for the time being, in the acute admissions ward of the hospital. I was given only ten minutes with the admitting doctor.

Subsequent reflection

I'm sure I would have had more time with the psychiatrist who admitted me had it not been that I just could not go through my story again in the context of feeling so utterly let down. I had told as much as I could to the medical director two days before. This further let-down, on top of what I had been going through already, was just one let-down too many. What was happening in this hospital was itself a further trauma. Later, in my clinical work, this experience was to become a powerful stimulus for being alert to the risk of repeating a patient's trauma.

I have since come to regard trauma as 'that which cannot be managed alone'. I was unbearably alone in that hospital, with no one at all to turn to. With our patients we can at least hope to be with them as they begin to face and to work through the experience of early trauma as this comes to be re-experienced in the course of their analytic work with us. But they do need to be sufficiently held, by an effective (and affective) relationship with us, for that to be possible. Also, they need to have begun to trust our analytic holding of them if they are going to be able to work through those experiences of trauma in the course of their work with us, as I have described with my burned patient (Mrs B).[7]

I was very angry with the medical director for having forgotten to make the arrangements he had offered. In fact, I felt too angry to speak to anyone until I had a chance to speak to him. However, despite my remaining totally silent on that Friday evening and all of Saturday, by the Sunday I had sufficiently recovered from the initial shock to be interested in the other patients on my ward, some of whom illustrated the diagnoses I had been learning about on my course. At least one patient was psychotic, one a manic-depressive, one an alcoholic who was having repeated epileptic fits while being dried out, and a severely depressed person having

---

7 *On Learning from the Patient* (Casement 1985: chapter 7, 1991: chapter 7) and further discussed in *Learning from our Mistakes* (Casement 2002: chapter 7). Although I shall not be describing my work with Mrs B in this book, I refer to it because that is the clinical work for which I have become most widely known.

narcosis treatment. This last person was being kept asleep for all but a few hours out of every 24, to give him a prolonged break from experiencing his most recent trauma.

On the Monday morning I met the medical director doing his ward round and asked him about the room he had promised. He simply announced I was not going to be allowed the private ward. He said: 'You are far too ill for that'. I had no idea what was the basis for this decision until a nurse later told me it was because I had remained not speaking for the whole of Saturday. Even so, while not understanding why I was being kept in the acute admissions ward, I settled down to have my week's rest. The strange life on the ward was extraordinary but also enlightening, though often noisy and sometimes quite shocking.

At the end of my first week, when I was making preparations to leave in order to be available for my fieldwork placement on the Monday, I knew I would need some time to clear my system of medication so that I could drive safely. But when I said this to the nursing staff I was told that I was not going to be allowed to leave. Only then did I learn that my Home Office training had been suspended; this without a single word being said to me about it, let alone any discussion with me about whether I thought this might be a good thing or not.

What nobody at the hospital had taken trouble to find out about, or allowed me time to speak about, was the fact that I was in a state of shock from the cumulative trauma in my personal life. I needed time to process these experiences. I also needed a chance to be talking these through with somebody who could help me to come to terms with them, and maybe also help me to understand why I had been so thrown by these experiences.

Strangely, even though the medical director knew (from the initial consultation) something of what I had been through, his treatment of me never reflected any knowledge of that. Instead I was treated as if I were suffering from endogenous depression, apparently requiring nothing more than medication. For much of the time I was so drugged I could barely walk, kept throughout as the only 'bed patient' on the ward.

On top of this I found that I was allergic to the medication, with the result that I swelled up all over with a body rash that began to drive me crazy. I even had to tie my hands to the top of the bed to prevent me scratching myself in my sleep, because I had sometimes woken to find that my nails had made me bleed. I was eventually given some antidote cream for this, which was fine until it ran out during a weekend. I was then told that no more could be prescribed until the Monday and no notice was taken of my pleas for a duty doctor to be called to attend to this unbearable allergic reaction. Foolishly, but in desperation, I turned to a supply of Piriton I had brought into the hospital with me. This had been previously prescribed for a hay fever allergy, so it occurred to me that it just might help to alleviate the rash.

I was already feeling quite suicidal, my life having anyway fallen apart. As well as what had been happening to me before, which had caused me to have such serious insomnia, now my Home Office training had been suspended. In addition, I was being treated as if I had no rights and no mind of my own. On top of that, I had this uncontrollable itching which was making me feel quite demented. During that night I continued to take the Piriton, with increasing doses, hoping that it might eventually do something to allay the irritation. Suddenly, nothing else seemed to matter. Finally, I felt it would serve the hospital right if I died. So I took the whole bottle which had been almost full.

This was my mistake. From that moment the medical director was able to use my attempt at suicide to justify keeping me in the hospital, whatever the original reasons for keeping me there might have been. I found myself trapped, unaware of my rights. Nobody inside or outside the hospital was fighting for me or troubling to find out what my rights might be. My life seemed to have come to a virtual end.

It was during this prolonged period of despair that I wrote to my former tutor, Harry Williams, knowing that he too had been through a time of breakdown. I still remember his reply. In his letter he said: 'The Good Friday experience can go on for a long time and it can feel as if it will go on for ever. But believe me, Patrick, in time you will come through this to your own Easter Day. And things will not be the same as before.' How right he was.

It was only towards the end of my time in hospital that I learned why I had not been allowed to have the private ward which had initially been offered to me. A Spanish nurse took me to one side when there was no one else around so that he could speak to me in private, saying there was something he had to tell me. He said that he knew I should never have been on that ward. He then explained that the medical director was well known for not being able to admit any mistake. He had forgotten that the private ward he had offered me was being decorated, but he could not admit this to me.

The medical director could have apologized. He could have offered me the choice of not coming into the hospital, perhaps with medication to help me sleep, or the option to stay on a more appropriate ward. Instead he had used my angry silence in order to justify treating me as 'too ill to be allowed to be in a private ward'. Continuing to conceal his mistake, he had informed the Home Office that I was apparently too ill to continue with their training. From that simple failure to admit a mistake everything else had escalated. It is not surprising that, following this, I came to be interested in mistakes; the need to acknowledge them and learn from them.

What the nurse had told me about the medical director was later validated by other observations. For instance, at some stage towards the end of my time as a bed patient the other patients brought me a letter they had written to the matron, which all the patients were being asked to sign. They were asking for the dayroom of this ward to be redecorated so that it could be made lighter. It was decorated in such a dark shade of grey-green that nearly all the light from the windows was absorbed, even when there was clear sun outside, so that it was not possible even to read in that room without artificial light. The other patients had ended this letter saying: 'It is hard to see how anybody could be anything but depressed in an environment such as this.'

Feeling more cheerful since the nurse had spoken to me, I too signed this letter. But as there was no room at the bottom of the page I put my name in the only space left, which was at the top of the list of signatures, adding: 'Yours all very depressed, Patrick Casement', followed by the other names. The result was startling. The medical director came storming into the ward, initially to me as he thought I had started all this (my name being the first on the list), saying: 'I will not tolerate my choice of decor being questioned.' He then turned to the whole ward and said: 'I am ordering every patient on this ward to have compulsory occupational therapy, so that you will not have time on your hands to be writing critical notes like this.'

The only experience of occupational therapy on the ward I had personally witnessed was seeing the master of an Oxford college (then also a patient on this ward) sitting in a corner, with his thick fingers like two bunches of bananas, struggling to make a basket

out of reeds. This task had been prescribed as apparently suitable
OT for him! At that time we did not hear anything of the much
more imaginative work that occupational therapists do elsewhere.

The patients' response to this new order was to state unanim-
ously that under no circumstances were they going to be sent to do
basket weaving. I don't know, how the patients actually dealt with
this as I was still a bed patient, but I heard that they had all 'gone
on strike' until the medical director took back this order.

The last that I heard about this medical director was some time
after I had been discharged. I returned with a friend to show where
I had been and, on meeting one of the staff I had got to know I
learned that the medical director had gone off sick with some kind
of breakdown shortly after I had left, from which he had not
returned. I was not surprised at this news.

Another bizarre aspect of my time in this hospital was that I
came to be used in somebody's research project. They seemed to be
wanting to show that mood might be changed if the body type is
changed. I had been reading about body types on my course, so I
knew I would initially have been classified as an ectomorph, those
regarded as 'the lean and hungry type'. The hospital therefore
insisted on making me eat extra food throughout my time there,
as well as giving me medication that kept me as a bed patient
for over three months. When I eventually left the hospital I was
seriously overweight, with a quite different body type called endo-
morph, the kind that is thought of as being 'fat and jolly'. But this
body change had done nothing whatsoever to stop me being
depressed and brooding about the value of life. I had certainly not
become jolly.

After I was discharged I was offered psychotherapy – my first
experience of this. I had already learned about the silent technique,
which used to be rationalized around an idea that the first things
said by a patient would be the most significant. As by a robot, I
was treated to that kind of silence. (I later discovered this therapist
was a psychoanalyst; that kind of psychoanalyst.) I refused to play
the game. My situation felt too dire to be playing games.

I was still extremely angry with the hospital, feeling they had
almost destroyed my life. This therapist was part of the hospital
staff, so my anger was being expressed at her through my silence.
Finally, after three completely silent sessions, during which neither
of us had said a single word, I told her that I regarded this as a
complete waste of time. By 'this' I meant the stalemate between her

and me, which was getting us nowhere. She just took me at my word, agreed with me and discharged me. She did nothing to enquire further about whether I still wished to receive some help, or even why I thought it a waste of time. She never even asked me why I had come into the hospital or why I had agreed to see her.

I left that hospital feeling that a successful suicide would be what they all deserved. What had they done except to make my life almost unbearable? But I also began to think that there must be better ways of treating patients. In the 17 weeks I had been an inpatient I had been allowed a total of 15 minutes alone with a doctor: ten minutes when I arrived and five at my discharge. For the rest of the time I was spoken to by the medical director only when he came on his ward rounds, always in the company of his junior doctors. The notion that somebody desperate enough to attempt suicide could be discharged without any further discussion or enquiry seemed extraordinary. I became determined to find something better than that.

After this I was required to see the late Dr Stewart Prince, then a Home Office consultant and Jungian analyst, to see if I was fit enough to resume my training. At the end of the consultation he told me that he preferred to believe *my* account of what had happened rather than the account he had received from the hospital. He saw no reason why I should not resume my Home Office training.

The otherness of the other

While still studying for the Home Office qualification, I had a chance to learn something important about the 'otherness' of the other. I had come to know a family strikingly different from my own and I had come to envy the children of this family for the freedom they had, from an early age, to make their own life decisions without their parents interfering or trying to control. This seemed to be how I wished my own family had been. But to my surprise one of the daughters had a breakdown and was admitted to a mental hospital.

As I had some experience of life in a mental hospital I was encouraged to visit her. There I was invited to meet the art therapist who had been treating this girl. 'Would I like to see some of her paintings?' I then saw that each painting had a muddled mess in the middle, from which – on every single painting – there were two parallel lines reaching out to the very edge. The art therapist suggested that the patient had been prematurely separated from her mother, made to be self-reliant before she was emotionally ready, as a result of which it seemed she was now reaching out to refind the lost umbilical cord.

Whether that was so or not I don't know. But the very idea was a revelation to me. Until then I had naively imagined that we all had to fight our way out of the clinging embrace of an umbilical cord if we were ever to achieve separation from our mothers. But here, it seemed, was somebody who had a completely opposite problem. Far from having to fight for her separateness she seemed to be trying to rejoin with her mother, to renegotiate her separation from her.

From this, I began to see the importance of realizing we cannot simply 'put ourselves in the shoes' of another person, for we are then likely to get some things very wrong. We may read others, in whatever situation, as it might have been for us had we been in their shoes. But each person has his or her own history, his or her own sensitivities, most of which will be quite different from how we ourselves have been or might have been. It was from this that I began to develop the notion of trial identification with the patient, whereby we can try to imagine how *that person* might experience whatever; not how *we* might. These are two very different experiences and represent a key issue in our attempts at understanding our patients. We are always confronted with the otherness of the other, though we may quite often fail to realize this as fully as we need to.

I also had the good fortune to marry someone from a family very different from my own. The members of her family were all real people, none of them having been caught in keeping up appearances, which had been such a feature in my own background. This chance to be with someone who was so truly herself helped me to continue my journey towards finding whatever was more real in myself. For so long this had been largely lost to me. And yet, all along, I had been trying to kick against the traces, trying to emerge, trying to find a way to be authentic, even amongst those who often seemed to be more concerned with fitting in and being accepted by others. No wonder I had been considered difficult.

So, by this strange and circuitous route, I became a probation officer. After three years of working in probation I changed to work as a family caseworker for the London Family Welfare

Association (known as the FWA), in an office that covered the East End of London. During my time there I trained to become a psychotherapist. In subsequent chapters I shall be describing some of that social work, from which I began to find further pointers to my subsequent understanding of psychoanalysis.

Psychoanalytic training

I have always felt it was a bonus not to have gone into therapy, or later into analysis, for any training purpose. I went into therapy because I needed it. My life was still in a confused and fragile state. Later, I went into analysis to deal with feeling a fraud as a therapist.

When I eventually applied to the London Institute of Psycho-Analysis for training, I was interviewed by Dr Clifford York and by Isobel Menzies (later Isobel Menzies Lyth). I made a point of telling each of them that my interest in psychoanalysis had originally grown out of my experience in the mental hospital. I needed them to know what I regarded as the worst about me. If I was accepted for the training, I wanted to know that nothing had been concealed from them. I wanted to be accepted as me, and not for any attempt at being what they might have been looking for.

Later, when I had qualified as a psychoanalyst, I wrote to Dr Stewart Prince to thank him for his help in extricating me from the tangle I had got into with the mental hospital, and to say I had since trained as a psychotherapist and then as a psychoanalyst. He wrote back saying that he was delighted and he wished to celebrate all of that by asking me out to dinner. He then raised a glass to my past, my present and my future. Some years later, when he died of a heart attack, I wrote to his widow who told me that, at the time of his death, he had my first book in his car. He had been reading this with the intention of writing a review of it for a Jungian journal.

Some reflections upon the journey so far

The progression of my life had certainly not been in the kind of straight line that my family might have preferred. It could look as if I had taken many detours, getting caught in a cul-de-sac or two on the way. But, looking back, I feel that every step of the journey came to play a significant part in leading me to where eventually I began to arrive.

I had experienced many pressures to become like other people. As well as being often rebellious I had also tried conforming. But I had never completely lost touch with the rebel in myself, which had helped me not to get totally lost in compliance. In the course of this journey I had begun to find my own voice. I had also found that I was strongly attracted to an open-minded approach to life, sensing and coming to value the otherness of the other, rather than still being caught into the constricting world of 'received truth' and dogma.

In parallel with this finding of my voice I also became able to speak in public. Up to that time I had been paralysed by stage fright so that I had been unable to speak in front of any large group. I had not even been able to ask a question at a lecture during my five years at university. I think this constriction was largely because until I had begun to find a mind of my own I could not yet speak with my own voice.

My way on, beyond training as a psychoanalyst, would lead me into exploring many of these matters further, especially in my clinical work. Whatever I had been discovering throughout that journey I have tried to share with others, in my teaching and my writing. But along the way I had to let go of much of my old thinking. This is surely what Harry Williams had meant when he spoke of an Easter Day that can lie beyond what (for me) I came to see as a necessary Good Friday. I now believe we cannot discover what lies beyond the brittle security of certainty until we can recognize how this is failing us. Perhaps only then can we become free to explore what lies beyond the known and the familiar.

Postscript

Throughout the time that I was being treated as a bed patient (over three months) I was so deeply medicated that I was barely able to register or remember any of the visits from my family, which fed further into my sense of isolation and abandonment at that time. Unfortunately, as my parents had grown up to believe that it was best not to speak of difficult things, my stay in that hospital was subsequently treated (as my mother's miscarriage had been) as if it had never happened, so I did not even know until many years afterwards that they had actually been regularly visiting me. It was later, in psychotherapy and psychoanalysis, that I began to find the freedom I needed to be fully open with someone and to face whatever needed to be faced.

Chapter 3

Finding a place for theory

> *And if I did not go in a rigorously straight line, with my system of going in a circle, at least I did not go in a circle, and that was something.*
>
> (Beckett, *Molloy* 1976: 85)[1]

Introduction

As I moved from my various training courses into social work, and later into psychotherapy and psychoanalysis, I encountered many clinical situations that seemed to illustrate theories I had been learning about. But I still had to find out how to apply them. Too often I was tempted to impose theory, making it seem to fit.

Anyone can slip into being driven by theory rather than being guided by an inner sense of what feels true. Of course, we aim not to be as absurd as I was being in the following example. But even in psychoanalysis it is possible for the practitioner to become absurd in different ways, applying theory too confidently. Analysts may feel proud of their skills of understanding while the patient may still not feel understood.

Applying theory straight from training

I shall never forget the first time I was asked to provide a court report as a student probation officer. I was on duty in court, along with my supervisor, when a man (I shall call him John Macmillan)

---

1 See Chapter 6: 111–12 for the context of this quotation.

was about to be sentenced for the latest of many offences. He was currently charged with minor theft. Standing in the dock he shouted at the magistrate: 'Give me a chance, guv. I've never had probation.' The magistrate remanded him in custody for two weeks, to allow time for a court report to be prepared. My supervisor allocated the case to me, my first case as a student probation officer.

I was given John's known details and previous convictions. He was aged 54 at the time and had been sentenced for 47 previous offences, the full list being provided. The first offence was for stealing blankets and this latest was for 'stealing a manhole cover valued at 12 shillings and sixpence'. Being straight out of college after my social studies course, which had included psychology and some reading of basic psychoanalytic theory, I was wondering about the possible symbolism of these offences. I determined to explore this when I met the client. I was given a note from my supervisor to allow me into Pentonville Prison, where John was being held in custody. My supervisor had written:

> The bearer of this note is Patrick Casement, a student probation officer under my supervision, who is required to provide a report on John Macmillan, at present being held in custody at Pentonville Prison.

The officer at the main gate of the prison took one look at this note and said: 'Casement, eh? We hanged one of you. Come in. There is surely room for another.'[2]

I was conducted to the cell where John Macmillan was being held. Outside his cell was a prison officer who was noisily turning the pages of *The Eagle*, a children's comic. The door was kept open throughout my time with John, making it even more difficult for me to conduct this, my first ever, social enquiry – feeling overheard by someone very likely to be critical of much that I had in mind to say to this prisoner.

The prison authorities had inexplicably chosen to see John as someone who might try to escape – he of all people! He had therefore been deprived of his trousers 'to make it more difficult for

---

2 He was referring to a distant relative of mine, Sir Roger Casement, who was hanged for treason in Pentonville Prison in 1916.

him to escape without being noticed'. So I had to interview this man while he was bizarrely sitting before me in his underpants. After some preliminaries, I got round to my grandiose idea of preparing a 'psychological profile' on this prisoner. Warming to my subject, I said to him: 'I see your first offence was stealing blankets. Were you in need of blankets at the time?' I felt primed by my training to enquire into this, as his first offence might have indicated some maternal deprivation. Perhaps he had lacked emotional warmth and/or security at home. John replied to my enquiry with well-deserved scorn: 'Don't be daft, gov. I used to sell them by the hundredweight.' I quickly abandoned any further idea of psychological profiling with this man.

Before the court hearing at which John was to be sentenced, I went to see the magistrate to discuss my recommendation. His name was Mr McGelligott, a name burned into my memory because of what followed. Trying to use the language of court to cover my shyness with this magistrate (the first I had ever had to speak to) I said: 'You asked me to see you after preparing my report on the man you remanded in custody two weeks ago; the man you might remember as an incorrigible rogue.' He replied: 'Maybe, but what is his name?' I, feeling flustered, said: 'McGelligott. No. I'm so sorry, sir. No. His name is *Macmillan*.' Fortunately the magistrate thought my slip of the tongue more funny than offensive.

I then explained that I had studied John Macmillan's history and found that, in the last 35 years, the longest time he had remained out of prison had been two weeks. 'So, if we are able to keep him out of prison for longer it might be some kind of progress.' Mr McGelligott made a two-year probation order, requiring John to report to me on a regular basis, at a frequency to be decided by me.

For the first three weeks John reported whenever I required him to. He was then apprehended again by the police, having stolen a large quantity of lead from a church roof. He had dragged this lead along Old Street, past the probation office where nobody noticed him, past the magistrates' court where nobody noticed him, to the door of the police station where he collapsed – unable to go any further. The police finally got the message. He was begging to be taken back into prison, the only place of security he had known during those many past years. He had stayed out for longer than two weeks, but was this progress?

I had a long way to go before I was to find the value in *discovering* connections between life and theory, rather than trying to apply theory by *making* connections. But I have found it useful to recall this misuse of theory as a caution against being too ready to apply theory to what I hear from patients.

Another absurd use of theory

Some years after this, when I had become a principal social worker, I had a consultation with my line manager on a matter affecting the running of the office. I was to discover that he had been deeply influenced by Kleinian thinking. I had been trying to explain an administrative matter for which I was seeking some practical help, bringing facts and figures in support of my request. Finally, instead of agreeing to any practical solution to the problem I had outlined, my manager chose to make an interpretation: 'You are projecting your impotence.' As I could not see how he had got to this, I challenged him: 'Where does *that* come from?' He replied: 'From the tingling in my fingers.' (Pause.) 'I always know that, when I feel a tingling in my fingers, the other person is projecting their impotence.'

I felt infuriated by this trite dismissing of the reality in my request and I no longer felt inclined to respond politely. I replied: 'Well that is most interesting. I thought the tingling I am now feeling in *my* fingers was because I have my elbow leaning on the hard arm of this chair. But, as you say, maybe you are projecting *your* impotence into *me*.' The end of this exchange was, finally, that my request for a practical solution to the problem was granted, but it had been hard work to get there.

This interchange left me with a useful suspicion of any theory that could be automatically applied. Another consequence was that I remained cautious about any use of the notion of *projective identification* (Klein 1946), until I was with a patient where this was the only way in which I could begin to understand what I was experiencing. That was in the example I have given before (Casement 1985: 77–80, 1991: 68–72) when I was feeling tears in myself that belonged much more clearly with the mother who had lost her two babies.[3] She had only been able to relate to me the details of those painful deaths, not showing any of her own feelings about them. I then came to understand that she was unconsciously provoking me

3 I return to this in Chapter 7.

to feel what she could not bear to feel, partly to get rid of her pain but also to communicate it in order to get some help with her own most painful feelings.

It had taken me a long time until then before I could accept the notion of projective identification as a real and useful concept. But it was worth all of that waiting, for me to have arrived at this understanding as clinically meaningful rather than routinely using it on the authority of others.

Pain that is beyond words

I came across another example of unspoken communication when a man came to see me for the first time. He said: 'You will not begin to understand me unless you realize that I suffered a severe environmental setback in my infancy.'

What this man was trying to tell me was that *his mother had died when he was two*. But what he was also indicating, in this stilted way of speaking, was that his feelings about his mother's death were still too painful for him to put into any experience-near words. It was only with jargon language, distant from what it was describing, that he was able to let me know at least the fact of that loss.

The historical fact of that traumatic death was being spoken of as something in his distant past. By contrast, his feelings about it were still too much for him to join up with, as yet. I think he was the kind of person that Winnicott (1974) referred to in 'Fear of breakdown' for whom some experiences can be too much, as an infant, for the mind to encompass. The details of the trauma are then registered in the mind while the feelings remain frozen, until some later time when it may become possible to join up with the feelings that had been too much to bear at the time.

Behaviour as communication

Long before I began to be interested in psychoanalytic matters I found myself discovering the importance of communication in behaviour. This was especially relevant in my work with juvenile delinquents, for these were often in the category that Winnicott regarded as pre-delinquent. He had the imaginative insight to recognize that some young people indicate, through their behaviour, particular needs that have not previously been met. He showed how the pre-delinquent will sometimes go in search of what has been missing, indicating this unconsciously and symbolically through stealing (Winnicott 1958: 10). What had been missing was sometimes in the area of affection and/or adequate recognition from a parent. Alternatively it might be the security of adequate firmness and containment that had been missing.[4] In his posthumously published paper, 'Delinquency as a sign of hope', Winnicott writes:

> At the moment of hope the child reaches out and steals an object. This is a compulsive act and the child does not know why he or she does it. Often the child feels mad because of having a compulsion to do something without knowing why.
>
> (Winnicott 1967: 93)

The case of Sam

While I was still a probation officer I was asked to do a social enquiry on a boy I will call Sam. He was 12 when I first met him. Sam had been found guilty of taking money from the milkman and had been remanded on bail for enquiries. From the record, I learned that he had been similarly charged about a year before, on which occasion he had been bound over not to offend again. I also noted that the probation officer who made the previous report had asked about pocket money. He had recorded: 'pocket money, sixpence a day'. (That would be something like 50p in today's currency.)

When I met the parents I learned that Sam was the eldest of four boys, aged 12 down to nearly six. During this enquiry I eventually returned to the matter of pocket money, asking whether this had stayed at sixpence a day. 'Yes. The boys all get the same. And I have a rule about pocket money. They have to spend it on the same day. They are not to save it.' As this seemed rather strange I asked about it. The father told me that his boys must never save their pocket money. You never know what they might then be spending it on.' He also tried to rationalize his rule by saying that he didn't want any child of his looking as if they came from a poor family. When other boys were buying sweets or ice creams after school he wanted his boys to be able to do just the same.

---

4 I return to this in Chapter 5.

The father explained his concern about being seen as poor. He had been disabled for some years due to a serious car accident. Money for the family had been short ever since. He also told me that if any of the boys needed money for something special they only had to ask. If he agreed he would let them have it. However, Sam had gone behind his back, having saved his pocket money to buy his mother a present on Mother's Day. The father had been furious about this, seeing it as 'deceit'. He had not seen how it could be important for Sam to find a present for his mother that he could pay for out of his own money, rather than having to ask his father to give him money for it. The father could only see that Sam had acted without his permission, outside his control.

The degree of control here worried me. Sam was one of four children in this family. How might he, and how might the others, develop within such a tight regime? I therefore thought it would be useful to have a reason to continue visiting this home, to see if the father could be helped to allow the children a more appropriate degree of autonomy according to their ages. I therefore recommended that Sam be put on probation, which would give me the right to visit the home regularly as well as seeing Sam on his own at the probation office. The father was furious about this. Sam had only stolen a few shillings. How dare I have him put on probation! Nevertheless, Sam was placed on probation despite the father's attempt at challenging my recommendation to the court. I arranged to see Sam on his own each week and I visited the home quite regularly too.

After about six months Sam was back in court, again charged with stealing money, this time from the dinner money at school. I went straight round to see the parents. Sam's father was beside himself. Not only had Sam been in court the day before but he had now run away from home. The father told me what had happened after the court hearing. He had summoned all four boys 'for a talking to' and reported having said to them: 'There is no place for a thief in this home.' The next morning Sam was nowhere to be seen, but there was a note on the table saying: 'You are right, Dad. There is no place for me in this home.'

During the two weeks before the next court hearing, Sam having been remanded on bail, I went to visit his home several times. I then learned that before this latest stealing Sam had been pestering his parents to let him get a job. He wanted to be a delivery boy, 'riding a bicycle with a big basket in front'.[5] He knew of some other boys his age who were allowed to do this, delivering for a local shop, but the father had absolutely insisted that Sam would never be allowed to ride a bicycle. He regarded cycles as too dangerous. Even though Sam had taught himself to ride on a friend's bicycle, he was not going to be allowed to ride any bicycle again.

I felt that this degree of protection probably reflected the father's anxiety about his own accident. He had been driving a car too fast for the conditions of the road. The car had got out of control and he ended up in a collision with another car. He seemed to think something like that would happen again. Sam might be just as careless as he had been, so he could not allow him to take that risk.

In the second week of remand I saw Sam's father again, Sam still having not appeared. The father was anxiously asking me where I thought Sam might be. I replied:

> If I know your boy, I think he is not going to get you into trouble with the court. He knows you have stood bail for him and he knows you would be made to pay a lot of money that you can't afford if he didn't appear in court for the next hearing. Instead, I think Sam is trying to get something across to you. Not only is he taking you at your word that 'there is no place for a thief in this house', I think he may also be trying to get you to see him in a different way.

I went on to say that Sam may have felt his father had been preventing him from having responsibility for his own money. It might be appropriate for him to have some money that he had earned, which could really be his own, rather than have money as an extension of the father's control – as with the pocket money that he was not allowed to save.

I also said I didn't know where Sam might be, but I thought it quite likely that he was trying to prove to his father that he could look after himself during these two weeks. I still felt confident he would turn up at the court, as required by the remand on bail. The father asked me how I thought Sam could be looking after himself.

---

5 The phallic symbolism of this did not escape my notice but I saw no reason to interpret it to the father.

He would have no money unless he stole some more. I replied that I didn't think Sam wanted to steal money. Much more important, I felt, was for Sam to be able to earn something that could be really his own achievement. My guess, I said, was that Sam had found somewhere to sleep. During the day I thought he might have found someone who would allow him to earn money by riding that 'bicycle with a big basket in front', which he had so much wanted to be allowed to do. The father thought this all most unlikely.

I then continued my round of home visits before returning to the probation office. When I got back I was greeted by a rather anxious senior probation officer. She had just had Sam's father demanding to see her. He was wanting to make a serious complaint against me, saying he was sure I was 'harbouring Sam'. I could not see how he could think that, but I was told the father had brought a note round to the office, written by Sam, which he said 'proved' I must be harbouring him. This note had been delivered by post just after I had been with the father. Sam had said: 'Don't worry Dad. I am looking after myself. I have found a job as a delivery boy so I can buy food. I will be in court on Friday.'

Fortunately, my senior was able to see how I had arrived at my guess. It was quite likely Sam was trying to demonstrate to his father that he needed to be treated as the age he was, not still protected as if he were much younger. It also looked as if he needed to be allowed an autonomy with money that had been denied him before. Sam did turn up at the court. His probation was extended and I continued to keep an eye on things. He was allowed to have a bicycle and he remained in the job he had found while he was missing.

When I was about to leave the Probation Service to work for the FWA I went round to see Sam's father for the last time. He was very proud of himself. Sam now had his own bike and only that day had had his first puncture. The father added: 'I knew I could have mended the puncture for him, which would not have taken long, but I let Sam work this out for himself.' As a result, Sam had taken the whole bike to pieces before he could find how to release the wheel in question. It had taken the whole afternoon, but at the end of this he had learned about every bit of the bike and how it worked.

The father saw this new step as his own discovery, that Sam could benefit from being allowed to do more things for himself. It was never mentioned, by him or by me, as something I had been trying to help the father to see. But I heard the father's account of the puncture-mending episode as his own way of saying 'Thank you' for the time we had spent in trying to understand Sam's needs and to see how they could be better met.

In the end it really did seem that Sam's stealing had been an unconscious attempt to win for himself a trust from his father that had been lacking. After this need had been recognized and had begun to be met, Sam did not continue to be a delinquent. I left feeling a quiet confidence that Sam would not re-offend.

This is just one story of many in which the communication was in the behaviour – and a key to understanding – where the young offender was unconsciously searching for some distress to be recognized, or some need to be met, symbolically expressing this through action. When that communication was adequately received and understood, the need to continue with that behaviour was reduced, often becoming redundant.

Communication through violent behaviour

Another probation enquiry concerned a boy who, along with others, had caused many thousands of pounds of damage in the park of a car sales showroom. The boys had gained access to this locked car park and found rows of new cars, each with the doors unlocked and the keys in the ignition. They had driven these cars around with increasing recklessness, bumping into other cars as if they were at a fairground. The damage had been appalling.

When I met the parents I was struck by the timid quietness of the father. He appeared to be a gentle soul, more feminine than masculine, and apparently lacking in aggression – as if he might be afraid of it. He and his wife were at a loss to understand how their son could have been involved in anything like this. I was told he was always a quiet boy, never getting into fights, always nice to people and never joining in with the rough lot at school.

I didn't yet have any idea why this costly outbreak of violent behaviour had happened, but I recommended a probation order so that I would have time to get to know this boy and his family, with the hope of understanding this better.

In the course of the son's time on probation I came to know more about the parents. I learned that the father had been in the Gurkhas. In fact he still had his Gurkha knife, which he sometimes sharpened just as he used to during the war. It was a knife for killing as well as for cutting a way through the jungle. When he showed it to me he became uneasy about keeping it in the house. Would I please take it away, to find a place of safety for it? He was now seeing his son in a new light, as perhaps capable of untold damage, even killing, which he had never before imagined possible.

I began to have a sense that this boy had grown up in a family where there was a marked split in relation to aggression. The father, once strongly identified with his Gurkha knife and all that went with it, seemed to have backed away from his own aggression. He now regarded any aggression as dangerous. At the same time, his continuing to sharpen the knife seemed to be a way of remaining connected with it. The atmosphere in the family was one in which all aggression had been taboo.

I felt the son may have been giving expression to some of the excitement in aggression that he could sense in his father, but which was always kept locked away just as the knife had been. So, along with others, the boy had reached beyond locked gates and become thrilled with the excitement he discovered in being destructive. I felt both father and son needed help with their aggression, to find it could become manageable and be kept within safe bounds, rather than disowned and repressed until it exploded.

Still needing to come to terms with my own aggression and my fear of it

There was an interesting sequel to this probation case, about which I continued to reflect and to learn. The father had got me to take away the Ghurkha knife, to find a safe place for it, but then I too didn't know what to do with it. For a long time I kept it in the door-pocket of my car until I realized that if a police officer ever caught sight of it there I could be charged with being in possession of an offensive weapon. I then took it into my rented flat where I put it out of reach on top of a wardrobe. (I was distancing myself from what this knife had come to represent for the father and then for me.) When I later vacated that flat I decided to leave the knife there, as if I had forgotten it, but my landlady found it and asked me to remove it. So I had the knife back in my possession, still not wanting to have it around me or knowing what to do with it.

I told the story of this knife to a colleague, a Jungian analyst, from whom I was then renting a consulting room. I discovered that he collected knives so the Ghurkha knife ended up with him – evidently being more at home with his aggression than I was at that time.

A knife in the consulting room

Years later I was supervising a student psychotherapist, who became pregnant during the course of her work with the case she brought for supervision. Her patient, as a child, had become seriously jealous towards his mother's next baby, whom he had experienced as displacing him when he was still very young. One day this patient came to a session with a knife. He said he was so angry with his therapist he wished to stab her in the stomach so that her baby would die. When the student reported this in supervision I felt a sense of horrified shock, parallel to what she had felt at the time.

The therapist naturally felt extremely threatened by this. When she had sufficiently recovered from the immediate shock, she used that session to acknowledge his anger towards her, for the interruption in his therapy that was going to follow in the later stages of her pregnancy. She also asked whether the patient felt safe with this knife, or did he feel he might actually use it? He wasn't sure he would not use it. She then said: 'Maybe it would be better if you let me have the knife.' The patient had agreed and it became easier for her and her patient to work with his phantasies about killing her baby without it coming so near to being enacted, quite literally, with the knife.

The patient became easier to contain. He had found somebody who seemed prepared to talk about his murderous feelings. But I was not sure to what extent the student therapist had allowed herself to remain engaged with these feelings, as still in the room with her even though they may now be hidden or denied. I asked her what had become of the knife, recalling my own difficulty with that issue those many years before. The student replied: 'It comes in quite handy in the kitchen. It's a very nice knife.'

I felt the actual knife should continue to be regarded as part of the therapy, kept somewhere safe but still related to the therapy, either in the consulting room or at least in the therapist's mind as belonging there, where it could stand more directly for the patient's hostility towards the therapist's baby. Having it converted into a useful kitchen knife might have helped the therapist to find a distance from the horrifying scene she had experienced in the consulting room, when her baby was being threatened. But subsequently I did what I could to help the therapist to engage with the continuing psychic reality between the patient and herself, still represented by the knife the patient had handed to her. He still needed her to work with his own hurt at being displaced, and his anger about this. In the end she managed this difficult case very well.

Insight for management

When I was working as a family social worker I was asked to see Miss A. In her present life Miss A had multiple medical problems. She was seriously diabetic. She also had scoliosis, a spinal deformity, one result of which was that she quite often felt unable to administer her insulin injection to herself, without which she could go into a coma. At such times she would take herself round to the nearest hospital, demanding to have the injection given to her. Then, if anyone showed a reluctance to take her at her word that she could not give this to herself, she would start screaming: 'Do you want to kill me?' Not infrequently this behaviour resulted in her being seen by someone from the psychiatric department of whichever hospital she had taken herself to. There, in each case, she was understandably diagnosed as paranoid.

Miss A had a most disturbing childhood history. She had been the first child born to an anxious mother, who had become seriously depressed after her birth. Early in Miss A's second year her mother was pregnant again, becoming even less available to this anxious child. According to the case notes, the mother had fallen down the stairs during this pregnancy, as a result of which Miss A had become even more clinging than she already was. The mother had died in childbirth and so had the baby.

My reading of this history was that Miss A may have come to believe, from various family comments, that she had been responsible for the death of her mother. It might also have seemed to her that it had been the intensity of her dependence on her mother which had caused her death, and that her jealousy might also have seemed to have killed the baby. She was now spreading her dependence across many people, as if no one would survive the full weight of it in a single relationship. With her dependency spread amongst many, she had set up a kind of insurance against loss. Some people might leave, one or two had even died in recent years, but while her dependency was spread in this way there would always be others to turn to.

This formulation made some sense with regard to the possible management of this case, but I decided definitely not to interpret any of this to Miss A. She had already been made to feel she had killed her mother. I could also see from the file that earlier attempts with this interpretation had only added to Miss A's unbearable sense of guilt, as if the previous social worker had been confirming her own conviction that she had been the cause of her mother's death. I therefore called a case conference of the people most involved in her continuing drama.

Over several years, Miss A had built up a network of some 12 or more social workers, who had each tried to deal with aspects of her multiple problems, and almost as many doctors or psychiatrists. Her drama had snowballed to such an extent that she had become a 'fat file' case in numerous hospitals, all this being very time consuming and costly.

At the case conference I suggested that I could be used as the principal worker in the care of Miss A, everyone else being invited to pass on to me whatever 'crisis' was brought to them during the week, dealing only with such medical states as might need immediate attention. I undertook to visit Miss A regularly every Monday at 2.0 pm (I still remember the time of those visits even after all these years), whether she was in crisis when I visited or not. I would then look at whatever problems had been reported to me during the week and try to understand what the underlying communication in each might be.

During the two years that I was seeing Miss A her claims upon the others, from whom she had previously been demanding so much attention, noticeably calmed down. She became containable with the regular contact she had from me. She was also beginning to find that her demands could after all be focused on one person without this either destroying me or driving me away.

However, Miss A managed to keep up a high level of drama. For instance, on one occasion I arrived for my usual visit to find pages of A4 plastered all over the door of her flat, a door that faced down a balcony where it could be seen by anyone walking towards the stairs at her end. She had written in huge letters:

KEEP OUT
EVERYONE HAS FAILED ME
(except Mr Casement)
I HAVE NO WAY OUT OF THIS
EXCEPT BY KILLING MYSELF

The proviso, directed at me, was in very small writing. The meaning of this notice, at 2.0 pm on a Monday, was very obvious. 'KEEP OUT' was clearly addressed to me, meaning 'COME IN'. I got the caretaker to open the door, through which Miss A appeared, screaming: 'Can't you even let me die in peace?'

I found that Miss A had spent the previous ten minutes trying to find a way of turning out the pilot light in her oven. Every time she tried to gas herself the oven had kept on lighting. She had not been able to get as far into her attempted suicide as she had wished.[6] Miss A knew that I would be there. She also knew I would not stay outside. I would come in. She knew we would then spend the time of my visit looking at the latest crisis that had brought her to make this suicide gesture.

I was later to regret that I did not oppose Miss A's plan to move to be near a friend in another borough. I knew her move would relieve me, passing the problems on to someone else. The gains made during those two years were then mostly lost and she became as uncontained in the new borough as she had been before I started working with her. I also think my acquiescence with her plans to move fed into her longstanding view of herself as too much for her mother, and therefore too much for anyone. For a time I had seen to it that I would not let her be too much for me, but in the end she had begun to be a burden I was glad to do without.

This experience subsequently led me to be very careful, in my analytic work, to do whatever is possible to survive the attacks and demands we are likely to get, especially when patients are testing us, driven by an inner conviction that they will be too much for anyone. I have always aimed to 'see it through' with a patient, seeking consultation to get support and help in surviving when necessary.

6 This was at a time when unlit gas could be fatal, before the introduction of North Sea gas.

In one instance, I came to think my continuing to be available to a patient (Mrs Y), regardless of how I was being treated, was possibly playing into some sadism towards me.[7] I felt it important that I set a clear limit to how much of this I would be prepared to tolerate. In the end I accepted the patient's own view that I seemed not to be able to help her any further, and gave her notice that I would not continue to be available. Much later this patient let me know that, however hurt she had been at the time when I stopped seeing her, she had subsequently come to realize that she had needed me to draw a line beyond which I would not let her go. That ending, she now knew, had been necessary.[8]

Missing a key point in an important enquiry

When I became principal of my FWA office, I had responsibility for supervising the casework staff and some of the students. On one occasion I heard of an anxious mother who had come to ask for advice about her 14-year-old boy. A neighbour was telling her that she was 'keeping him a baby' because she held his hand across the road every day, to and from school, even waiting to collect him in case he got out before she arrived. This mother was convinced this protection was necessary because the roads are dangerous. Her question to the student caseworker was: 'Am I right or is the neighbour right?' The student had been careful not to give advice, but she had not sufficiently understood the issues raised by this question. She had ended by saying: 'I suggest we talk about this some more next week.'

In supervision I expressed my concern about this. What did the dynamics seem to indicate here? Yes, the roads are dangerous – particularly if one has not yet learned to cope adequately with that danger. So, what if this mother were to take the advice being given by her neighbour? She had clearly infantilized this boy, continuing

---

7 Mrs Y, in agreeing to this material being published, made the following useful comment: 'In my rage at you, I was the child. (I don't lose my temper in normal circumstances.) I was expressing the rage I had never been allowed to express. What I didn't realize was that it may be a child's rage, but it gains immeasurably in force when expressed by an adult. Children are not being sadistic when they rage at their parents. It is only sadism, I believe, when one enjoys it.' I completely agree with this.

8 I return to this in Chapter 10.

to be his 'eyes and ears' for safety, rather than helping him to develop that function for himself. If she were to withdraw that protection before he had developed his own road sense, he could be very much at risk. Also, we needed to be aware of the possibility that, in her overprotection of her son, she might be indicating something of her own ambivalence towards him. She could be projecting some of her own hostility towards this dependent child onto the world around her, the cars being seen as carrying that projection, in addition to the danger of traffic in its own right. Therefore, if she were to withdraw that protection prematurely, she could be allowing her own aggression towards the boy to be enacted for her by the traffic. I therefore suggested that the student and this client should look carefully at the task ahead, for the mother to teach her son sufficient road sense before he be allowed to do the journey on his own.

Unfortunately we were not given another chance. The client, still looking for advice, took the only advice being offered – the neighbour's. Against her own judgement, she had told her son to go to school and back on his own. On *the very first day* he had been knocked down by a car. He very nearly died.

We always need to listen beyond the immediate surface of what is being told us, or is being asked of us. There is often some other communication that is being expressed, even though it might be concealed.

A further cautionary tale

Another student, this time in the probation office where I had previously worked, had gone round to see a depressed woman who had asked her to visit. The door was open at the arranged time but there was no answer when she knocked. The student had then called out but still got no answer. As she felt it would be wrong to enter uninvited she left, intending to write about the appointment not being kept. However, before any letter could be sent, news came to the probation office that this client had been found dead a few hours later. It seemed that she had taken an overdose just before the planned visit. We had a hard time supporting the student over this, confirming that she had behaved correctly. But for another time I felt we would need to be more ready to read the signs for what they might be indicating. Later, when working as a psychotherapist, I was glad to have had the chance to learn from that occasion.

Waiting for a patient to arrive[9]

I will not pretend that what I shall now describe is how I always spend the time waiting for a patient, but it is how I would usually spend it during difficult times in an analysis or therapy. When a patient was late, unless I had allowed something to divert my attention, I would always register this and think about it, though not necessarily comment on my thoughts when I saw the patient. I would keep the absence in mind and wonder about it. But when the lateness was uncharacteristic of the patient, I listened more specifically for what could be communicated by it.

One particular example comes to mind when a once-a-week patient had not turned up. She was usually either exactly on time or early. By five minutes into the session I was beginning to feel anxious. My mind went back to a year before, when this patient had been referred to me from a psychiatric hospital. She had been discharged after a suicide attempt. I then recalled that she had been more depressed in the previous week than at any time since she had started working with me.

By ten minutes into the session I was beginning to sense there could be something seriously wrong. I wondered about ringing my patient's flat, where she lived on her own. Of course she might be on her way, perhaps delayed by public transport, so it would not matter if I phoned when no one could answer. However, if she was still in her flat she might feel intruded upon by my ringing her there. I felt in a dilemma, but decided it was better to ring than to risk a suicide.

When I rang, the phone was continually engaged. I then asked the telephone exchange to check whether this was 'engaged speaking' or not. They reported that the phone was off the hook and there was no one speaking. I therefore asked the telephone engineers to connect me to the patient's phone (which in those days they were able to do) so that I could call out her name. After doing this for a while and getting no reply, I telephoned the GP to say I thought there was a risk of suicide here. He immediately went round to the patient's address and after getting help to gain entry found the patient unconscious after a serious overdose. In this instance, listening to my patient's absence had clearly helped to

9 This example is taken from Casement (2002b: 29–32).

save her life. There had been a very serious communication in her unusual absence and my 'starting the session without the patient' had helped me to pick this up.

Since then, when a patient has not come, I have often sat in my consulting room noticing whatever comes to mind, in thoughts or feelings or images, in relation to that absence. It has been surprising how often this has helped to alert my listening to some unspoken communication from a patient.

An invitation to collude

While I was still with the FWA we sometimes had visitors come to see us, interested to learn more about how we worked. During one of those visits we put on a live supervision, a member of my staff bringing some work I had not previously heard about, work with a couple she had been seeing.

I was told that my colleague had been offering marital therapy, husband and wife coming for joint sessions. Then the husband had stopped coming. For a time my colleague had been holding to her contract with the couple, being reluctant to see the wife on her own, writing to the couple to encourage them both to come back, to talk through what had been getting in the way of them coming together. After several failed appointments my colleague felt she had no choice but to see the wife on her own, especially as she was now saying she needed some particular help from her caseworker.

During the interview that was presented for this supervision, the wife had been putting pressure upon my colleague to help her with an application for divorce. The wife was saying she had given up on the marriage and was now wanting to divorce the husband. Therefore, as my colleague knew her situation quite intimately, the wife said it would help her case against her husband if she would give evidence in her divorce. Would she agree to this? My colleague was able to resist, saying she would like to see the wife again the following week. My colleague was now asking me what she should do.

As I was listening to this presentation a number of things stood out as unusual. My colleague knew I was most unlikely to be giving her advice on what she should do about her client and yet she was asking me to tell her. Her client also knew that her caseworker didn't usually give advice. So what was going on?

As we looked at this, it became clear that the wife was putting pressure on my colleague to enter into a collusion, to give evidence on her behalf even though the therapeutic contract had been with the couple. Also, why would the wife need to have support in making her case? She was an intelligent woman, well able to stand up for herself. So why was she behaving as if she could not do this on her own?

Gradually, we came to see that the pressure on this caseworker was probably motivated by the wife's continuing indecision about the marriage. Was she really as single-minded about proceeding to a divorce as she was claiming? Maybe she was wanting the case-worker to side with her against the marriage in order to silence her own uncertainty about ending it. Perhaps she didn't altogether wish to end it. We were then able to see that this wife might still be looking for help with the difficulties in her marriage, even though she was acting as if it was all over.[10]

After this discussion my colleague felt able to make a clearer stand on behalf of the marriage. Perhaps she had unwittingly begun to take sides with the wife and this could have been picked up by the husband. This may have been part of what he was communicating by staying away. Was there any point in him coming for these joint sessions if his wife was more readily heard than he was?

The caseworker felt able to write a letter to this couple that stated again her wish to be there for both of these clients, resisting the pressure on her to take sides. The husband then began to feel he was once more being taken into account in this marital work and he came back. The couple got through this difficult phase in their relationship and the marriage continued.

We might have missed the clues here if we had not been listening to the communication implicit in the wife's behaviour and in the husband's staying away, which seemed also to be reflected in some parallel process engaged in by the caseworker and myself in the supervision. It was only after we had sufficiently refocused our attention on the couple, not only on the wife's side of things, that the marital counselling began to be fruitful again.

---

10 I have sometimes thought of such talk of divorce as a kind of 'suicide threat' on behalf of a marriage. It can be as if there is a view being expressed in a marriage that things cannot go on as they are. If they cannot change then it must end – *unless someone can find a way to help things to change.*

Recognizing the past in the present

I remember an occasion when I recommended to members of my casework staff that it was time we began doing some family therapy, rather than just reading about it. We were, after all, working in an agency dedicated to working with families. This was at a time when family therapy was in its infancy, some people just beginning to try it out. None of us in my office had so far worked in this way, having rationalized our continuing delay on the grounds that we had not yet found a suitable family to whom we could offer this kind of therapy.

As I was supervising the casework staff I came across a family that seemed to be crying out to be seen together. I was supervising both the mother's caseworker and the caseworker seeing the teenage daughter. This is how I knew that there was also a much older daughter, who had trained in psychology, and a father who was mostly away at a university where he held a professorial chair.

What had alerted me to there being a shared problem here was that, for the past several years, the four members of this family had hardly ever been under the same roof. Usually it was the father who was absent. But whenever he came to visit, either one or both of the daughters would absent themselves until he had left. What was going on here? Why could they not be together?

I suggested we work towards an exploratory meeting with all four in this family. But before that I offered to see the father and the older daughter separately, so that each member of the family would have someone they had already seen before the proposed meeting. When I saw the father he told me that he had reluctantly agreed to come to this exploratory meeting with the family, 'but only as a hostile witness'. I didn't know what he meant by this, nor did he explain. He said he had been 'fed psychology up to the back teeth' by his elder daughter, so he would not tolerate any 'psychological stuff' from us. He insisted there must be 'no interpretations' or he would just walk out of the meeting and not come back.

We eventually met this family late on a Friday afternoon, to fit in with the father's schedule. We were all anxious and I, in addition, was feeling my hands were tied by the father's demand that none of us should interpret. The father then began attacking his wife until he had her in tears. Eventually, through her tears, she managed to say: 'The trouble is that you have never wanted either of our daughters – from the day they were born.' The father shouted back: 'Correction, from the day they were conceived.'

We then learned that the father had not wanted any children. The couple had been together for five years without children, seeming to get on all right except for the fact that the mother was desperate to start a family. In the end she had tricked her husband into making her pregnant by pretending still to be taking the pill when she was not. She had similarly tricked him into the second pregnancy. So the father was right when he corrected her, that it had been from the moment they had been conceived that he had resented the children.

At the end of this exchange the father had his children in tears, as well as his wife, and both of my colleagues by this time had become paralysed into silence. I too was beginning to wonder what I had initiated in setting up this exploratory meeting. At this stage it seemed to have been a complete disaster. So that it would not feed into the family conviction that they could never be together, I ended by saying:

> I think we have all found this meeting painful, but I believe that it would be a serious mistake to leave things like this. I therefore suggest we plan to meet again, all together as for today. In the meantime, it might be helpful if each of you meet with your individual social workers.

The father said that he at least would not be able to come. He was going back early on the Monday morning and he certainly would not be travelling down to London again for another such meeting as this. I therefore asked the father when we would need to meet so that he could still catch his train on the Monday. He said we would have to meet no later than 7.30 am, if he was to catch his early train (he knew the office hours were 9.0 am to 5.30 pm). I said I would open the office early so that we could meet at the time he mentioned, 7.30 am.

On my way home from this traumatic encounter I went through two phases of reaction to this father. I have two daughters of my own, and I was wondering what had so turned this man away from the chance of having the rich experience that is possible for a father with daughters. But, most powerfully I was feeling angry with him for having attacked his children before our eyes, stating so violently that he had never wanted either of them. How could this have come about?

So that I could let go of this stressful experience over the weekend I created an imaginary scenario that could, for the time being at least, seem to offer some explanation of this father's relationship to his wife and his children.

On the Monday the father arrived punctually for our meeting. I started by saying that I had left on the Friday feeling very angry with him because of what he had been saying in that meeting. I had therefore needed to make up a story about him so that I might have some way to make sense of what had happened, rather than remaining angry with him. I then explained to him that I had a further problem because he had told me that he would not tolerate any interpretation, or anything psychological, to be said about this. I then said:

> I am glad that I know absolutely nothing about you, or about your childhood, because I realize that the worst thing I could do would be to try being clever with things about your history. So, without knowing anything about you, I would like to tell you the story I had made up so that I would not spend the whole weekend feeling angry with you. I would like to tell you this story and then you can tell me where I have got this wrong.

So far, the father had not interrupted me. Feeling emboldened by that, I continued:

> The story I made up is that you were, I think, your mother's first child. I also suspect that your mother became pregnant much too quickly after your birth, so that (in this story) I think you may have begun to lose your mother before you had ever really had her.

The father still remained silent, so I went on:

> If there is any truth in this imaginary story, I think that what may have happened when you got married was that you were at last with a woman who could be there just for you, in a way that your mother may not have been. And, for a while, you did have her just for you.

> But when your wife managed to get a pregnancy out of you, I don't
> think you experienced that pregnancy as really being a child of yours.
> Instead, I think you may have experienced this as a repetition of your
> mother's pregnancy, as if you were losing your mother all over again
> to another baby.

The father's mouth had fallen open by this time and for a while he
remained quite speechless. After some time he said: 'How did you
know?' He then went on to tell me that everything I had said was
true. His mother was pregnant by the time he was only two months
old, and she gave birth to his first sister when he was 11 months.
A second sister was born about 18 months after that. So it was
true, he had experienced the births of his daughters as if they,
like his sisters, were 'stealing' from him the only woman who really
mattered to him.

We looked quite deeply into this in the time we had remaining
on that Monday morning. The father then asked that we see him
with his wife and daughters for several further meetings, which we
did. After just a few meetings these four people had become a
family, as if for the first time. They began to sense belonging to
each other and could begin to enjoy being together. The father
subsequently made a significant donation to the FWA, which is
a voluntary agency, saying his family had gained so much from
this experience that he wanted to help others to benefit from that
work too.

All of this grew out of those feelings stirred up by the scene we
had witnessed in the father's attack on his wife and daughters.
Even though my initial response had been to be caught into angry
criticism of this father, once I had recovered some analytical
curiosity about what had been happening, I began to listen further
to my response to what had been enacted before us.

Finding a limit to understanding

I was very influenced by that last experience. In particular it helped
me to realize that we often get into being critical of others when we
are losing sight of the need to understand. In my new clinical work
then as a psychotherapist, and in my continuing work as a social
worker, I was often able to turn a corner in my understanding of
people, whom I would otherwise have been wanting to criticize,

through recovering my analytic curiosity as to what might lie behind their difficult behaviour. But it does not always work like that.

Before ending this chapter I wish to share my experience with a man I shall call Mr C. It was while I was seeing him I had to learn that we cannot use any particular approach as if it is going to fit all cases – however useful we may have found this to be elsewhere.

In my capacity as social worker, I had been seeing a family with a really terrible-sounding marriage. The wife was being kept seriously short of money while struggling to look after several small children. The husband seemed to do nothing to help her, either practically or financially. I also learned that he was quite well off, but he continued to keep his wife very short of money. Meanwhile he remained engrossed with his shares, and how to make more money, seeming to be totally self-absorbed and uncaring of anyone but himself.

Wondering about this man's selfishness, but wanting to understand it, I had been trying to find out about his childhood for any clues that might help to explain his behaviour. But however much I looked for clues, I was finding nothing that threw light on any of this.

One day, when I was visiting the home, Mr C was yelling at those around him while doing absolutely nothing to help his overwrought wife with the children, or with anything that needed to be done in the flat. At the same time he was letting off steam about his stockbroker who, he said, had missed the chance of a lifetime for making a considerable amount of additional money for him. He had missed the optimum moment for selling shares before they had suddenly crashed in value. He became so excited while telling me about this that his false teeth fell into his lap. At this point my analytic curiosity became exhausted. I just found this man utterly despicable. I could not wait to leave the home, wishing that I would never have to meet him again.

I knew that Mrs C had, on a number of occasions, expressed similar feelings to me about her husband, so I was not surprised that I was responding to him in this way. But I continued to wonder about the dynamics here and what they might be indicating, thinking that I might still be able to make some sense of this.

Before I was next due to visit this family, I received a message to say that Mr C had continued to be highly excited about having lost that opportunity on the stock market. But when he was once more shouting at his stockbroker he had collapsed with a heart attack and died. I now had a completely different therapeutic task. How might Mrs C be now that her openly expressed wish, to be rid of her husband, had seemingly been granted? I went round to see her as soon as I could. To my surprise she was not upset by any of this. She felt as if God had taken care of her. She was at last free of this dreadful man. She would also be better taken care of now that he was dead. His money, for the first time, would be available to the family.

I still worried about the possibility that Mrs C might fall into depression, perhaps even a melancholic depression, or she might suffer guilt over her husband's death. But, though I visited her several times in the following months, she continued to be transformed by her release from this terrible husband. Even the children seemed to be happier now that there was no longer the constant fighting and tension in the family. I didn't see the family for long enough to know how lasting Mrs C's recovery was, but this experience did make me think more carefully about applying theory in any universal way. Perhaps some people really do not react as theory suggests to us that they might.

I know that much of what I have been describing here may be more directly of value to social workers or counsellors, but I believe that the matter of applying theory, and of listening to behaviour for what it communicates, is also a central issue in therapy and in psychoanalysis.

Chapter 4

Learning to say 'no'

> *Whosoever shall compel thee to go a mile,*
> *go with him twain.*
>
> (St Matthew 5: 41)

Introduction

One of the recurring problems I have encountered, not only in
social work but also in psychotherapy and psychoanalysis, has
been linked to my wish to be generous with my time and what I am
willing to do for those I am responsible for. But I will not pretend
that this is altogether born of altruism.

I think that many of us in the helping professions may be
motivated by a wish to provide a better experience for those less
fortunate than ourselves. Yet this may also be linked to our wish to
be liked, and to the pleasure it may give us in feeling good through
giving to others. Self-interest is found to be linked into much
of what we do. Over the years, I have come to believe that the
Achilles heel for many of us in social work, and probably also in
psychotherapy and psychoanalysis, can be found in the wish to be
the 'better parent'. Also, there are some schools of analysis where
the notion of 'corrective emotional experience' continues to be a
guiding light in the clinical practice.

A problem with that style of analysis or therapy, which aims to
provide curative experience, is that evidence can be provided to
suggest that patients appear to become better because of the 'good
experience'. Patients may begin to feel more confident, more positive about themselves, and in various ways appear to be flourish-
ing. Analysts or therapists can then congratulate themselves on the
benefits which seem to be growing out of this style of work, and it

cannot be denied that some benefits do become manifest. But from another point of view it has to be asked how radical and how lasting such changes are likely to be?

It took me a long time to learn the importance of saying 'no' in my work with clients and later with patients, learning to set limits when these are necessary. But this is often more productive than either doing too much for others, as can sometimes happen in social work, or in thinking that patients can benefit from being explicitly cared for by the analyst or therapist.

I, like many others, have wanted to be liked. It so happened that I had not been helped to get beyond this by my first therapist, who seemed to have the same problem. It was only when I got into analysis, with an analyst who did not have this problem, that I began to find my way beyond this.

The appeal of charismatic 'cure'

I had clearly benefited in some ways from the experience of being in relationships with people I admired. Likewise, in my national service and while working as a bricklayer's mate in Sheffield, I had found that people worked with me or for me much more willingly when they felt liked by me. Also, the experience of being in a special relationship may lend value to the person receiving this special attention. Yet this often does little to change the internal world of that person, or the more basic levels of self-image and self-esteem.

Self-esteem by association

During my time as a probation officer I was still attracted to the idea that people could be changed through association, through being treated better by someone new than they had been treated before. I can now see how superficial those changes probably were, compared to the kind of change that can become possible in psychotherapy or psychoanalysis. I have come to see that 'going the extra mile' may mean 'seeing it through with a patient', going through the worst with a patient and allowing oneself to be used to represent the worst in the patient's internal world, rather than trying to provide some superficially better experience.

I saw the problem of 'self-esteem by association' in my first analytic training case. This patient, from a poor working-class family, was someone who had a profound problem with self-esteem. She had married a professor and for a while she felt lifted up by association with him. She had become 'the professor's wife'. Gradually, however, she came to believe that it was only because of this reflected glory that she seemed to be treated well by others, whereas in herself she felt that this new esteem did not really belong to her. She felt inferior to her husband, still feeling herself to be a kind of nobody.

This patient left her husband and set up home with the plumber who had come to fix the bathroom. It was he who now felt lifted up by his association with the professor's wife, and she could thus feel superior to him. She then began to feel a somebody. However, we had a lot of work to do on her real sense of self before she could begin to find a value in herself, as compared to the former sense of value by association with, or in contrast to, others.

Some examples will illustrate my initial reluctance to move beyond the idea of cure by association. James had been placed on probation for a serious offence, for which he could have been sent to prison for at least two years. He had been making some progress in his life during this probation and had begun to take his responsibilities to his wife and child more seriously. He had then committed another offence, minor compared to the offence for which he had been placed on probation. This time he had stolen money from a cigarette machine. He was being held in custody in a Midlands town.

I felt that James should be allowed to continue the progress he had been making, but he might be sent to prison as he could still be sentenced for the original offence, this being a condition of the probation order. I therefore decided to attend the further court hearing to present my report in person. Because I was going to attend the court I had not sent in my report. Unfortunately, on the day before the court hearing I had some dental treatment that had gone wrong. An extraction had failed, with a root from the tooth escaping into an antrum cavity. I was told I must go immediately to a dental hospital to have this root removed. But I would then not be able to attend the court hearing, which could be a disaster for James.

I decided to postpone the hospital treatment and drove up to the Midlands the night before, to be there the following morning for the hearing. However, the next day I was in great pain, the wound in my jaw having become infected. I clearly looked quite ill, which was noticed by James, so I explained what had happened. I then made a personal statement in court, in support of my report, and James was allowed to remain on probation. As soon as I got back to London I was admitted to hospital and operated on the next day.

When I recovered from the anaesthetic I found James sitting at the foot of my bed. He had telephoned the probation office to ask how I was. Upon hearing that I was in hospital he had insisted on being told which one. When he arrived at the hospital, he ignored the nursing staff who tried to insist that he wait until visiting time if he was going to see me. Instead, he found his own way to the ward and just sat there, refusing to leave, until I came round. He had come to say 'Thank you' for my having gone to such lengths to save him from being sent to prison.

I give this example as it could seem that this experience had been an important one for James, and I believe it had been. He had a new sense of being taken seriously and clearly benefited from this. But it was not a helpful model for me to learn from. I came to feel it might be through such extraordinary steps, which we can take on behalf of a client, that we are able to get across something important to them. Even though this may be true, the question remains how far does that experience really go?

When we act in some obviously caring way we may come to be regarded as an exception; 'not like other people', not like the more usual people in authority for whom delinquents have often developed a deep distrust and dislike. But how much is changed in their *inner* world, in which authority is more generally regarded with suspicion? The good experience we provide can so readily be split off from the other's usual way of seeing the world, seen as not really relating to the world as they usually know it. I believe that we have much to learn in connection to this kind of issue.

Engaging with hostility

Robert was another person I saw as a probation officer, who was also in danger of being sent to prison if he failed to keep to the terms of his probation order. He stopped coming to see me, which was a breach of his order. He also moved his address without notifying me, another breach of that order. I therefore had to apply for a warrant for him to be brought back to court, and I did not have any grounds for asking the court to let his probation order continue. He was therefore sentenced for his original offence and sent to prison for six months.

When the magistrate pronounced sentence, Robert stood in the dock, glaring at me with eyes of utter hatred, and spat out towards me: 'You wait. When I get out I will ******* kill you.' This caused some consternation in the court, the clerk consulting with the magistrate to see if they should deal immediately with this threat, charging him with the further offence of making threats. Instead the magistrate told me I should report it immediately if this man ever made any further threat to me.

I thought Robert would probably assume that I would wash my hands of him as soon as I no longer had any official responsibility for him. But rather than leave things in that state, I wrote to him. I said: 'I know that you are very angry with me. I am therefore going to make arrangements to come and see you in prison, so we can talk this through face to face.' When I got to the prison I was expected by the prison officer at the gate. He had heard of me from Robert. As a result I was not going to be allowed to see him on my own. He might attack me. I was given a bodyguard who stood in the cell while I was seeing this man who had threatened to kill me.

Robert was amazed I had come to see him. Yes, he had been extremely angry, but he knew I was doing my duty. He also knew he had brought this on himself. What he could not understand was that I had taken the trouble to come and see him. That was not part of my duty, and why would anyone come to see him after he had made threats like that? In the end Robert was genuinely grateful I had gone to see him. Something did seem to have been achieved in that visit. But again, how lasting would it be? I don't know.

Saying 'no'

The first time I had come to see the positives that can come from saying 'no' was when I was a student probation officer in Coventry. Before seeing any clients, I had plenty of time to read the files of those cases I was to be responsible for. One of these was someone I shall call Bill. He had been placed on probation about 12 months before and there was another year to go. During this time he had several times been to see his probation officer, claiming he needed money for his rent. He had given various excuses for being in need of this. On each occasion the probation officer had handed out just enough to cover a week's rent, not wanting this man to be evicted.

Each time was to be the last, but this had not stopped Bill from turning up with further requests for money.

I could see it was highly likely that Bill would try the same thing with me. I therefore decided that the first thing I would do when I saw him was to go through the history of these requests for money. I would point out that this had not helped him to budget his money any better. In fact it looked as if this repeated handing over of rent money had allowed him to think there would always be an easy way out. I would warn him that if he allowed himself to run out of money again he would have to find a way out of this for himself. He could even get a job, there being plenty of work available in Coventry at the time.

My plan seemed sensible enough. What I had not catered for was Bill turning up the very next day with his familiar request for money already in place. He claimed that he had borrowed money from a friend who had suddenly asked for him to repay it. Having paid back his friend he now could not pay his rent. 'You will just have to bail me out again. Otherwise I will lose my digs.'

I stood firm on my decision not to repeat the easy way out allowed to Bill by the previous probation officer. I pointed out that other people were working in order to pay their rent, which was something he too could do. I would not give him more money as he now seemed to have the impression there would always be someone else to take over his debts. I added:

> If you are going to make more of your life than you are doing at the moment, you will have to learn that you have to be responsible for your own actions. This time it is going to be *you* who gets you out of this problem, and maybe another time you will think twice before allowing yourself to get into a similar problem again.

Bill was furious. He shouted at me that I was failing him as his probation officer. I was meant to help him. I was meant to sort out his problems for him. I was meant to keep him from further crime. Now, if he stole money to pay his rent, he would tell the magistrate that I had made him do that. I had refused to give him rent money when he needed it. I was no use as a probation officer. He would make sure the magistrates heard about this.

Bill stormed out of the office, my first case there. What had I done? Was I wrong to have taken a tough line with him, even without warning him that this is what I would do? What might he do next? It was two weeks before I heard from him again. When Bill came back to see me, it was mainly to tell me again how useless I had been. He said:

> You did nothing to help me. I lost my digs, which I said I would. I had to sleep on the floor in a friend's room. I then couldn't get benefit money as I didn't have a proper address. Even when I got a job I had to work a whole week before I could pay for new lodgings. You did nothing for me.

Some time later Bill was able to refer back to that interchange. He said that more than likely he would never have got off his backside to find a job if I had agreed to him being handed out 'easy money' yet again. Now he had a job, had a room he was paying for and more money to spend on himself than he'd had for years. 'I suppose I should thank you for that, really,' he said, with a slightly embarrassed smile.

That experience of standing firm, and caring enough about the outcome to take the anger and see it through, was something that helped me at other times when I needed to stand firm. There were many other occasions when I had to do something similar and I never regretted taking that harder way. Only then might some change begin to be possible, whereas the easy way in the past had often removed the incentive to move on.

Whose problem is it?

Some time later, while still a probation officer, I found I was not getting to sleep because I was worrying about a client. I had several times found accommodation for him but each time he had messed things up with his landlord or landlady, with the result that he kept on being given notice to leave. This had happened at least three times and now I was being told that I would have to find him yet more accommodation or he would become homeless.

It was understood that one of a probation officer's responsibilities was to help find accommodation when this was needed. But this was not easy, especially to find landlords who were prepared to take the risk of having this kind of person as a tenant. Who could I turn to now, having exhausted the contacts that I already knew?

When I thought about the anxiety I was feeling, it dawned upon me that the man on probation was probably sleeping well in his bed while I was awake worrying about him. Whose problem was this? I then realized I was picking up in my gut a sense of my own impotence in this situation. I could not keep on protecting this man from himself. No wonder I felt anxious when I was faced with something I could not do. I began to see that I should be facing this man with his own responsibility for finding accommodation. If I were to be trying to do this yet again I would be spending hours I didn't have just to get this man out of his own mess. He, on the other hand, could spend all day trying to find his next room if necessary.

Once I had recognized that this did not have to remain my problem, that I could hand it back to the man who had been creating the problem in the first place, I was able to sleep. Then, the next day, I clarified to this man that he would have to find his own room and maybe he would be more careful not to lose it this time. He spent a difficult two days looking for his next digs but he then became more careful about keeping to the conditions set by the landlord. He kept those digs for as long as I continued to see him.

Recognizing the perverse strength in a marriage

When I was working as a social worker I was asked to see a couple I shall call Mr and Mrs Smith. They had applied for help because they were having difficulties in their marriage. In the absence of suitable office space in the area, I was asked to see this couple at their home, which was a quite usual practice in social work. This was actually an advantage, as it happened.

The time with the couple started quite normally, with three chairs in a balanced triangle. But as the time passed the couple got increasingly agitated and excited. They even began shifting their chairs away from me, ending up with the husband standing over the wife, shouting and gesticulating, while I was being totally ignored. They did not leave any space for me to contribute. Eventually, from my position of being left completely outside of the action, which was now taking place at this new distance from where I was left sitting, I held up my hand and said very loudly over their shouting:

> I don't know if you want to make use of the time left to us, while I am still here, or not. Whether you do, or don't, I want you to know that I will be here for the remaining ten minutes and then I shall leave.

The couple continued to ignore my presence, so at the end of my time I said:

> I am not convinced that you have been wanting me to help with any of what has been going on between you. I am therefore not going to offer another time. If, however, you reach the point of knowing you do want some help with your marriage, you can get in touch with my office and I will offer you another time. I will leave it to you. I am now going. Goodbye.

I formed the impression that this couple had not really wanted help. Rather, I think they were demonstrating a perverse strength in their marriage, strong in the sense that it was the way it was and no one was going to be allowed to help change any of it. They would probably go on in this way, perhaps even boasting that they had asked for help but it hadn't been any good.

There was an interesting sequel to this. The following year I happened to be in the same district, at a function with local social workers, when I found myself talking to someone who worked in the area where I had been asked to see this couple. I briefly described my experience of trying to help someone there, outlining a bit of what I have described above. This social worker asked me if the couple had been called Smith.

It turned out that this social worker had been seeing Mr and Mrs Smith for the past six months, achieving no more than I had. He hadn't recognized the sense of their 'demonstrating the state of their relationship', even the perverse strength in it, defying anyone to be able to help with it. But hearing me describe their relationship in this way, this social worker felt he could see exactly what I meant by this. He wished he had found out before that I had seen them. It seems that some people really do not want to be helped, or to change.

The setting of limits: a belief in growth

I am including here two examples that have been previously published, as they relate so clearly to the theme of this chapter. The main issue here is that of two very different kinds of caring. There is an insecure kind of caring, which some people show when they are trying to prove their love for someone by keeping everything nice, and as far as possible without conflict. There is a quite different kind of caring that is shown when someone cares enough to engage with conflict, as when they are able to say 'no' to unreasonable demands, even if that 'no' (as in the examples already given) is met with anger, hate and accusations of not caring.

The first example is from my work with a child whom I was asked to see for what was described as 'remedial reading combined with a psychotherapeutic approach'. She was referred to me by her mother's analyst. I have described my work with this child in my second book, in a chapter called 'A child leads the way' (Casement 1990; 1991) I will describe here only that part of my work which relates to the theme of this chapter.

Joy had an older brother and a younger brother. She was six and a half when I first started seeing her. I learned from the referring analyst that the mother had found it very difficult to accept Joy being a daughter. The mother was described as being openly affectionate to the two boys but cold and rejecting towards Joy. I also heard that the mother could not bear being made to feel her hate for this child, when Joy was being hateful to her.[1] Therefore, instead of setting appropriate limits, and being 'there' for the tantrum rages that followed when she said 'no' to Joy, the mother indulged her. Joy was allowed to do whatever she wanted and to have whatever she wanted. She had become a seriously 'spoiled child'.

Not surprisingly, in my work with her, Joy tested me quite severely and she became very demanding with me too. When I said 'no' she would get angry. Indeed, she sometimes became so angry she would start kicking me or trying to bite or scratch me.

Fortunately, I had the mother's permission to be firm with Joy so she was prepared to hear her screaming, which sometimes she did. (I was seeing her in a room set aside in the family home.)

---

1 Winnicott was very clear that it is normal for a mother to hate her children at times. He says of this: 'A mother has to be able to tolerate hating her baby without doing anything about it. She cannot express it to him. . . . The most remarkable thing about a mother is her ability to be hurt so much by her baby and to hate so much without paying the child out, and her ability to wait for rewards that may or may not come at a later date' (1947: 202).

Then, on several occasions, I had to hold Joy through her rage until she quietened.

I discovered that I could hold Joy in such a way that she could not kick, scratch or bite me. At such moments she would then shout: 'Let go, let go!' Each time I calmly replied to this: 'I don't think you are ready to hold yourself yet, so I am going to hold you until you are ready to hold yourself.' Whenever this happened, and it happened several times during the first months of my seeing her, Joy would scream: 'Let go, let go', but each time with less determination. I would then say to her: 'I think you may be ready to hold yourself now. But if you are not, then I will hold you again.'

After this Joy would calm down, and each time we had been through this sequence she would become cooperative and begin to do something creative. After going through this several times she showed that she had begun to find a new kind of security with me. Whatever had seemed to be uncontrollable in her, which her mother could not manage, she felt I *could* manage. She was then able to take something from my holding of her that helped her to hold herself. Her view of herself was beginning to change, and with this her behaviour also changed.

Comment

I should perhaps clarify here that the above example is taken from a time before I had trained in psychoanalytic ways of working, when I was asked to work as a remedial teacher not as a therapist. It is also taken from a time when such physical holding of a child by a teacher, when deemed necessary, could be recognized as appropriate rather than suspicious. The point illustrated in this case is that there are times when limits are essential for containment. The same is true in psychoanalysis. But in analytic work we have to find ways of containing a patient through words, and through the nature of our attitude and presence in a session, without having to resort to physical measures.

Here is a further example, taken from a paper with the title I am using for this section (Casement 1969).

While I was with the FWA I came across many examples of insecure parenting. For instance, an insecure mother (whom I shall call Rita) had been trying to fend off her children's demands by giving them almost whatever they asked for. Even though she could not afford it, she would buy them expensive gifts – trying to show that she loved them. However, she had regularly spent money on presents even though she needed that money for paying the rent and other essential expenses. As a result she had got into serious debt and was about to be evicted because of the rent arrears.

I had been called in to see if I could prevent this family from becoming homeless. I therefore had to sort out Rita's debts. To that end, I had been able to obtain a small grant from a charity to clear some of what she owed in order to bring the rest of her debts to a point where she could deal with them herself through weekly payments. The situation thus came to be stabilized and for quite some time this mother was paying her own way and her debts were being reduced.

However, having been helped with her debts in a way that seemed so easy to her, Rita was tempted to get into further spending. She told me of an additional expense she was planning, claiming that this was so important to her I would have to get money from the charity, or she would get into more unmanageable debt. However, I stood firm and clarified to her that if she added again to her debts in the way she planned, she would have to deal with them herself. I would not again be providing her with any easy way out.

When I next visited Rita she was ready to challenge me. Despite what I had said, she had spent the money as she had planned, having borrowed money for this additional expense. She said I would therefore have to get that money for her, otherwise she would definitely be owing more money than she could manage to repay. She and her children might again be in danger of becoming homeless, and it would be my fault if they were evicted. I reminded her that I had made my position very clear to her. She would have to deal with this new debt herself. But I assured her that I would still visit her as her social worker.

Rita then became violently angry – throwing things at me. Nothing actually hit me, but the shoes and whatever else she found to throw were all flying past my head. It was a major crisis in my relationship with this very deprived mother. I therefore kept calm and simply repeated that I was still not going to change my mind, however angry she was with me. But, as I had said, I would continue to visit her as I knew that the time ahead was going to be difficult for her, especially now that she had this new debt to deal with.

Many months later, I noticed that Rita's old habit of trying to win 'peace at any price' with her children had changed. She was no longer buying them sweets and ice creams as a way of shutting them up whenever they were annoying her. Christmas had also come and gone without the excessive buying that had been her usual practice. This time she had only given the children what she could afford, rather than the extravagant presents they had usually had before. She had also managed to clear all of the recent debt from her extravagant spending earlier in the year.

Rita was feeling pride in her achievement and told me how she had managed her money during this year. She recalled the occasion I had said 'no' to her when she had demanded that I get more money to help with her new debt. She added:

> I then got very angry with you when you stuck to what you had said, that you would not pay for it. I even threw things at you, but that did not stop you coming to see me. In fact, all of that helped me to see you really cared.

She went on to say it had also helped her to realize that she could now say 'no' to her children, even when they shouted at her and said they hated her, just as she did to me. A bit later she said:

> I have a new sense of what loving means. It means being able to bear difficult times with the children, rather than always giving in to them in order not to have those bad times.

She ended by saying: 'I have now realized it was that kind of love they needed from me rather than more ice cream or sweets.'

When I went to say 'Goodbye' to Rita before leaving the FWA, she referred back to that time and said:

> I want you to know that if you had given in to me, when I was shouting and throwing things, it would not have helped. *I would then have been unable to believe anything that you said.* Instead, you kept to your word. I am so glad that you did.

Rita was an unusually insightful person. She had been able to see that she had been spending money on giving treats to her children when she was doubting her own capacity to love them when things were difficult. We too find that it requires a real caring for us to be there for the anger that can come at us from patients, especially when we do not fall into the temptation to appear to be good and caring – as in trying to be the better mother or better father than they seem to have had.

Chapter 5

Hate and containment[1]

What do I mean by hate?

Hate usually means some intense dislike. It can be rational, as in hating the unknown person who has broken into the family home and wrecked it. It can be irrational, as in a child hating spinach because of its colour. It can also be quite complicated, as in hating to be let down by someone we had trusted – when we may also be hating ourselves for having been taken in by someone who was not trustworthy.

The hate we feel can range from flash moments of hating to a hatred that may go on for a lifetime, or even for generations. Brief moments of hating can be such as when a child is not getting its own way. Ongoing hate may be what someone feels for a rival who is threatening an important relationship. And there can be that ongoing and usually irrational hatred that some have for a particular group of people, or for a particular nation or race.

We may hate some people for being *too much like* ourselves, for they may take attention away from us when we are wishing to be regarded as unique. Equally, we may hate other people for being *unlike* ourselves, their personal ways or customs being strange to us – upsetting our sense of what we regard as proper ways of behaving or being. We may, in particular, hate some people because we are seeing in them what we are not wanting to see in ourselves.

---

1 An earlier version of this paper was written for the 11th East European Psycho-analytical Summer School in Kiev, Ukraine, in June 2004.

What do I mean by containment?

When we are children we need to find that there are significant others, especially parents, who are able to manage what we are not yet able to manage in ourselves. This includes our anger, our destructiveness and our hate. If our parents are not able to provide this containment, we will probably go in search of this from others. If we do not find the containment we need from others, we are likely to grow up believing that there is something in us that might be too much for anyone.

There are two particular ways in which a child may develop in response to a failure to find adequate and reliable containment from others. A child may begin to get out of control, becoming increasingly difficult for anyone to manage. Here the unconscious search is for a firm containment that has not yet been found, a containment that might eventually be sufficient and able to manage what no one before seems to have been able to manage. Winnicott regarded such a child as being unconsciously still hopeful of finding what is needed.

A different outcome can be when a child gets into a false-self development, as a result of coming to feel that it alone should be responsible for containing what others seem not to be able to manage. What is meant here by 'false self' is the public mask that is sometimes developed by an insecure child, behind which it becomes able to hide what is most truly thought and felt. Instead of being more spontaneously difficult, the child becomes compliant, anxious to please and thus unnaturally good. This kind of child seems to have given up the hope of finding what has been most deeply needed from others. Such a child can become afraid that the parents might not survive unless they are constantly protected from anything in the child that it feels could be too much for them. The child is then, in its own mind, 'taking care' of the parents who may only appear to be taking care of the child.

Hate in relation to containment

When children feel hate, their hate is often experienced in much more total and concrete ways than most adults feel it. Children tend to swing between total love and total hate. This is what we adults can calmly call 'ambivalence'. But a child cannot be calm about this. The young child often feels it necessary to keep these two states of mind separate, because it cannot cope with the conflict between such opposite feelings being felt for the same person.

A great deal depends upon how a child's hate is understood and how it is received. One of the really difficult things for a mother is to find herself hated and treated as if she were a bad mother, when she is actually doing her best to be a good mother. For instance, as with Joy,[2] when a child is demanding to have its own way it will need a parent who knows when to say 'no'. But a child who is not getting what it wants will often get into a tantrum in order to break down the parent's attempts at firmness. With more shouting or screaming the parent may give in.

Such tantrum behaviour is often aimed specifically at making a parent feel bad, in order to increase the chances of getting what is being demanded. It can therefore take much more confidence for a mother to be able to hold on to her own love for a child at such a time, especially when she is being made to feel as if she were not loving the child. A mother's temptation to give in to her child's tantrums is often because she wishes to appear loving and to feel loving, whereas deep down she may be driven by a wish to shut out a sense of hating, either in herself or in the child – as with Rita.[3]

When parents or carers give in to a child's tantrums too readily, this can only ever be a hollow triumph for the child. Such children may come to rely upon repeatedly getting their own way as a kind of proof that they are loved. But this never works as it cannot substitute for the experience of being more profoundly loved, and being loved by a parent who is also able to bear being hated. Often, it is precisely this firmness and containment, when a parent is able to set limits, that is unconsciously looked for in tantrums and in other forms of difficult behaviour.

Unfortunately, instead of finding this necessary containment, a child may develop a growing sense that there seems to be something in its behaviour that the parent cannot cope with. Rather than a parent taking on and helping to contain what can begin to feel like an uncontrollable 'monster' in the child, a parent may seem to be trying to buy this off by giving in to the child's demands. Such a child is then deprived of feeling loved in the more

2 In Chapter 4.
3 In Chapter 4.

fundamental ways and deprived also of the security that goes with a firm but caring containment. It is then likely to feel that there really does seem to be something bad inside itself, maybe its own anger or hating, that seems to be too much even for the parent to be able to manage.

Some relevant theory

In this section I present some concepts I have found especially useful in clinical work when this is concerned with such issues as hate and containment. I am quoting Winnicott a fair bit here, but this is not because I am trying to apply his theories to clinical work. Rather it has been that, in following my patients, I have quite often been led back to Winnicott. The same has often also been true in relation to some writings of Bion.

First, I wish to return to Winnicott's concept of *the antisocial tendency* (see Chapter 1). As well as seeing this in relation to stealing, he saw it in relation to the destructiveness whereby a child may be in search of something missing: a containment that can allow for a fuller aliveness than had previously been safe to express.

The important thing about these forms of pre-delinquent behaviour is that there should be someone who can recognize the unconscious search; someone who can then go to meet what Winnicott calls 'the moment of hope' (1956: 309). By this, he means that a child (such as Sam in Chapter 3) needs to find someone who can recognize the unconscious search expressed in difficult behaviour, the unconscious hope being that this behaviour can be understood but also that there may be someone able to meet the need it expresses.

When this moment of hope is met, the need expressed in difficult, even hateful, behaviour can begin to be attended to and, because of this, the difficult behaviour may gradually become redundant. This is because the containment that had been missing, and which had been unconsciously looked for, is now being found.

However, when this moment of hope is not met, we can expect the difficult behaviour to escalate and become increasingly problematic. The unconscious search then begins to include others outside the home such as teachers and perhaps even policemen. But we may also find that the world outside the home begins to be punished for failing the pre-delinquent child, and this behaviour may then develop into true delinquency and sometimes serious criminality. The ultimate containment, if it is found at all, may eventually be found in some institution such as a hospital or prison, rather than in relation to a person.

Winnicott also reminds us that a growing child, and in particular an adolescent, needs to seek out *confrontation* with parents or other adults. Of this he says: 'Confrontation belongs to containment that is non-retaliatory, without vindictiveness, but having its own strength' (1971: 150). He warns us that if parents abdicate in response to the demands of a growing child, he or she arrives at a false maturity. Instead of becoming a mature adult, the adolescent is in danger of becoming a tyrant, expecting everyone to give way to him or her.

In 'The use of an object' Winnicott (1971) writes further about the *potentially creative aspects of destructiveness*. There he describes how a child may in phantasy[4] 'destroy' the object in the mind. What is then needed is for the external object (i.e. the real parents or the real analyst) to be able to survive that destruction. The parents or the analyst can then be found to have their own strength, rather than only that strength which, in phantasy, has been given to them by the child, or by the patient, to protect them from all that had been assumed would be too much for them to bear.

Some readers may, however, find the word 'object' strange in this context. When analysts speak of a patient's 'internal object', they are referring to a phantasy view that a person might have of another person, or indeed anything. Qualities are attributed to this object in the mind that reflect how we imagine the other to be, whom we then relate to in terms of these usually unspoken assumptions – just as I did with Mervyn Stockwood in Chapter 2. But the other person will always be, in some ways, different from this. In his paper 'Hate in the countertransference', Winnicott says:

> The analyst must be prepared to bear strain without expecting the patient to know anything about what he is doing, perhaps over a long period of time. To do this he must be easily aware of his own fear and hate. He is in the position of the mother of an infant unborn or newly born. Eventually, he ought to be

4 I continue to use this spelling to distinguish between unconscious phantasy, as in Isaacs (1948), and fantasy which can be a conscious imagining.

able to tell his patient what he has been through on the patient's behalf, but an analysis may never get as far as this.

(Winnicott 1947: 198)

I have also found Bion's description of *containment* very useful in the consulting room. In 'A theory of thinking' (1962) he makes it clear that it is important that a mother can take into herself the distress of her infant's state of mind. She needs to be able to bear being in touch with that which the infant cannot bear, so that the infant can eventually receive its frightened state of mind back – made more manageable by the mother being in touch with this and being able to bear it.

Bion also discusses the *failure to contain*. If a mother is not able to be in touch with her infant's unbearable state of mind, or if she too cannot bear it when she is in touch with it, then the infant does not receive back its state of mind made more manageable. Instead the infant's experience is made worse by the mother also having been unable to bear it. The infant then comes to experience a 'nameless dread' (Bion 1962). This dread may perhaps one day be named, but only when somebody else can bear being in touch with it.

It is not such a rare thing for patients to bring into the analytic relationship something of this *nameless dread*. The patient then needs the analyst to be able to bear the impact of what is being communicated and to be truly in touch with it. But patients may take a long time before it seems safe to believe that this containment by the analyst is real and not merely imagined.

A clinical example

Mr D's mother had conceived him in her mid-forties, an only child after an unplanned pregnancy. She had not wanted children, being preoccupied and stretched in her work. His father was by then an alcoholic who was seldom, if ever, available to support the mother in looking after the child. The father died when the patient was in his teens.

Mr D had grown up feeling afraid of making any demands upon his mother. However, when he had sometimes dared to take his distress to her, he had often found that she seemed to be unable to bear even that most natural need. As a result Mr D came to feel that he had become too much for his mother. So he tried to protect her from what he felt and, in particular, from any pressing needs that he had. He often hated her but pretended to love her. He felt likewise that his mother often pretended to love him whereas it felt to him that she really hated him. He came to imagine that she wished he had never been born.

To avoid the terrifying consequences of his own hate, and what he assumed to be hers, Mr D had learned to be a good and helpful child, even though this felt superficial and false. Mr D came to be afraid of being needy. He also came to be afraid of ever being critical of others, and he was especially terrified of his anger. He had come to feel this to be lethal.

In relation to this I had been told a key memory from when Mr D had been aged four. He remembered hating his parents most intensely when they were fighting. On one such occasion his parents had been fighting in another room and he had begun to think they were going to kill each other because the fighting sounded so bad. Then, when the fighting suddenly stopped, it was followed by a deathly silence. Mr D immediately thought that he had killed his parents by having hated them so intensely while they were fighting. In a panic, he had run to a neighbour to get help, saying his parents had both died. He remembered being severely punished by his parents for having involved someone else in what was going on in the home.

For a long time in this analysis, Mr D obsessively monitored my face each day when he came into the consulting room. He would also listen closely to my voice during a session for any signs that might indicate what my 'mood' might be. It soon became clear that he was almost always expecting I would be critical of him, rejecting of him, impatient, angry and much else. However warmly I was feeling towards him (though I was careful not to reassure him by telling him this), he never dared to believe I could feel well disposed towards him.

One day, during the third year of this analysis, Mr D suddenly exploded at me during a session, speaking to me (or at me) in a startling new way:

> I have come to realize you are completely useless as an analyst. I have gained absolutely nothing from this analysis. It has been a total waste of time. You are a rubbish analyst; to me at least. You might be of some use to other people, but you have not been of any use to me.

Mr D continued in this way for much of the session. He had never spoken to me in this kind of way, nor had I ever heard of him speaking to anyone else like this.

In the process of my internal supervision I noted (in my countertransference) two very different responses. I heard what Mr D was saying as a quite devastating attack upon me and I realized that I could easily feel seriously insulted. I might also find myself hating somebody who was so profoundly attacking my sense of myself as an analyst. But, alongside this, I also began to feel a sense of clinical optimism. This patient had spent most of his life relating to people through a false self. He seemed now to be speaking from somewhere in himself that felt much more real. Perhaps this could be the beginning of a breakthrough.

I remained silent for most of the time left in this session, taking this attack as it came and being careful not to defend myself. Shortly before the end I said to him:

> I must take very seriously what you are saying. It is possible I have been letting you down in the ways you say, so I must think on this very carefully. But, at the same time, I can't help noticing that you have been speaking to me in ways that I don't think you have ever felt able to speak to your mother or, as far as I know, to anyone else.

Mr D was silent for a while and then he replied: 'Yes, that is true.'

In the next session Mr D said he had felt a great sense of relief when I had allowed him to speak to me as he had. He had never imagined I would be able to take it, but I hadn't collapsed and I hadn't retaliated. His father would have collapsed. His mother would have retaliated.

I will now describe parts of two sessions from the next year in this analysis. These sessions were in a week when I was going to be away on the Thursday and Friday. The manifest content of these sessions revolved around a theme I shall call 'the dripping pipe'.

In one session, after some initial silence, Mr D began to tell me about a longstanding problem he had been having with his flat. There had been a dripping pipe keeping him awake at night but nothing had been done about it. Unfortunately, the landlord lived a long way off so he hadn't seen the problem for himself. He had only heard about it from the patient.

At last it had looked as if the problem was going to be attended to. A plumber was meant to come to see to it before the weekend, but the pipe was still dripping. He did not know whether the plumber just failed to turn up on Friday, or whether he had come but failed to see where the problem was. Mr D knew there was a window that was stuck, so if the plumber had tried to look out of the window he would not have been able to. It would then not have been possible for him to see where the problem was – or that there was still a problem.

Mr D had been in touch again with the landlord who said he would tell the plumber to come back. The patient then went silent, clearly waiting for me to say something. During this silence I was wondering what Mr D might be alluding to in the analysis; if there was more to this story than just an account of recent problems in his external world. I therefore settled for what I think of as 'unfocused playback' of the main theme in what he had been telling me and said:

> There seems to be a theme here around something that has been wrong for quite some time, still needing to be attended to, with nothing – or nothing effective – being done about it.

It seemed to me to be a rather lame response to what he was saying. But Mr D surprised me, even shocked me, when he took it up with some enthusiasm. 'Yes,' he said emphatically. 'I think it goes back to the "no" that I have needed you to understand.'

Mr D was referring back to a time in his late adolescence to which he had frequently returned during this analysis. He had been involved with a girlfriend I will call Sarah. They had talked of getting married. Then Sarah had gone on holiday without him, at a time when he could not leave his degree course to go with her. During the time she was away Mr D had found himself becoming so intensely jealous of Sarah that he had felt compelled to follow her to where she was on holiday. Some time after this, he had begun to feel what he described as a completely new kind of 'no' rising up inside him. He just knew that he would not be able to marry Sarah. He also knew he must say this new kind of 'no' to her. But instead, he just let the relationship fade away. Ever since then Mr D had been feeling bad that he had not been able to say the 'no' he had felt so deeply. That 'deep no', he told me, had made him feel real in himself, in a way he had never experienced before. But he had missed the chance of saying it.[5]

We had often before talked of this 'no' in relation to Sarah, I wanting to think we had got somewhere near to an understanding of it. For instance, we had explored the possibility that he had been alarmed at his feelings of jealousy, perhaps needing to protect himself from ever feeling such intense jealousy again. Or, another time, I had wondered whether it was the degree of his dependency upon another person that had seemed to be so dangerous, leading then to those feelings of jealousy. Or was it his need not to be defined by another person, as by Sarah beginning to believe they would be getting married? Or was it his need to say 'no' to commitment, etc. It had seemed to represent many important things, including the 'no' that a child needs to be able to express to a mother, and later to a father, in the process of becoming separate. But here Mr D was saying he thought the matter being spoken of as 'not dealt with' might refer back to this 'no'.

At first I felt almost annoyed to hear Mr D going back to this 'no' yet again. What was it about this that I had not been understanding? Why was he still going on about it? But I knew I would need to be very careful not to be influenced by my countertransference. Mr D continued:

I was not able to say to Sarah the 'no' from inside me because I felt that *it would have destroyed her*; leaving me alone, frightened and unbearably vulnerable. It seemed much safer for her to get the message gradually, that it was not going to work. But I had failed to say to her this 'no' from inside me. And this 'no' that I had found inside myself had felt like the only real experience I can remember.

---

5 Mr D, in approving this text for publication, made the following interesting observation: 'I remember that, prior to this episode, it had been on my mind for quite a while that I wanted you to understand about the two "nos"; I wanted you to understand what I meant by this, and I also wanted to understand it better for myself, with your help. But I felt that you couldn't and wouldn't understand, and therefore I had to keep it at the back of my mind, unsaid. It was only by your open interpretation of the "dripping pipe" (which then reminded me of the "no" that couldn't be expressed to Sarah which hadn't been understood by you) that I felt the door was opened for me to try again to explain it to you – even at the risk of annoying you.'

I now found myself recalling that Mr D had recently been making several references to Winnicott, saying that he felt *he* understood the early experiences of children in a way most other people seemed not to. So I was wondering how well was *I* understanding Mr D's childhood experiences? I then found myself associating to Mr D's fear of destroying Sarah, recalling what Winnicott had written about a child's need to 'destroy the object' – to be able to find that the object has survived being 'destroyed'.[6] I said:

> I think that a key here is in the thought that you might have destroyed Sarah with that deep down 'no', which you had found inside yourself. This reminds me of what Winnicott has said about this; that a person needs to be able to destroy the object in his or her mind, to find that the object has survived being destroyed.

(I would not normally use analytic jargon or theory in a session, but I felt it was an available way of addressing this issue with Mr D as I knew he had been reading on this.)

Mr D said: 'Yes, it *does* feel something like that.' Then, after thinking some more about it I replied:

> I believe you had not been able to risk destroying either your mother or your father, in your mind, as they may have seemed too fragile to be able risk that with them. I think this may have left you feeling that they would only survive if you were constantly protecting them from everything in yourself which you had come to believe would destroy them.

Mr D agreed with this and went into exploring this further. His father had felt like a collapsed man almost throughout his childhood. His mother's survival had also felt fragile to him as she had seemed only to have survived by retaliating. I had often heard of her explosive rages whenever he had dared to stand up to her, or in any way made demands upon her. He had always felt that he had to keep her propped up, so that she still appeared to survive as a mother. In fact, he came to believe he had kept her surviving by

---

6 I am referring again to 'The use of an object' in *Playing and Reality* (Winnicott 1971).

fitting in with her, by being good, by being compliant and by not standing up to her. We then came to a point in the session when I said:

> I think it has been very important that you have continued to stand up to me on the matter of this 'no'. I think you have needed to go on pointing out to me that I have not yet understood the most important things about this.

Mr D said: 'That's true. I don't think you have understood this yet.' I replied:

> So, it may be that you have had to find a way of saying 'no' to me, to stand up to me, and to risk not protecting me with any suggestion that I might have nearly understood this. It is now clear that I have not been understanding this in the way you have most needed me to. And I think you have had to dare saying this to me, even though you may have feared I would not be able to take it, or that I might retaliate in some way because you have been telling me this.

Mr D agreed. A bit later in the session, towards the end, I commented that we might now be able to see how relevant his opening thoughts had been. I added:

> There really has been something not dealt with, still needing attention. Something that the absent 'landlord' or the 'plumber' might assume to have been attended to. Now we have got back to this most central thing you have been trying so hard to get me to understand. (Pause.) Fortunately, you have dared to take whatever the risks seemed to be for you, in going back to this as often as might be necessary, until I might begin to understand it better.

After some further exploring of this, Mr D said: 'Strangely, I feel today that you have begun to understand.'

On the Wednesday, which was the last session of that week as I was going to be absent for the next two days, we got into the following sequence:

Mr D: I feel very hostile towards you today – very angry. I don't know why.

PC: There is a lot to be angry about.

Mr D: Yes. Why have you not understood this before? *And* you are going away.

PC: I can see that it really is very bad timing that I am going away just now.

Mr D: I had to protect mother and I kept on protecting her. Maybe I didn't have to. But it would have been such a waste of time and effort if it had not been necessary.

PC: I think there is a problem here as in 'sun dancing'.

I am here referring to something I had pointed out to Mr D before, using an analogy taken from anthropology. I had told him that there used to be a primitive society in the South Sea islands where, for generations, the community would get up early each morning to do 'sun dancing'. This was because they had come to realize that without the sun they would all die. So, each morning – before sunrise – they would get into sun dancing; and it never failed. The sun always came up over the horizon for another day. I had used this analogy as a way of trying to point out how Mr D had the unconscious phantasy that without his constant protection the impact of his inner reality would (he assumed) be too much for the other person to survive. The session continued:

PC: So much of your life has been given over to protecting the other person. You have come to see the other as always needing this protection from you, all of the time. But what if it has not been necessary? I can see that it could face you with a dreadful sense of so much time and effort having been wasted.

Mr D: Yes, and I've been protecting *you* all this time from that 'no'.

PC: So, you may now be wondering what if I haven't needed to be protected by you? That too could seem like such a waste of all that care and effort that you have shown towards me.

At this point, and for the rest of the session, Mr D was in tears – for the first time in this analysis. Finally, he managed to say: 'Some things can't be put into words.' I replied: 'Tears can sometimes communicate what words cannot say.'

I could not assume we had now dealt with this essential experience. At best we might only have begun to see it differently. But at least Mr D had found a way of prompting me to rethink what we had so often thought about before. This time we were able to reach a point where we could see the problem had come directly into the analytic relationship. I was now clearly the person who needed to be faced with his 'no'. He was now daring to say to me: 'No, you are *still* missing the point with this. You are *not* understanding this most essential thing.'

But with this beginning it became possible to revisit Mr D's central relationships and to see how, in different ways, they had each seemed to need to be protected by him from his 'no', which he had felt they would not survive.

Both Mr D's mother and father had seemed to be on the verge of not surviving. So how could he ever dare to test out that most natural and common phantasy of children, that the parents might seem to be vulnerable to what feels like omnipotence in the child? It is only when this phantasy can really be tested, with them (or the other person) surviving without collapse or retaliation, that it can become possible to find a new kind of relating where the world is real. Only then are the parents (or the other person) found to have a strength of their own, not just a strength that seems to be given through being protected from what is assumed to be too much for them.[7]

So in the analytic relationship Mr D was beginning to get more into this process of testing me. He had been saying 'no' to my attempts to understand, until eventually something of this inner-most 'no' could be brought into his relationship to me. The test I was being put through was to see whether I could recognize this: whether I could now attend to it, or might I continue to bypass what we most urgently needed to engage with? It seemed there was now a chance that the dripping pipe, and what it represented, might at last begin to be properly attended to.

---

7 Mr D also offered the following useful footnote to be inserted here. He said: 'Perhaps one of the consequences of not feeling free to destroy the object in phantasy is that the child will not find the reality that Winnicott talks about, and may therefore invest (ironically) much of his later life in phantasy, rather than in reality, like a Walter Mitty character.'

Chapter 6

Samuel Beckett's relationship to his mother tongue[1]

Introduction

The paper that I am republishing in this chapter had an interesting inception. It was prompted by a paper by Professor Christopher Ricks, on 'Beckett and Death', which I heard him give to the Applied Section of the British Psycho-Analytical Society in about 1980. I had never read any Beckett, but I found Ricks' paper so fascinating it inspired me to comment.

Professor Ricks had shown us that Beckett had needed the freedom he found in French before he could get past a writing block that had seriously troubled him while he had been trying to write in English. I therefore wondered if this move to another language might have reflected something of Beckett's relationship to his mother, English being his mother tongue. Then, when we heard (from Ricks) of the richness that was later revealed in Beckett's translation of his work from French into English, I sensed something of a parallel to what analysts often find when working with a patient's dream. It was as if the French had been like a *dream text*. The subsequent translation of this into English then seemed to be rather like the work of interpretation in an analysis, whereby the latent content that lies disguised beneath the manifest text of a dream may come to be revealed. Professor Ricks replied that he thought I was 'definitely on to something'. He suggested I look into it.

---

1 An earlier version of this chapter was published in *International Review of Psycho-Analysis* (Casement 1982a) and subsequently republished in *Transitional Objects and Potential Spaces: Literary Uses of D.W. Winnicott*, ed. P.Rudnytsky (1993: 229–245).

Eight or nine months later the BBC telephoned, my name having been given to them by Professor Ricks, who was preparing a programme on Beckett and wanted to include a contribution from me. Would I be willing to be interviewed? I had not taken up Ricks' suggestion to look into the ideas I had expressed during the discussion of his paper, so I was not at all sure. This felt like jumping in at the deep end but the challenge appealed to me. 'When is the programme due out?' I asked. It was to be in about three months' time. Having then agreed to be interviewed, I responded to the challenge by writing the paper that is now reproduced in this chapter. It was based on my reading of all the Beckett novels that were then in print (which did not include his novel *Company*) and the biography of Beckett by Deirdre Bair (1978).

Writing it also gave me an opportunity to put into words some of what I had gleaned from Winnicott about the importance of finding an emotional space, free from interference, within which it becomes possible to play with one's own thoughts and creativity. That space had been denied to Beckett. It really did seem that he only began to find this space when he had another language in which to express his previously unthinkable thoughts.

Beckett's writings abound with allusions to mothers and many of these allusions are contemptuous. In Deirdre Bair's extensive biography of Beckett (1978)[2] we also find frequent references to Beckett's complicated relationship with his mother, which appears to have continued to be full of conflict until she died. It would be simplistic to assume any direct biographical links between Beckett's relationship to his mother and the 'mother' in his writings. Equally, we should not assume that what we find in his writing is merely an expression of his internal relationship to his mother.

We might consider whether Beckett uses his writing, and in particular his writing in French, as a 'potential space' (Winnicott 1971) in which he is able to play out something of his own unresolved relationship to his mother alongside the 're-created' mother of his literary art. I do not here wish to be specific as to the interconnections between these three mother relationships (the internal, the external and the re-created). I prefer to let Beckett's text speak for itself, to let it pose questions that may invite further

---

2 All the undated page numbers in the text of this chapter belong to that biography (Bair 1978).

investigation, rather than to offer premature answers in the limited brief of this chapter. I should add that I have concentrated on Beckett's novels, not his plays.

Various reasons have been offered to explain Beckett's use of French as his primary literary language, adopted by him, so it is said, in order to escape the richness of the Irish speech rhythms. When asked about this, Beckett is said to have replied that it was easier to write in French 'without style' (p. 149).

When Herbert Blau (co-director of the San Francisco Acting Workshop) asked Beckett about this use of two languages, and suggested that by writing in French he was avoiding one part of himself, he replied that there were a few things about himself he didn't like and French had the right 'weakening effect' (p. 516).

When writing in French, Beckett took great care that no sign of his English origins should be evident. Apart from any question of literary style, there is evidence quoted in the biography which suggests that Beckett's careful elimination of any trace of his mother tongue may have expressed his need to escape from his turbulent relationship with his mother. He had spent the first 29 years of his life, until the break with his mother in 1937, trying to free himself from her hold upon him. She had bound him to her almost as much from afar as when in her presence. It seems that his mother's influence intruded into him so relentlessly that it began to make him ill. It also threatened to make him unable to write, a problem that Beckett referred to as his 'verbal constipation' (p. 94). He tried to suppress his problems. Perhaps he also tried to seek refuge in forgetting:

> Memories are killing. So you must not think of certain things, of those that are dear to you, or rather you must think of them, for if you don't there is the danger of finding them, in your mind, little by little. That is to say, you must think of them for a while, a good while, every day several times a day, until they sink forever in the mud. That's an order.
>
> (*The Expelled*, in *Four Novellas*: 33)

If this can be taken as an allusion to Beckett's own thinking, what was he trying to forget? What was he trying to avoid? From the biography we learn that from an early age Beckett and his mother were at loggerheads. Her stubborn wish to rule and overrule was equalled only by his determination not to be possessed by her (pp. 194, 259ff). From this backdrop to his adult life Beckett's sole ambition to be a writer emerged, an ambition that left no room for any other meaningful use of his life. But to become a writer he needed time, he needed room to breathe and the chance to wait upon his reluctant Muse (pp. 159ff). Against this were his mother's constant attempts to have him brought to heel, if possible to enter the family business like his elder brother, or at least to be settled (if necessary to be crushed) into a 'normal job' (pp. 154, 157, 214). For Beckett this would have been a fate worse than life, to be trapped forever in a place devoid of meaning, waiting for death – or perhaps for Godot.

Beckett was born in 1906. Of his childhood he offered the enig-matic comment: 'You might say I had a happy childhood . . . although I had little talent for happiness. . . . My father did not beat me, nor did my mother run away from home' (p. 14). In the biography we find that it was his mother who beat him and his father who was absent (pp. 15ff). The manner of this absence included his father's failure to stand up to this strong woman who used her explosive rages, as well as her clutch on the purse strings, to bend her children to her will (pp. 137, 250). His father, whom he loved, would secretly give him financial help beyond the allowance officially limited by his mother (p. 142). But this clandestine support, behind his mother's back to keep the peace, was not enough to rescue Beckett from her overriding influence.

Beckett paid a dear price for this kind of peace. Among his psychosomatic ailments he suffered from physical sensations of suffocation and choking (p. 136). He was frequently laid low by cysts and boils, which in their way would erupt with the suppressed venom of feelings for which he had not yet found other forms of expression. It was as if his mother's attempts to control him threatened to kill the only seed of meaning to his life that he had discovered. To survive at all he may at times have brooded upon her death. If so he was later able to express this venom, better than his boils could, by allowing the characters of his novels to speak out his own unthinkable thoughts: 'I'm looking for my mother to kill her, I should have thought of that a bit earlier, before being born' (*The Unnamable*: 395). Elsewhere he has Molloy wonder hopefully whether his mother might be 'already dead . . .? I mean enough to bury' (*Molloy*: 7).

After his father's death in 1933, Beckett's elder brother Frank was the only remaining ally in his embattled relationship with his mother. It was to Frank that he would cling for protection from the night terrors which began to plague him. He tried to avoid sleeping because he was afraid to dream (pp. 174–175). He seemed to be close to a nervous breakdown. He was becoming unable to find escape even in writing. Visits abroad always led ultimately back home. Drinking offered only temporary oblivion. On his blackest days, it is said, he would enclose himself in his room curled up in a foetal position, with face to the wall, allowing no one near him (p. 135).

However, he maintained such lifelines as he had in his intimate correspondence with Thomas McGreevy (pp. 159, 169) and in long discussions of his problems with the late Dr Geoffrey Thompson, his longstanding friend from Trinity College, Dublin (pp. 169–170).

It was Geoffrey Thompson, himself later to become a psycho-analyst, who recommended that Beckett should receive psycho-analytic treatment to relieve himself of these increasingly crippling ailments. Eventually he went to London where he was treated by Bion, who was then working at the Tavistock Clinic (pp. 177ff). This at least clarified the problem that Beckett was gripped by a fiercely ambivalent attachment to his mother. He could neither be with her nor could he, for any long period, keep himself away (p. 202). If analysis were to be able to release him from this pathological attachment to her, it would take longer than Beckett felt he could afford. Time as well as money were pressing issues for him. Is Beckett speaking of himself in *Molloy*?

> And of myself, all my life, I think I had been going to my mother, with the purpose of establishing our relations on a less precarious footing. And when I was with her, and often I succeeded, I left her without having done anything. And when I was no longer with her I was again on my way to her, hoping to do better the next time. And when I appeared to give up and busy myself with something else, or with nothing at all any more, in reality I was hatching my plans and seeking the way to her house.
>
> (*Molloy*: 87)

When after two years Beckett left his analysis, he told Bion that he was returning home to Dublin and that this was because he 'owed' so much of himself to his mother (p. 212). His attachment to her still remained complex and deep, and again there seem to be echoes of this in *Molloy*:

> I took her money, but I didn't come for that. My mother. I don't think too harshly of her. I know she did all she could not to have me, except of course the one thing, and if she never succeeded in getting me unstuck, it was that fate had ear-marked me for less compassionate sewers. But it was well-meant and that's enough for me. No it's not enough for me, but I give her credit, though she is my mother, for what she tried to do for me.
>
> (*Molloy*: 19)

Without his mother's money Beckett could not support himself while he remained unacknowledged by publishers and public alike. His first novel, *Murphy*, had not sold well and his second novel, *Watt*, was rejected 44 times before being accepted for publication. But with his mother's money he was still her captive. Either way his own ambivalence held him to her:

> For in me there have always been two fools, among others, one asking nothing better than to stay where he is and the other imagining that life might be slightly less horrible a little further on. So that I was never disappointed, so to speak, whatever I did, in this domain. And these inseparable fools I indulged turn about, that they might understand their foolishness.
>
> (*Molloy*: 48)

Elsewhere in *Molloy* we seem to be offered a further glimpse of Beckett's struggle to resist the lure of this fated, hated tie to his mother. Could anyone have held him back?

> Could a woman have stopped me as I swept towards my mother? Probably. Better still, was such an encounter possible, I mean between me and a woman? . . . I once rubbed up against one. I don't mean my mother. I did more than rub up against her. And if you don't mind we'll leave my mother out of this.
>
> (*Molloy*: 56)

Something occurred in the autumn of 1937 about which Beckett remains silent (p. 262). Its significance can be estimated from the fact that it enabled him to make the break with his mother that previously had seemed impossible. Again he went to France, this time to stay. As if to reinforce his need for separation, he turned to French and disowned his mother tongue. Simultaneously then, from this newfound distance, he could allow himself to be surprised by moments of unsuspected affection for his mother, which formerly he had kept hidden even from himself (pp. 280, 292ff). The two sets of feelings for her could be allowed to emerge and to coexist. In *Molloy* too we find:

> I called her Mag, when I had to call her something. And I called her Mag because for me, without my knowing why, the letter 'g' abolished the syllable Ma, and as it were spat on it, better than any other letter would have done. And at the same time I satisfied a deep and doubtless unacknowledged need, the need to have a Ma, that is a mother, and to proclaim it, audibly. For before you say mag, you say ma, inevitably. And da, in my part of the world, means father.
>
> (*Molloy*: 17)

Beckett here plays with the syllable 'Ma'. In his wish to hide the allusion to his mother he chooses the letter 'g' as 'better than any other', and it is better by far than 'y', which would instantly have revealed his mother by name, for her name was May.

In the same passage Beckett makes a passing reference to his father, as if to remind us that it was to the land and language of his Huguenot forefathers that he turned to escape from the siren call that had so frequently threatened to wreck him. Was he seeking there the paternal influence that his father, in life, had been unable to provide for him?

From his refuge in France, and in French, Beckett could begin to achieve the separateness and freedom from his mother's 'savage loving' (p. 263), which nothing else had made possible. He could then succeed through language where other attempts had failed.

In the Addenda to the novel *Watt*, his last novel for many years to be written directly in English, Beckett writes: 'The maddened prizeman . . . for all the good that frequent departures out of Ireland had done for him, he might just as well have stayed there' (*Watt*: 248f). But in *Molloy* we find the following:

Perhaps they haven't buried her yet. In any case I have her room. I sleep in her bed. I piss in her pot. I have taken her place. I must resemble her more and more. All I need now is a son. Perhaps I have one somewhere. But I think not. He would be old now, nearly as old as myself.

(Molloy: 7–8)

As in so much of Beckett, this piece of writing is filled with the *unlogical logic* that dreams are made of. If then we think of Beckett as the dreamer of this (and he was after all the writer of it), we may sense an unconscious hopefulness that some life could conceivably exist for him beyond the still-to-be-fathomed deep that lay ahead in the writing of the *Trilogy*; beyond the despair, the death, and the dying of it.

At the time of writing *Molloy* Beckett was already self-exiled in France and into French. By leaving his motherland and by finding another language he had found freedom enough to write. Yet strangely it was only upon his later return to that once abandoned mother tongue that he seems to have been able to lay to rest the suffocating influence on him of the mother who had so dominated his life.

Paradoxically too it was only when Beckett allowed his own language once again to resemble that of his mother that he could establish himself as separate from her, and most fully alive. I believe that here, even in the French, we can foresee the time when Beckett would find his own mother's son – the son who was that Self which for most of his life until then he had not been able to be.

In order to be able to write Beckett needed psychological space. Without this his creativity remained inhibited, as did his anger. In 1932 he had forlornly hoped that his Muse might erupt, that he might be able to excavate a poem 'one of these *dies diarrhoeae*' (p. 155). But, unable to vent his anger, and without the space he needed to become free in himself he seems to have turned in upon himself, and reached an impasse. The Unnamable says of himself:

I must have got embroiled in a kind of inverted spiral, I mean one the coils of which, instead of widening more and more, grew narrower and narrower and finally, given the kind of space in which I was supposed to evolve, would come to an end for lack of room. Faced then with the material impossibility of going any further I should no doubt have had to stop, unless of course I elected to set off again at once in the opposite direction, to unscrew myself as it were, after having screwed myself to a standstill.

(*The Unnamable*: 318–319)

As so often in his writing Beckett may be describing himself here by proxy. He had intimately known this strangulation of his creativity from which there was no way on but back. He could not write while there was no room for creative play, yet it was particularly in the ability to play with words and with language that his genius ultimately lay.

Let us examine this area of creativity *in statu nascendi*. To be free to enter into imaginative and creative play, a child needs a space between himself and the mother over which he has the autonomous rights of initiative. Given this space, which has been described by Winnicott (1958) as 'being alone in the presence of the mother', the child begins to explore the creative potential of this space. But this requires of the mother a sensitive reluctance to enter into this play area uninvited. If all goes well the playing child can put into it the products of his own imagination – being free to 'include' her into or out of his play.[3] He can use the mother's 'absent' presence or her 'present' absence as the warp and woof of his play. He can 'create' or 'uncreate' her at will, and thereby enjoy the magic of playing God and King over his own playrealm. The seeds of later creativity are sown and nurtured here. Of this Winnicott writes: 'It is in playing and only in playing that the individual child or adult is able to be creative and to use the whole personality, and it is only in being creative that the individual discovers the self' (1971: 54). So, to be deprived here is no simple deprivation, as it threatens the very essence of the child's creative potential. For Beckett, it was to be suffocated and choked in a central part of the self to the point of inwardly 'dying'. If the inner life be dead why should the body tarry so? In this light we may be able to understand Beckett's preoccupation with death as a wished-for state. He had near-

---

3 The notion of a child including the mother's presence 'into or out of' the play is not as contradictory as it might sound. It is only if the mother is intrusive that she might need to be excluded. If she remains a benign presence, alongside a child's playing, the child can use her presence in his playing or he can use her background presence in whatever way he chooses. He can even use it as an absence, which is also part of the play. Thus he might 'include her out' of his play.

glimpsed this and had longed for the other kind of dying. He has Malone say: 'I shall soon be quite dead at last in spite of all' (*Malone Dies*: 179).

Thus, when all is not well for a child, he may not be able to play because the potential play area has become a sterile or persecutory world. This may occur if the mother is too long absent, leaving the child too depressed or too preoccupied to be free to play. Or, nearer to Beckett's experience, the space may be so dominated and intruded upon as to be effectively unavailable to the child. Faced by this threat, a healthy child will resist his mother's invasion of his mental space to preserve his own essential aliveness. The less vital child may collapse into a capitulation to these pressures, and in this compliance he abandons the stirrings of his own creativity. This was Beckett's particular dilemma. He urgently had to fight back, to preserve from suffocation his creative ability, for to give in to these pressures would have been to succumb to the worst kind of death. He would have become dead in himself, entombed within a body that had the perverse audacity to go limping on through 'life' until a some-other-time death, which never seemed to come. It was touch and go who would come out on top, he or his mother's misguided determination to act in Beckett's assumed best interests: 'And when you cease to want, then life begins to ram her fish and chips down your gullet until you puke, and then the puke down your gullet until you puke the puke, and then the puked puke until you begin to like it' (*Watt*: 43).

At times it must have seemed much easier to capitulate, to give up any aspirations of becoming or being a writer. Without access to the necessary mental space within which to play with the tools of his genius, Beckett felt that he had screwed himself to a standstill.[4] He alludes to this sense of sterility in a playfully irreligious question in Molloy: 'What was God doing with himself before the creation?' (*Molloy*: 168).

Beckett had earlier begun to use his writing to prove that though it may be 'hard to kick against the pricks' it was not impossible, choosing the title of his first collection of stories to proclaim this, *More Pricks than Kicks*. He seems to use this book to give an account of his experience of purgatory in life. It is no accident that he gives the hero of this book the name Belacqua, which Beckett

4 I am using Beckett's own expression here, as elsewhere in this chapter.

takes straight out of Dante's *Purgatorio*. His opening words are: 'It was morning and Belacqua was stuck in the first of the canti in the moon. He was so bogged that he could move neither backward nor forward' (*More Pricks than Kicks*: 9).

In *Murphy*, which Beckett worked on from 1934 until it was accepted for publication in 1937, his hero begins and ends strapped into his rocking chair in which he escapes from the world by rocking himself into an orgasmic ecstasy:

> He sat in his chair in this way because it gave him pleasure! First it gave his body pleasure, it appeased his body. Then it set him free in his mind. For it was not until his body was appeased that he could come alive in his mind. . . . And life in his mind gave him pleasure, such pleasure that pleasure was not the word.
>
> (*Murphy*: 6)

In the mad patient, Mr Endon, Murphy meets another who sought escape from the world and has found it more successfully than he can: 'The relation between Mr Murphy and Mr Endon could not have been better summed up than by the former's sorrow at seeing himself in the latter's immunity from seeing anything but himself' (*Murphy*: 171). He envies Mr Endon's impenetrable insanity, the perfect mental state – beyond the reach of anyone. But, unable to forgo his own sanity, Murphy sees himself as a failure and returns to his room to rock himself into a final explosive oblivion (*Murphy*: 172ff).

Watt was Beckett's next novel, his first after leaving Ireland, written in France during the Second World War. He spoke of the writing of it as 'only a game, a means of staying sane, a way to keep my hand in' (p. 327).

In psychoanalysis we are familiar with the way in which a prolonged experience of an intrusive relationship can come to be internalized as a 'persecutory object'. This internal persecution, if succumbed to, can lead to mental illness, or it can be resisted and expelled. In Beckett's subsequent writing in French he increasingly developed this theme of expulsion and of spitting out all that belonged to this former invasion of him, and he calls one of his short stories 'The Expelled'.

Beckett's part in the war, in France, may also have given him relief from his internal battle and offered him some diversion and hope. Having joined the Resistance, he had a chance to deal with those other invaders and to survive. For this work he was later to receive the Croix de Guerre.

It was during the war that he began writing exclusively in French, and in this adopted language Beckett could start the purgation of his more hidden thoughts. He could thus begin to achieve in writing what his body had expressed symptomatically. L. Janvier, co-translator of *Watt*, said: 'the "dark he had struggled to keep under" was ultimately to become the source of his creative inspiration' (p. 351). This seems true throughout his writings. 'Look at Mammy. What rid me of her, in the end? I sometimes wonder. Perhaps they buried her alive, it wouldn't surprise me' (*Molloy*: 81). Now with the new freedom of his French, Beckett could be more hopeful and his words could vent the suppressed 'pus' of his feelings. 'The truth about me will boil forth at last' (*The Unnamable*: 352).

The former crippling ambivalence, which had so bound him to his mother, Beckett was now able to allow into the open:

> I forgive her for having jostled me a little in the first months and spoiled the only endurable, just endurable, period of my enormous history. And I also give her credit for not having done it again, thanks to me, or for having stopped in time, when she did. And if ever I'm reduced to looking for a meaning in my life, you never can tell, it's in that old mess I'll stick my nose to begin with.
>
> (*Molloy*: 19)

Later in the *Trilogy*, while Malone is eagerly anticipating death, he remarks: 'Let me say before I go any further that I forgive nobody. I wish them all an atrocious life and then the fires and ice of hell' (*Malone Dies*: 180).

With this new language Beckett could contemplate the circularity of his life and a possible exit from it's engulfment:

> And having heard, or more probably read somewhere in the days when I thought I would be well advised to educate myself, or amuse myself, or stupify myself, or kill time, that when a man in a forest thinks he's going forward in a straight line, in reality he is going in a circle, I did my best to go in a circle, hoping in this way to go in a straight line. For I stopped being

half-witted and became sly, when ever I took the trouble. . . .
And if I did not go in a rigorously straight line, with my system
of going in a circle, at least I did not go in a circle, and that
was something. And by going on doing this, day after day, and
night after night, I looked forward to getting out of the forest
some day.

(*Molloy*: 85)

Typically, here, Molloy is trying to find his way back to his mother.
We know that Beckett would often do this too. Equally we get the
impression that his relationship to his mother was circular and
encircling, as was the forest to Molloy. So maybe this could offer
to be for Beckett his way out of that maze. By doing his best to go
in a circle he could hope to be able to find something that would
not be a circle, 'and that would be something'. Thus, in the course
of this circular way of proceeding, Beckett found in France, and
later in French, the asylum that he looked for where at last he
could begin to be free in himself and in his writing.

How close Beckett may have felt he came to inner annihilation
we can perhaps judge from his description of near extinction in *The
Unnamable*:

Perhaps that's what I feel, an outside and an inside and me in
the middle, perhaps that's what I am, the thing that divides the
world in two, on the one side the outside, on the other the
inside . . . I'm in the middle. I'm the partition, I've two surfaces
and no thickness, perhaps that's what I feel, myself vibrating.
I'm the tympanum, on the one hand the mind, on the other the
world, I don't belong to either.

(*The Unnamable*: 386)

In 1950 Beckett's mother died, he having done what he could to
establish a more amicable relationship with her, but he took no
possessions of hers with him when he returned to France. He seems
to have preferred to remain unencumbered by further links or by
associative ties (p. 406).

I don't believe it was by chance that Beckett only began to
translate his French writings, as it were 'back' into English, after
his mother had died. It is as if a taboo upon his mother tongue
had been exorcized with her death. The process of translation
seems always to have been difficult, Beckett at first using a

translator to work with him. Later he began to translate his own work without this assistance. Of this process Seaver remarked, when co-translating *The End* with Beckett, 'what we ended up with was not a translation but a complete re-doing of the original. And yet, even though it was completely different, he was totally faithful to the French. It was a completely new creation' (p. 438). Bowles, co-translator of *Molloy*, similarly recalled that Beckett had stressed 'it shouldn't be merely translated; we should write a new book in the new language' (p. 439).

Why such care to create a new work upon his return to the once abandoned English? Of course the literary artist in Beckett required of him as much care to avoid traces of French style remaining in the English as in the reverse when working in French. But if, as the translator Janvier had intimated, there were dark elements of himself concealed in the French, then these would have had to be faced by Beckett when beginning to relinquish the defensive aspect of his initial flight from English. A further clue to this is indicated when Beckett turned on his artist friend Pierre Schneider who, I think, got too near to the truth for comfort when he had suggested that, for Beckett, writing in French was not so much an evasion as an attempt to state his darkest thoughts without actually confronting the inner sphere in which these thoughts were located (p. 516). When Beckett had begun writing in French this may well have been true. He had needed to deaden that in himself which had been deadening him. Maybe the work of translation included working at this delayed confrontation with himself.

If we compare the French and the English, some remarkable things emerge. The French is often bland whereas the English by comparison reveals a freshness and a new liveliness of language that seems absent in the original text. It has been suggested that Beckett may be a different person, or a different kind of writer in the two languages. Is it due to the years that had elapsed between the French and the English? Or does it reflect second thoughts about what he had written, not necessarily dependent upon the passage of time? May it be due to differences inherent in the two languages? All of these are possibilities, but I would like to explore yet another.

Let us go back to a passage already referred to and compare it with the French: 'The truth about me will boil forth at last, scalding, provided of course they don't start stuttering again' (*The Unnamable*: 352). In the French we find 'D'une seule coulée la vérité enfin sur moi me ravagera' (Les Editions de Minuit 1953: 127). Although this clearly suggests the ravage that such an outpouring of self-truth may entail, the French falls short of the allusive fullness of the English version. There we find that Beckett chooses the phrase 'will boil forth', which links immediately to his own years-long trouble with boils. He then moves on from 'boil forth' to 'scalding' (cf. the French 'la coulée'). But it would also be entirely like Beckett to sense here a play upon the phonetic link between 'scalding' and 'scolding', with its reminders of childhood correction from a hotly correcting parent. It is typical of his translation that this short sentence alone is able to evoke such a plethoral image of internal turmoil. We get a glimpse of long-suppressed feelings that half-hopefully look forward to a someday cathartic outpouring. Alongside this we can see the caution of habitual doubt that anything so fulsome could be achieved, with the pessimistic fear that instead it might result in nothing more than an impotent stuttering, which would continue to hold back just as violently as it strains to speak out.

We also find this filling out with associative nuances in my next example: 'Ah the old bitch, a nice dose she gave me, she and her lousy unconquerable genes. Bristling with boils ever since I was a brat, a fat lot of good that ever did me' (*Molloy*: 81). In the English we again find reference to boils, whereas in the French Beckett uses the word for 'pimples' ('boutons') instead of using 'furoncle' (boil) or 'clou' (carbuncle), either of which in the French would have been nearer to a description of his own troubles. This might be because Beckett chooses in the French to write 'away' from himself, and this would be consistent with what we know about his need to get away from his past while writing in French. It is only in translating this that Beckett allows more of himself to emerge into the English text.

We find a similar associative richness around his choice of the word 'dose', which is absent in the French: 'Ah elle me les a bien passées, la vache, ses indéfectibles saloperies de chromosomes. Que je sois hérissé de boutons, depuis l'âge le plus tendre, la belle affaire!' (Les Editions de Minuit 1951: 107). In the English there is a double entendre with Beckett's use of the English slang for 'VD', which is further supported by his use of the word 'lousy'. The French 'saloperies' with its allusion to 'salope' (trollop or slut) has a similar connotation, which Beckett typically extends in the translation. Having allowed us to sense the risks of contamination from too close an intimacy, this idea is then left to argue with the contrary thought that Molloy's troubles were inherited from his mother. We are thus left with the impression that either way there was no escape, for what was to be gained by avoiding contact if the fateful effects of being the son of your mother follow you still just as inevitably?

Before leaving this example we may wonder whether there might be an implied sarcastic reference to a 'dose' of medicine that is supposed to be good for you. Much of the unchangeable attitude of Beckett's mother toward him had been intended by her to be for his own good, as envisaged by her for him. A fat lot of good it had ever done Beckett to have had his mother's unconquerable good intentions for him or, for that matter, to have had his own boils bristling with the boiling of his own inner resentment against this. Either way there had seemed to be no winning or escape.

When Beckett did find release from what had bound him, it is much more than just the release of his suppressed resentment that follows. He discovers a new freedom of expression in his writing:

> Personally I have no bone to pick with graveyards, I take the air there willingly perhaps more willingly than elsewhere, when take the air I must. The smell of corpses, distinctly perceptible under those of grass and humus mingled, I do not find unpleasant.
>
> (*First Love*: 8; cf. Les Editions de Minuit 1970: 8)

> . . . a pair of venerable trees, more than venerable, dead, at either end of the bench. It was no doubt these trees one fine day, aripple with all their foliage, that had sown the idea of a bench, in someone's fancy.
>
> (*First Love*: 14; cf. Les Editions de Minuit 1970: 18)[5]

In these examples we find a playfulness that is absent in the original. I shall indicate only a part of what is evident here: (a) the associative allusion to a boneyard and 'I have no bone to pick with graveyards' is entirely absent in the French: ('Personellement je n'ai rien contre les cimetières, je m'y promène assez volontiers . . .

---

5 I am indebted to Professor Christopher Ricks for drawing my attention to the last two of these examples of Beckett's translation from the French.

quand je suis obligé de sortir'); (b) the play on the word 'must', sliding into its other English meaning as it leads on to 'the smell of corpses', is also absent in the French; (c) again a new fertility of thought is introduced when the trees 'one fine day, aripple with all their foliage . . . had sown the idea of a bench'. The French has only 'qui avaient suggéré . . . l'idée du banc'.

We can see a re-emergence in Beckett's translation of that capacity for self-expression and for creative play in writing, which I believe had been formerly inhibited and nearly destroyed.

Let us look at how Beckett refers to this in what he writes. For instance he has Malone think upon death as providing him at least with an opportunity for play: 'Now it is a game, I am going to play. I never knew how to play, till now. I longed to, but I knew it was impossible. And yet I often tried to' (*Malone Dies*: 180). Frequently, in the translating into English, we find Beckett playing with language, playing with words, bringing familiar words into new conjunctions, infusing a fresh vitality into metaphor, phrase and cliché which had been long dead without a proper burial. Beckett, who seems to have regarded himself as one who had 'never been properly born' (*Watt*: 248), breathes new life into them. Through this return to his mother tongue, which now he can use afresh as his own, Beckett is able to pass beyond his own unnamable death into a new aliveness.

In this escape from a half-life choked by his own mother tongue, via his sojourn in another land and another language, with his eventual 'translation' of himself 'back' into English, we find what Winnicott speaks of as the essential need to recover a capacity to play. Winnicott regarded this as a central part to any successful analysis and of this he says: 'The person we are trying to help needs a new experience in a specialized setting. The experience is one of a non-purposive state, as one might say a sort of ticking over of the unintegrated personality' (1971: 55). Compare this with Beckett writing in *Watt* where he says: 'Having oscillated all his life between the torments of a superficial loitering and the horrors of disinterested endeavour, he finds himself at last in a situation where to do nothing exclusively would be an act of the highest value, and significance' (*Watt*: 39). As if to echo this, Winnicott continues:

> There are patients who at times need the therapist to note the nonsense that belongs to the mental state of the individual at rest without the need even for the patient to communicate this

nonsense, that is to say, without the need for the patient to organize nonsense. Organized nonsense is already a defence, just as organized chaos is a denial of chaos.

(Winnicott 1971: 56)

Thus an opportunity for creative rest is missed if the therapist needs to find sense where nonsense is. This recalls how Beckett ends his novel *Watt*: 'No symbols where none intended' (*Watt*: 255).

So we come, like Beckett, full circle. It is as if the French text emerged as a dream does within the dreamer. The French seems to be thrown up from the unconscious, disguised and overdetermined, often hiding as much as it reveals and yet containing the seeds of that which can be later revealed by interpretation. Beckett then works on his own text in much the same associative way as occurs in the work on a dream in an analytic session. At first Beckett needed a translator to work with him, for there was much 'interpretive' work to be negotiated between the original text and the resultant richness of the new works brought finally to birth into English. Once freed from his mother, Beckett becomes 'mother' to himself and his return to English is much more than going back to what he had discarded. His circle does not bring him back to where he was before but to where before he couldn't be. So, with French en route, his formerly deadened self 'dies' as it were into life. On this Al Alvarez comments:

His [Beckett's] move into French is also part of that spirit of negation he has so persistently explored. It involves a cat's cradle of complications which Watt might have been proud of: an Irishman living in Paris, writing in French about Irishmen, then translating himself triumphantly back into English. And genuinely transforming himself in the process: through his translations from his own French he has emerged as a master of English prose, which he certainly was not when he wrote only in English. In other words, even his creativity begins with a refusal, a denial of everything he had been up until that moment at the beginning of middle age when he began to write in a foreign language.

(Alvarez 1973: 47)

I think it appropriate to end with words from Beckett himself, words he gave to Moran in the closing passage of *Molloy*:

I have spoken of a voice telling me things. I was getting to know it better now, to understand what it wanted. It did not use the words that Moran had been taught when he was little and that he in his turn had taught to his little one. So that at first I did not know what it wanted. But in the end I understood this language. I understood it, I understand it, all wrong perhaps. That is not what matters. It told me to write the report. Does this mean I am freer than I was? I do not know. I shall learn.

(*Molloy*: 176)

A sequel

This paper was first published in the *The Bulletin of the British Psycho-Analytical Society*, prior to my presenting it to the Applied Section of the British Psycho-Analytical Society. Amongst those who responded to it was Masud Khan. He wrote me a letter in which he said he had noticed my paper in *The Bulletin* and wished to discuss it with me, with a view to recommending it for publication in *La Nouvelle Revue de Psychanalyse*. 'Arrange a time with my secretary.' The letter was signed: 'Prince Masud Khan'.[6]

Flattered by this attention, I duly made an arrangement with Masud Khan's secretary. When I arrived I was kept waiting for about three-quarters of an hour.

Eventually, I was admitted to the presence and initially treated as if I were a scholar worthy of his attention and interest. However, when I explained how I had come to research and write this paper, having no prior knowledge of Beckett, his tone changed. He decided that he would need some changes to my paper before he could recommend it to the editors of *La Nouvelle Revue*. The issue of this journal, for which he wished to recommend it, was on the topic of 'Thinking'. He therefore suggested that I change the title to 'Beckett: his own unthinkable thoughts', which he had taken from my text: 'Change the title, and give all the quotes in the original French (with references) and give me this paper, in four copies, by three weeks today and I will recommend its publication in *La Nouvelle Revue*.'

---

6 Roger Willoughby (2004) gives details of Masud Khan's escalating narcissism which eventually led to this grandiose form of address.

Still under his spell, I spent every spare moment of the next three weeks in finding the French texts that related to my quotations. I then had to find my way through the French to find each and every quotation I had used. But that was only the beginning of my task. I then had to type in every quotation, accurately and with every accent, as instructed. But this was before computers were widely used, so I had to retype the entire text in order to include these quotations, using an old-fashioned typewriter.

I duly delivered to Masud Khan the text that he had required of me. Several weeks later I received a curt acknowledgement: 'Although I like your title' (which he had chosen) 'your paper does not sufficiently address the subject of this title. It therefore does not represent a work of sufficient scholarship for me to recommend it for publication in *Nouvelle Revue*.'

Chapter 7

Mourning and failure to mourn[1]

Introduction

It is my belief that bereavement counselling provides a crucial service to a vulnerable group of people at a time when the rest of their life can be at stake. How well, or how poorly, people cope with a bereavement may mark all of the life that remains to them. Some, if they have had no help, may never quite recover. The death of a significant person brings into sharp focus the relationship that had been, the good things and the bad. There is work to be done in connection to each.

What I describe here is mostly drawn from my work as a psychoanalyst. I cannot claim to have had the wide experience of working with the bereaved as bereavement counsellors will have had. However, in the course of seeing patients in psychotherapy and in psychoanalysis, I have encountered bereavements of many kinds. I have also had patients who have come to me because of a previous failure to mourn. I have had the opportunity to learn from these patients something of what has helped them in their mourning and what has not helped.

Death in life

Just as none of us can ultimately escape from our own death, we cannot be protected from the deaths of those around us: our parents,

1 An earlier version (Casement 2000) was published in *Fort Da*, the journal of the Northern Californian Society for Psychoanalytic Psychology 2: 20–32. It was originally prepared for the Westminster Bereavement Service, London. Also published in *Insikten* 5, 8: 10–15 (1999, Sweden).

our friends, sometimes a brother or a sister, and it can be the death of a child. I should add, there are also those who mourn for other kinds of losses, a mourning that is not always recognized by others; for example, those who have had an early hysterectomy or who have had a miscarriage. Even changing a job, and certainly retirement for some – or moving house, can lead to a mourning reaction.

At the time of a significant death it can feel as if life itself has come to an end, all that mattered in life having ceased to be. Yet life has to go on. It is therefore important that the bereaved redis-cover purpose in life, even without the person who more than any other may have represented that purpose. Life therefore has to be put together again, built upon different foundations, and for some that can seem to be an impossible task.

We naturally invest a great deal of ourselves in those we love, and in our relationship to them. So when such a person dies, it can feel as if we have also lost something of ourselves in them, even as if something of ourselves has died with them. It may seem as if we can never really come to life again apart from them.

How can we go on living when a part of us has died? That question lies at the heart of the process of mourning. Not only do we need to become able to get over the loss of that relationship, but also to receive back from it all that most fundamentally belongs to our selves and to our own aliveness. Without this we can remain *as dead*, and mourning may fail to become the constructive and recreative process that it needs to be. Life can be reduced to that of the walking dead, stuck in a state of meaningless pain, or of numb-ness in order not to feel that pain. It is to help people not to be lost in a half-life that we need to find ways to help them to mourn creatively towards this refinding of life.

Bereavement and identity

We are all, in some measure, the person we are because of our significant relationships. We are the child of those parents, we are the brother or sister of that sibling, the mother or the father of that child, and the life partner of our life partner. So, who are we when that person has died?

When a parent dies, for instance, we no longer have that parent to turn to as we may have done before, to seek comfort from or to be interested in us, to draw upon their experience of life and their counsel, or even sometimes to quarrel with and to argue with. We can miss that too. Also, when both parents have died, we may find that we are no longer protected as before from having to face our own mortality. Moreover, we realize that we are no longer somebody's child. We may find that we no longer have the home of childhood, literally or emotionally, in the parents who were that home. Siblings too can be extremely important, whether as the rivals they have sometimes been or as the companions of childhood with whom we have shared important stages in life.

The death of a spouse is for many people the most difficult adjustment to negotiate, particularly when children have left home or when there are no children. The constant presence of a life companion is then replaced by an absence that can seem relentless; and that absence can in its own way become a painful 'presence' which never quite goes away.

The death of a child is an excruciating experience. A nurse who had worked with the dying over many years wrote about the different kinds of death that nurses encounter.[2] With the old there could be some sense of relief, especially when the patient had been suffering. With younger patients it was always more difficult to make sense of their deaths, as they had not yet lived full lives. But she said that the most painful death, for most nurses, is the death of a child. And she was speaking of the death of someone else's child. How then might it be for parents to have their own child die? We can only imagine what that could be like for someone else. Mostly it will still remain beyond our imagination.

Those who have suffered the death of a child sometimes indicate that their pain is beyond description, and we need to understand that. They can never truly tell it to another person even though they may need to try. They are constantly reminded of what had been and what might have been. Other people's children can become a tormenting reminder. So may the home, now depleted of the life that had once been there. That emptiness is constantly present at first and can threaten to remain for ever.

Attempts at replacement and substitutes

In my clinical practice, I have probably had more experience of those who have lost children than I have had of other kinds of

2 Charles-Edwards (1983).

death. But much of what I have learned can be applied in some measure to other bereavements. It is not without significance that perhaps the most common feature I have encountered amongst the patients I have seen over the years is that of a child who died in the patient's childhood. Their parents had never quite recovered from that experience. In the family there had remained a sense of a dead child somewhere, perhaps never talked of, perhaps never even acknowledged. But there had been a shadow cast over the child-hood, even of a sibling not yet born. Often an attempt had been made to recover from that particular kind of loss by seeking comfort in the birth of another child as soon as possible, to fill the unbearable gap. It is then the 'replacement' child who may absorb the distress of the family. But he or she can never successfully be that replacement.

Mourning has to do with being able to let go and being able to carry on with life afresh. It is not about replacement. Nor is it about creating shrines to the dead, as one couple had to realize when they were planning to buy a family grave for their dead child so that they could eventually be reunited in the one grave. That might be a solution for some but it was not for this couple. For them it was important (even though harder) to plan a more separate burial as a focus for their grief, leaving their child where they could not so literally join him. To be able to achieve that different resting place they had to be able to see that in due course they would need to be more rooted in life, hopefully with other children, with a home amongst the living, rather than be emo-tionally joined with their dead child in his grave. But to achieve that step they needed to be given time, not to be rushed, and they needed to be able to begin to see that a day might come when their lives could be focused not on the death of their child but elsewhere.

Listening to the bereaved

Some time ago I had a patient who did not have any children. Her most recent pregnancy had also failed, this time when her baby died during premature labour after medical procedures to test for abnormalities. Knowing her, I had some idea of what that loss might mean to her. She had already had several miscarriages, all of them very early, and she had tried for years to hold a pregnancy successfully. At last it seemed she had been able to manage that.

But now her child-bearing years were passing her by. This could have been her last chance to have a child.

Friends had tried to be of assistance to this woman but she did not find them helpful. Some tried to divert her with talk about other things, but all she could focus on was her baby who had died. Others had tried to help her by saying that they knew 'just how she felt', particularly those who had also had a miscarriage. But their trying to put themselves into her shoes was failing her, because that was too exactly what they were doing. It was their own experience that they were talking about and she needed to be able to talk to somebody about hers.

For the woman I am writing of, it was yet more difficult because she felt great guilt that she had not been able to keep her baby safe, and that she had allowed a procedure which indirectly ended her healthy baby's life. She shared this sense of guilt with her husband but felt unable to talk to him about it for fear that he would feel blamed by her, as she blamed herself. So she talked to me.

When this patient was with me for the first few sessions after she had lost her baby, I said very little. For most of the time she just poured out her pain. She wept so bitterly I was tempted to try to quieten her, or in some way lower the intensity of her distress. But I knew that she was expressing her own emotional reality of that time, and I knew she needed me to be able to bear being in touch with it. I also knew that, had I in any way tried to divert her from her distress or tried to lessen the intensity of her crying, it would almost certainly have been more in order to protect myself. It was almost unbearable to be faced with this degree of distress.

Personally, I felt completely helpless. I could say nothing to alter what she was going through. But professionally I know it is the pain which cannot be shared that remains most unbearable. If no other person can bear it, how can the bereaved person bear it alone? It could seem as if the bereaved person's pain is experienced by others as dangerous, especially if they manoeuvre to protect themselves from it. So I have learned to stay with what patients bring me of their pain and to let their pain reach me. I believe that if they are eventually to become able to bear it on their own, it helps if they have had the experience of being with somebody who is able to bear it with them.

To this patient, after a long time of my listening to her in silence, I said: 'I know that there is nothing I can say to make any of this feel less devastating for you. The only thing I feel I can do is to be here for you in your distress, and to go through it with you, for as long as may be necessary.' She replied: 'I know you can't take this away from me; in fact I would not want you to take it away. But it helps that you are there. It also helps that I can see in your face that you are prepared to feel my pain along with me.' A bit later she added: 'Your eyes have said to me all that matters.'

I had not tried to hide from her the fact that there were tears forming in my eyes too while she had been crying so desperately, but I had also been careful not to draw attention to this by any movement to wipe a tear away. It was her pain that should remain the sole focus of my attention, not what this might be doing to me.

What I have tried to describe here, of my way of beginning to help this bereaved mother, is a very simple example of trying to go through the unbearable with somebody in acute distress. It is not meant to be an example of how to do it. There can be no right way for this kind of therapeutic endeavour. We each have to learn to use ourselves in whatever way is natural and honest, and as far as possible to remain non-defensive. We will find that people are very different. However many bereaved people we have seen, we still have to learn from each new person what helps and what does not help.

Some examples of pathological mourning or failures to mourn

Mourning can fail for very different reasons. Some people may so defend themselves from the impact of a death that they carry within themselves feelings which threaten to overwhelm them, so they keep these feelings severely in check whilst still being unconsciously affected by them. Others may fail to mourn even though they may grieve greatly. This is because they fight never to let go of the lost relationship, so they are never able to move on from their loss to any kind of life beyond that death.

Miss W was in weekly psychotherapy with me when her mother died. Outwardly she coped too well with this death. Six months later she went to her yoga class and in the course of this she went into a sudden psychotic breakdown, as a result of which she was hospitalized. I have described this sequence in some detail in my first book (Casement 1985: 147–153; 1991: 123–127), but I hope that it will bear some repetition in this present context.

When I saw Miss W in the mental hospital, she was still psychotic and talked in bursts of words, not all of which were intelligible or coherent. But from this staccato communication I was able to pick up the following:

> Yoga. . . (Pause) Falling . . . everything falling . . . no stopping. (Pause) Being held . . . Yoga teacher holding me . . . (Pause) In pieces . . . They wrote to me . . . the yoga class . . . (Pause) Six months since . . . hadn't been since . . . I'm falling again . . . I can't stop the falling.

In the course of this strange communication it began to dawn on me that Miss W had managed to fend off the emotional impact of her mother's death until she had visited her yoga class for the first time since her mother's death. It seemed that she had suddenly become a child with no mother, falling into an intense regression which seemed to represent the experience of no longer having a mother to hold her through her emotional pain. After a while I said to her:

> I get the impression that this was your first visit to the yoga class since your mother died. I think you then came to realize that the last time you had been there *you still had a mother*. So, you may have suddenly become aware of yourself as a child with no mother, leaving you with the sense that you were falling, with no one there to stop the falling.

After saying this to her she began to quieten. And then, after a few minutes of being silent, she replied:

> The falling has stopped now . . . You are there to hold me together . . . You have stopped the falling.

There was, of course, much more work to be done in helping her to mourn. But at least the process had begun and she could find that it could begin to be manageable, with appropriate help available.

This work with a patient in a psychotic breakdown is somewhat different from bereavement counselling. However, I hope it shows something of the fragile state that can exist beneath a surface of coping when there has been no adequate acknowledgement of the feelings of loss at the time of a death. I wish now to discuss a form of mourning that is failing to be productive, even though the feelings may be clearly evident.

Melancholic mourning

What I shall be saying here is familiar to all psychoanalysts and psychotherapists. However, there are others for whom it might be useful to have an explanation of the dynamics of melancholia, as Freud (1917) understood them. We speak of melancholia when mourning seems to go on indefinitely. The analytic understanding of this, as a response to a death, is that the relationship to the deceased had been in a state of acute and unresolved ambivalence – both loving and hating the other person. Then, when the other person dies, the survivor seems to be unable to recover from the bereavement. Often there is a reaction which can be seen by others as specifically self-destructive. Often too there are indications of the bereaved having become in some significant way identified with the person who has died, taking on the symptoms of whatever had contributed to the death, or their mannerisms. There is often also a lot of self-attacking and self-reproach in melancholic mourning.

Analysts have come to see these typical melancholic reactions in terms of the negative side of the ambivalent relationship, now split off from the person who has died and attached to some aspect of the bereaved person's own self. The dead person can then be idealized and protected from the former ambivalence, as if the relationship had no flaw. The bereaved person becomes the object of the attacks which may, in life, have been a major part of the relationship.

Unconscious guilt

Often we wish people dead (as in the Oedipal situation) but not really truly, and we are horrified when what we thought in our wish seems to have been granted. Therefore, when a bereaved person feels in some way responsible for a death, this can lead to unconsciously driven self-punishment. Even though the bereaved person may not be able to see it, to an observer it may be quite obvious that they are struggling with an unconscious sense of guilt.

How are we to help someone with unconscious guilt? I have come to believe that when guilt is based on unconscious false connections (as with magical thinking) it is important that we do not appear to believe that the bereaved person *should* feel guilty, as if the guilt were a rational response rather than an irrational and false connection.

While I was a family social worker with the FWA, I was seeing a couple for marital counselling. I was seeing the wife, a colleague was seeing the husband, and sometimes we saw them together. My client was often very outspoken in her despising of her husband. In her eyes he seemed to have no good qualities whatever. She didn't know why she had married him, why she had stayed with him, or why she was bothering to have marital counselling. She would be so much better off without him, she thought. In fact she often wished him dead. Whilst Mrs J was thus preoccupied with her despising of her husband, he had a heart attack and died. She then became transformed into a deeply grieving wife who sounded as if she had always adored her husband. She arranged the most elaborate and expensive funeral and she spent most of the time I was with her in praising her husband.

However, Mrs J was clearly in a profound depression. Very soon after the funeral she developed a skin irritation that was driving her demented, for which the doctors could find nothing that would help. She was constantly scratching herself and her arms were becoming lacerated. It was painful to witness.

Being then a student psychotherapist, I felt sure that I was witnessing a guilt reaction to her husband's death, with the irritation she had before been so vocal about now being expressed somatically. It was as if her attacks against her husband had been turned against herself, as if he had quite literally got under her skin. I foolishly tried to offer an interpretation of this, but the more I tried to suggest that she might be feeling some unconscious guilt, the more she felt I was accusing her, as if I were suggesting she should feel guilty. The way I was talking could certainly be heard in that way. She became very angry and refused to see me again, and I don't blame her.

In a subsequent case discussion, when I described my clumsy attempts at trying to interpret to Mrs J, a colleague reprimanded me by saying that in her opinion I had been merely 'adding insight to injury'. She was quite right.

Nowadays, if I had felt it appropriate to approach this problem of unconscious guilt with Mrs J, I would have tried to take a position of not understanding. I might have drawn her attention to the way in which her scratching was beginning to look like some kind of self-attack, as if she were punishing herself, but not being clear what this might be for. If she were ready to look at her feelings of guilt about her attacks upon her husband, she might have tried to make sense of this with me. Then, perhaps, we could have begun to see how her previous attacks upon her husband, which she knew I had often witnessed, seemed to have been turned against herself. Then, maybe, she could have dared to get back in touch with some of her anger against her husband, even her anger at him for dying. Once it could have been spoken about more openly, I think she might have been able to find some relief from that self-attacking which was so tormenting her in the skin irritation. We have to learn from our mistakes, but Mrs J alas was not the one to benefit from my learning.

A further example of a failure to mourn but with a positive outcome

Mrs T was referred to me for psychotherapy because of a problem of gynaecological pain, which no doctor had been able to account for. This had been so severe that it had prevented intercourse for five years, and was threatening to break up the marriage. However, it soon became clear to me that this was a case of a failure to mourn.[3]

In her first consultation with me, Mrs T described her experiences of having had two babies (each of which had been deemed normal at birth) but each had begun to be in pain from the age of six months. This led to unbearable screaming at all times except when they were medicated, and both babies died before they were one year old.

Mr and Mrs T had then gone for genetic counselling where they were told that there was a 50:50 chance of them having the same abnormality in any subsequent pregnancy. Mrs T was therefore advised to accept sterilization, which she did, and she learned after the operation that there had been a third foetus which had also been removed. So she had lost three babies.

All of this dreadful account was told to me without Mrs T showing the slightest sign of emotion. Her face was entirely

---

3 This case was the subject of discussion in a previous paper (Casement and Lewis 1986) and in Casement (1985: 78–80; 1991: 68–70).

without expression and wooden. I, for my part, was close to tears. But I knew that if Mrs T had been more appropriately in touch with her own tears I would not have felt so intensely upset on her behalf. It was as if I were inwardly crying *for her*. This helped me to realize that her gynaecological pain might well be due to a failure to mourn. This initial impression seemed to be confirmed when I asked whether she had cried after her babies died. She told me that she had never been able to cry, with either death, not even at the funeral.

I now felt almost sure that her body was expressing her psychological pain, *as if it were physical*, because she had been unable to be adequately in touch with her feelings about the death of her babies. It was also not without significance that it was precisely that part of her body which had been most associated with their births which had since become the focus of that unexpressed pain. I therefore recommended to Mrs T that she see me regularly for a while and that I would like her to tell me in detail about her experience of each baby's illness and death.

In the course of seeing Mrs T, I learned quite a lot about how her family had mistakenly tried to help her by diverting her attention from her tragedies. After the first funeral she had wanted just to go home alone with her husband, to be able to offer such comfort as they could to each other. But her mother had decided that it would be better if the more immediate family came back from the funeral to have something to eat with her. When Mrs T said she had nothing in the home to give to them, her mother sent her off shopping for provisions. She suggested that it would be good for her daughter; it would take her mind off the funeral.

Mrs T had felt numbed by the whole experience of nursing her first baby through his last months, and now the funeral and the funeral tea. But she was comforted at the time in knowing she was already pregnant with a second baby. But then the whole process was repeated, and after the second funeral Mrs T again could not cry. She just felt dead inside.

After the sterilization, Mrs T fostered two children – trying to fill the gap left by her dead babies. In due course she and her husband adopted these children, so her mind was always kept busy, but inside she still felt dead.

After some months of encouraging Mrs T to tell me about her babies, and her experience with them, she began to be more in touch with her feelings and she began sometimes to cry. In parallel

with this, her gynaecological pain became much less and intercourse was resumed. It now became apparent that, even though she
was again able to allow intercourse, Mrs T could not yet allow
herself to reach orgasm. Something held her back from this. I
sensed that she might still be afraid to allow herself to get more
fully in touch with the feelings that had been so closely related to
the conception and birth of her babies. One day she did reach
orgasm. Then we discovered more of what she had been defending
herself against. After that climax she fell into the deepest anguish
she could ever remember experiencing. She had a vivid memory of
a nurse in the hospital trying to take her dead baby from her,
forcing her fingers away from holding her baby, making her let go.
That, more than anything, was the memory she had been shutting
off. But having reached it, she began to recover.

The marriage became alive once more and intercourse could
again be satisfactory for both of them. Nevertheless, for some time
she still cried deeply after climax, which was all part of her
mourning. So the mourning, which had been so drastically cut
short, was now *in process* – after all those years of delay.

I saw Mrs T for a comparatively short time, about nine months
in all; the length of a pregnancy, as it happened. She wrote to me
the following year. The progress had been sustained and she was
much happier in many respects. She was also much less driven to
be busy.

To conclude

Mourning has ultimately to do with letting go. What I have not
discussed is the essential counterpart to letting go that is a refinding
of the internal relationship to the person who has died. Recovered
memories can go a long way towards re-establishing a sense of
support from within, which before had mostly come from the
external relationship that has been lost. To a surprising extent, an
internal relationship to dead parents or a dead partner can change
over time. Often, an angry relationship can gradually give way to a
more forgiving one; a blaming relationship to a more understanding one.

Chapter 8

Internal supervision in process: a case presentation

For about 20 years, I conducted a series of clinical workshops on the theme of 'internal supervision in process'. I started each workshop by presenting a session, inviting the participants to work with this clinical material. I always used the same material because it proved to be useful as a learning experience for all of us, using the record of a session from a student who had once presented at a clinical seminar I had been conducting.[1]

Before working with this session in these workshops, I would outline some of the ideas that I use in relation to the process of internal supervision. I would also give some history of the concept and of how I had often noticed people using too much of someone else's thinking in a session, especially after a supervision. I would say that instead we need to develop a process of internal supervision so that we can draw upon our own thinking more readily when we are with a patient.

I believe that once we are familiar with this process it can become largely subliminal to our listening. We can't take time out for this. It should not distract our attention. We certainly don't want it to be like attending to another voice in our thinking, as can happen when a student family therapist gets some instruction through an 'ear bug' from the actual supervisor, who is watching through a one-way mirror.

I encourage *abstracting themes from the detail*, so that we can get a better sense of the *shape* of possible meanings that emerge, over

---

1 I would have much preferred getting permission to publish this material from that student himself, but I no longer know his name. Instead, permission to publish has been given by the training organization where that student had trained, the original clinical work having been some 20 years ago.

time, in a session. I also advocate what I have come to think of as *listening with both hands*. By this I mean that, on the one hand we can hear what the patient is saying, perhaps in a literal way, whereas on the other hand we can hear something quite different that might also be in the patient's communication.

I would also speak about needing to have (as it were) *two heads* in a session, rather like when there are two therapists in family therapy or marital therapy. We can then allow one part of ourselves to be drawn quite deeply into some dynamic with a patient, while with another part we continue to reflect on what is happening and why.

I also suggest that we can learn to *practise with clinical material*, trying different ways of understanding it. This can be useful at any time. The emphasis is then less on how the therapist might have dealt with a session, as if criticizing, but more on considering how we might do things a bit differently another time. This kind of discussion is really not meant to be a criticism of the therapist. Rather it can help us to become alert to different possibilities. We are all likely to find ourselves in similar situations sooner or later, so I think that it is useful to practise in relation to clinical vignettes in preparation for such a time.

I think of this practising as similar to a musician who undertakes the discipline of playing scales, or other technical exercises. These exercises are of course never played in concert, but they can help to develop a fluency in the fingers, to enable the musician's playing when in performance. Similarly, in clinical work we can learn to develop a fluency in our processing, so that we can hear more readily the different possibilities and implications in what we might say, for another time. We might then have a greater fluency in our thinking when we are in session with a patient.

Also central to the practice of internal supervision is *trial identification with the patient*, listening to oneself from the patient's point of view, from moment to moment in the session, before speaking and after.

I also remind the workshop of the concept of *unconscious supervision*[2] and my idea of *unconscious criticism* by the patient: by

---

2 The notion of *unconscious supervision by the patient* grew out of Harold Searles' paper 'The patient as therapist to his analyst' (1975). However, I first came across this being articulated in these terms by Langs (1978).

displacement, by contrast, by introjective reference, or by mirroring. (For a fuller description of these see Casement 2002d: 21–24.)

Before proceeding with a discussion of the clinical material to be presented, I always stress that we should be mindful of what Racker (1957) calls *indirect countertransference*, when the analyst or therapist is being affected by something that is not directly to do with the patient. This can be especially pertinent when someone has been asked to present to a clinical seminar.

The presenter in the session I am about to share with you was almost certainly affected by knowing he would have to write it up. He could then not be alone with the patient in his usual way, as he was also trying to remember the detail and sequence of the session. He was therefore not responding to his patient as he might have done if he had not known he would be presenting. We thus get a vivid sense of the therapist being caught up in this way, particularly at those times when we would expect him to have responded to the patient's multiple cues. But keeping in mind this notion of indirect countertransference helps us to be more understanding of the therapist's lapses, and grateful to him for the honesty with which the session has been recorded.

In these workshops I would present clinical material, reading just a little at a time, inviting participants to respond to my prompts and questions about it. This way is nearer to how we experience a session. Of course, there is much value also in being able to take a session as a whole, which we more often do in a clinical seminar. But here I work with the session from moment to moment, to illustrate how much we can pick up from each bit of a session when we have the time to practise in this way.

An example of how a typical workshop would go

PC: I shall be reading verbatim from the notes prepared by a student therapist. From the presentation given to me we hear the following: [1]

Male therapist; female patient. The patient has been in therapy for three months. Predominant themes: multiple hospitalizations from six months of

---

1 Italics are used throughout this chapter to indicate when I am quoting from the therapist's own record. He refers to himself as 'the therapist'.

age due to a congenital foot deformity. She has already had previous counselling with a woman which she complains bitterly about. She sees the present therapist three times per week: Monday, Thursday and Friday. The session below is a Friday session.

At this point I encourage the workshop to tune into this material from what we are given.

PC: What are we hearing here? Also, what areas of particular sensitivity in the patient can we notice?

GROUP: Separations. Absences. Being left alone in a strange place.

PC: Yes indeed. We might also wonder about this being a second attempt at getting help.

GROUP: She is likely to compare this therapist with her former counsellor. She may idealize this therapist alongside the bad counsellor. She may be anxious about whether this therapy will work or not.

PC: Yes. In particular we need to be careful about splitting between the bad out there and the good in here, the former counsellor as the bad one.

We now hear some more:

For the previous session the therapist had been a few minutes late in answering the door to her.

PC: So if you are this patient, with her background, what might you be feeling outside this closed door?

GROUP: Rejected. Shut out. Not wanted. Anxious. Thinking something has gone wrong. Wondering if I have got the time wrong.

PC: Yes. And when you pick up that she might feel anxious, at what age might she be experiencing that anxiety?

GROUP: It might link back to those times when she was left in the hospital.

PC: True. And she was very young indeed when that kept on happening. So, if she were to experience this at that early level, 'a few minutes' might feel like for ever. The notes continue:

This session, the patient turns up an hour early.

PC: Now, if you are the therapist and your patient turns up an hour early, what do you do? There is something that needs to be clarified.

GROUP: I'd say: 'You are early.' I'd say: 'Please come in and wait in the waiting room.' I'd say: 'I think there's been some mistake about the time.'

PC: The patient does need to know that you were not expecting her, or that there has been some mistake about the time. But if I say: 'You are early' and you are the patient, how might you hear this?

GROUP: I would feel criticized.

PC: Yes. I think this could equally link with times when somebody has said: 'You are late.' These are different forms of not being on time, so it could feel like the same kind of thing. If, instead, we simply acknowledge that there seems to be some mistake about the time, we are not so likely to be heard as being critical of the patient.

And what about the idea of the patient being invited to go to the waiting room, and waiting for an hour? What if there is another patient due at this time? You could have two patients in the waiting room together. Or, if you manage to get one into the consulting room, you could still have the distraction of knowing that there is another patient waiting. Also, your patient might hear noises from the next patient and feel anxious about being over-heard.

I'd probably say: 'I would prefer it if you could come back a bit nearer to your time.' I would not be telling her to. I would just be stating a preference. The patient might anyway offer to do that, so I might not even need to say this. But if she doesn't take the hint, as I regard the preserving of boundaries as my responsibility, I would then ask her to come back later because of what I have already said (to you) about having one patient already in the waiting room while seeing another.

One more point here. We can notice that the patient, in her mistake in coming early, brings to this session an issue to do with time. This could link back to the previous day. The notes continue:

As the therapist is free he makes a snap decision to see her now. The patient seems quite unaware of her 'over-punctuality'.

PC: What is missing when we make a snap decision?

GROUP: We haven't left time to think.

PC: Exactly. And what is also missed out here, with this snap decision, is the matter of making it clear to the patient that this is not her time. If she knew this, she might prefer to come back for the time usually set aside for her. Here we learn that she does not seem to realize she is early, which could give the therapist an unfair advantage over her. He then knows something she seems not to know. Also, the therapist records this in a strange way, calling it her 'over-punctuality'. I am not sure what to make of that, just yet. We then hear:

The patient lies on the couch and starts talking straightaway and rather rapidly.

PC: We can see, from the way the patient is described, that she is almost certainly anxious. Let's see how she goes on.

Patient: I've been thinking about last Thursday (not yesterday) when I felt that I just could not get through the day.

PC: She says she is not thinking about yesterday. This is a nice example of *negation*. The thought crosses her mind to refer to yesterday, but she immediately tries to cross it out of her mind. The therapist says nothing. It could be OK to say nothing here, or he could have said that there is 'something about yesterday' that she seems not to want to be thinking about. The patient goes on:

That feeling of not being able to get through the day. . . Yesterday, at work, I kept feeling that if I stopped for a moment, I might just fall to the floor and not be able to get up again. Just stop breathing. It made me panic a bit. I just had to keep on going. Today, it's not so bad.

PC: The patient is speaking of not being able to get through the day. She also brings this forward to yesterday, having tried to disconnect her thoughts from yesterday. But what about her saying 'if I stopped for a moment'? She had previously stopped for a moment in this session, during which the therapist had said nothing. I think he was busy trying to remember how this session had started, his attention probably being on the notes he'd be writing up afterwards, rather than on the flow of the session. So the patient stops for him to say something. When he says nothing she is left to manage on her own. The patient then tells us she is afraid she might fall to the floor and not be able to get up again. Why do you think she's afraid she might fall to the floor?

GROUP: It could be because of her foot deformity, being unsteady on her feet. Or it could be that she feels there is no one there to hold her.

PC: Yes. I think she may be telling us that she is having to rely on self-holding, as when she was in hospital, and this might fail. In the meantime she just has to 'keep on going'.

The patient ends by saying that 'today it's not so bad'. Then the therapist reports:

After a pause, she goes on: 'But I've got a pain in my arm.'

PC: That is a typical form that we find in relation to negation or denial. For example, we often hear things like: 'I am not feeling angry (about whatever) but . . .'. The denial in her saying that today it's not so bad isn't altogether working. Why do you think the patient now has a pain in her arm?

GROUP: It might be the arm she used for pressing the bell when she came yesterday.

PC: That is possible. But why do you think she has a pain that is now physical? It might be that the emotional pain of yesterday, which she tries not to think about, has become somatized. Maybe it feels easier to have a physical pain, which she can try to look after; rather than the emotional pain which someone else may be failing to attend to. The patient goes on:

I didn't sleep very well last night. I couldn't go off. It's still here. (Rubs her arm.)

PC: Although she has tried to convince herself, or the therapist, that it isn't so bad to-day, the pain is still with her. She rubs her arm. This too may be a form of self-holding, trying to deal with the pain herself, which her therapist doesn't seem to have noticed yet. She also makes it clear that the pain, whether physical or emotional, is still here. She goes on:

I've been reading a book by Anna Freud. I read it to and from work. It fills the time. My mind is blank now. (She moves restlessly on the couch.)

PC: Why do you think she is reading a book by Anna Freud?

GROUP: It is a book by an analyst. It is a book about therapy. It's a book by somebody who knows about children. She is not so alone when she is reading the book.

PC: Exactly. And I think it may highlight how alone this patient has been feeling, perhaps especially since the previous day. Has her therapist recognized the level of her anxiety when she was shut outside his door? Does he recognize how the child in her may have been reactivated by that experience, as a child feeling alone with no familiar person to turn to? It is also interesting that she happens to tell him about this book just now, as she is probably feeling alone in this session too. Is he hearing her now? He still hasn't spoken.

The patient ends here with 'My mind is blank now', and she moves restlessly on the couch. I see this as the clearest prompt yet that she needs to hear something from her therapist.

Now, before knowing what the therapist says here, I want us to keep in mind that we all sometimes spoil an interpretation by saying too much. I will therefore give the therapist's interpretation in two forms. First, I will say the bit that was appropriate to the moment.

Therapist: You say that it's not so bad today and yet, in the way you are talking, I get the sense that you are quite anxious here at the moment . . .

PC: Whatever else the therapist has picked up from the session so far, or missed, he has at least noticed that the patient is anxious.

If I practise with this bit, I would prefer to say that she is 'anxious' rather than 'quite anxious'. This would leave it for the patient to add, for herself, *how* anxious she feels. I would not say 'very' here. She could say that, which could also allow her to own it more clearly rather than just agreeing with my description of her as 'very anxious'. But, similarly, I would not limit it to 'quite', which suggests only a little anxious.[2]

---

2 I understand that 'quite' in America can mean 'very', which could be confusing here.

If you were this patient, I think you could feel heard in this bit of what the therapist said. Whatever else has been around, not yet picked up, at least the therapist recognizes that she feels anxious. Now I will read to you this interpretation in full, as recorded by the therapist.

Therapist: You say that it's not so bad today and yet in the way you are talking I get the sense that you are quite anxious here at the moment, and as if you are having to fill up the time here somehow.

PC: Once again, I invite you to be the patient. How do you feel when you hear the rest of this interpretation?

GROUP: I now feel that the therapist has not picked up any of the earlier signs of anxiety, even panic. Saying that the patient has been just 'filling up the time' feels terribly dismissive of everything said up until now.

PC: Yes, I agree. But let's remember we have had the privilege of listening to this session with time to consider it. We have not had the added burden of trying to remember the session for a clinical seminar. Nevertheless, what is not being acknowledged here is the patient's near collapse, her not being able to think about yesterday, her anxiety about this therapy, and that this might fail her too. None of that has been picked up yet by her therapist.

The patient is showing us (at least unconsciously) that she has already begun to look for another therapist, telling him just now that she is reading this book. But I can see that this might be especially difficult for a student therapist to pick up. The last thing he is likely to want to hear from his patient is that she might leave this therapy. He would probably have to start over again with another training case. So we might be seeing some of the therapist's own defensiveness here, in not picking up the signals she is giving.

The patient replies: I suppose it hasn't gone yet.

PC: As I interrupted the flow, 'it' here initially referred to the pain. I notice that, in her first response, the patient picks up the one bit in the therapist's comment that does not cause her a problem. She agrees that 'it', now referred to as her anxiety, hasn't gone yet. But she goes on:

I was wondering this morning how I would get through the day.

PC: She is still in a very shaky state, not sure how she is going to get through the day. I think we are seeing that she is anxious about whether her self-holding might still break down, in which case she could be in even greater need of being with somebody who is in touch with how shaky she feels. She goes on:

I had a dream last night. I was talking to a friend and she said that she could introduce me to Anna Freud. That she sometimes goes to a pub in Hampstead and that if I got there at 8.00 sharp she would introduce me.

PC: Of course it is much too early to attempt an interpretation of the dream we are beginning to hear, but we can think about bits of it as we are hearing it, much as we might in our internal supervision in a session. So far we are hearing more about Anna Freud. In her dream there is a possibility that the patient could be introduced to her, somebody who might understand how children feel.

We also hear something about time, that the patient could be introduced to Anna Freud if she gets there at the stated time, here described as '8.00 sharp'. The dream continues:

My friend said that when I finished therapy with you perhaps I could start to see her (Anna Freud), which is funny because Anna Freud is dead. (She laughs.)

PC: So, what are we hearing now?
GROUP: The patient is talking about when she finishes therapy with this therapist.
PC: Yes. We do seem to be hearing of the patient's anxiety about this therapy. She might need to find someone else to go to when she stops seeing this therapist. Even though we hear that she laughs here, let us remember that laughter can be a defence against tears, or against anxiety. The patient goes on:

So I went to the bar and Anna Freud was there. I talked to her for a few minutes but then an ex-patient of hers came in and she went off to talk to her.

PC: What link do you notice between this bit of dream and what has been around in the day before; some possible 'day residue' which may have prompted this dream?

GROUP: I notice that the patient refers to 'a few minutes'.

PC: Exactly. We can also note that Anna Freud seems to be represented in two forms. In one she is the therapist who will be there when she says she will be, as someone reliable. Alongside this we hear of her as having divided attention. After a few minutes she leaves the patient *to be with someone else*. It looks as if Anna Freud is represented here as being reliable in a way that her therapist had failed to be. But there also seems to be this further reference to yesterday, in that Anna Freud in the dream then attends to someone else and leaves the patient unattended to, which she may feel is what had happened the day before. Perhaps the therapist was attending to someone else.

We might also practise here with the name Anna Freud. If we stay with the manifest detail, her actual name, we are hearing of an analyst who is no longer alive. She might represent some idealisation of an analyst. She might represent someone who knows about children. But, in the literal sense, this patient and the therapist both know she cannot go to see her. However, if we abstract from the detail of Anna Freud's name, we can also hear this as the patient thinking of going to see 'someone else'. That is a real possibility. If we hear it in this way, that it has occurred to her she might really go to someone else, we might see how much more of a threat that could be to this student therapist. The patient ends by saying:

That was the dream. I woke up feeling unsafe, like I was falling apart.

PC: We now hear of the patient feeling unsafe, as she may well feel if she is afraid that she might be with a therapist who isn't reliably there for her. We also hear more about her self-holding. Here this seems to be represented as 'falling apart', which happens to be one of the most primitive anxieties that Winnicott speaks of; that and 'going to pieces' or 'falling for ever'. The child in her could feel close to collapse, unable to go any further on her own. She continues.

I've been thinking I can't wait to get back home tonight to be on my own again.

PC: That's very interesting. Why do you think the patient is feeling she can't wait to be on her own again?

GROUP: She might feel safer there. She might feel able to look after herself in ways she can't in the consulting room.

PC: Yes. She might be able to turn to other ways of trying to comfort herself, or trying to make herself feel safe, perhaps in having a hot bath or in getting into bed, or in having something to eat. It is interesting that she seems to feel that she will have to meet her own needs rather than turning to the person she has come to see for therapy. She seems to be giving repeated prompts for the therapist to recognize how traumatized she has been, because of the incident at the door.

We also need to keep in mind that this patient could well be reliving some of her own early trauma of being shut out of her home, being left in a strange place where she was unable to reach the only person who might be able to help her with what she was feeling. We know that she had been frequently hospitalized from a very early age. The notes continue:

Therapist: Perhaps you are drawing our attention to not feeling very safe here with me at the moment.

PC: I would like to make a brief teaching point here. It may often be appropriate for us to be tentative in what we say to patients, as we are usually not in a position to be really sure. So we offer an interpretation and invite the patient to work with us towards some better understanding.

There is, however, one particular time when we need to be more sure than tentative, and that is when we are being given signs that the therapy could be in crisis. Here is a time for being more definite than this therapist is being. I would therefore prefer him to be saying something more along the lines of: 'It seems clear that you are not feeling safe with me.' The patient could then know that the therapist is picking up how critical the situation feels to the patient.

I would not include 'at the moment' in this interpretation, as the patient's anxiety might feel timeless to her, linked as it seems to be with her childhood anxiety, and I want to be careful not to minimize how anxious she may feel with me. It may not just be a temporary matter for her. The notes continue:

Patient: It has taken me a long time to find you. I don't think I could go through all that again.

PC: I think this is also very interesting. The patient says that it has taken her a long time to find this therapist. We can hear this in more than one way. It has taken her a long time, in the sense of having already been through a time of counselling that failed her before coming to see this therapist.

We can also hear this in the context of this session, in that she has been communicating her distress to him throughout all of this session, which we have had an opportunity to be tuning into. It is only now that she is beginning to find her therapist showing some awareness of what she has been saying. It has taken her a long time to reach him *in this session*. It is part of the richness of unconscious communication that we can hear these different meanings. I wouldn't, however, interpret this latter point. The question about whether this therapy might also be failing her is much more important. The notes continue:

Therapist: And yet the dream seems to be indicating something about finishing here and seeing Anna Freud. (Pause.) One thing that strikes me about the dream is having to be somewhere at 8.00 sharp and it puts me in mind of yesterday's session when I didn't answer the door at 10.30 sharp for our meeting.

PC: We have another example of an interpretation in which the therapist says too much. There are two different issues in this, each of which needs time for proper attention.

The first issue is about the possibility of leaving this therapist. The patient needs time to respond to this and to have a chance to work through some of that with her therapist. Here we find that he doesn't give her that time. Instead he deflects her from the idea of finishing with him, immediately directing her attention to this other issue.

If we practise further with this vignette, I would like to find another way of introducing the next detail from the dream. Here the therapist says: 'One thing that strikes me about the dream', which can be heard as if the other matter (of perhaps finishing this therapy) is of little or no significance. Instead, and only after attending to the first part of this, I would say something like: 'Another thing that I notice in the dream', which puts it more clearly alongside the other, each being treated as important.

We might also practise with the therapist's choice of words. True, he uses the patient's own words back to her. But in this context how might it feel to her? If you are the patient here, what might you feel in response to hearing your therapist remind you that he had not opened the door 'sharp' on time?

GROUP: I would feel criticised. I would feel shamed. I feel that I am being told that I am making a lot of fuss about this; that it was only a few minutes. I feel blamed for making so much of it.

PC: Yes, indeed. So, let's try to find another way of referring to that moment. How might you feel if I were to say, in this context: 'I am hearing about *punctuality*, and I am reminded of yesterday when I failed to be punctual for you.' Where is the criticism focused in that?

GROUP: I feel completely different in hearing it put that way. You are making it clear that you understand that it is your responsibility to be punctual for my sessions, and you seem to be accepting this without being defensive that you had failed me in that. You leave me free to be critical of you.

PC: That is why I think it can be so useful to practise with things like this. It gives us a chance to realize the value of monitoring how we put things to a patient, listening to it from the patient's point of view. The more often we practise this, like now, the more readily we can spot the implications in how we put things to a patient. So, even though I am sounding critical of this therapist at different points in this presentation, it is all in the service of helping us to get a better fluency in our listening for another time. In fact I am very grateful to this therapist for the session going the way it is going, including his mistakes, and for recording it so honestly. We all have a lot we can learn from this. The patient goes on:

I was wondering whether it would be the same today.

PC: What might be the same as yesterday?

GROUP: She might be afraid to find the therapist again not answering the door.

PC: Yes. Having found herself left outside, which may have become linked in her mind with her repeated experiences of hospital, she might be expecting to be left again. Her being left outside, yesterday, might be thought of as belonging to an unconscious set in which this keeps on happening.

It might be useful if I make a further teaching point here. Matte Blanco (1975) pointed out that the unconscious mind makes links between things once experienced together, as in a trauma, as if they belong to a *set* that comes to represent the trauma. Then, if one or more elements of that *set* are experienced again, the mind begins to expect a similar trauma. It is a way of being better prepared than at the time of the original trauma, to be on guard against the possibility that it might be about to happen again. Through being prepared, there might not be the same shock of surprise as there had been before. The patient goes on:

I couldn't see your car. I thought maybe you'd gone out. Or maybe you'd had a car crash. (Laughs.)

PC: Why might the patient think the therapist may have been in a car crash?

GROUP: Because she has been feeling murderously angry with him.

PC: Yes. But it may also tie in with the patient's experience of being left in the hospital. Why was her mother not there? A child left in hospital can't make sense of the mother's absence. She would surely be there if she could be. Maybe something terrible has happened to prevent her from being there. Which of course can tie in with the child's fear that her anger at the mother, for leaving her, might have harmed her. She goes on:

But you did give me some extra time at the end of the session. Maybe it's not important.

PC: We hear that the therapist had made up the missed time in the previous session. If you are the patient, does that make up for the missed time?

GROUP: Well, she does get the time she is paying for – the full 50 minutes.

PC: But how might it affect you as patient, that the time was made up?

GROUP: I could feel that my anger about the late start has been bought off. I might feel that I shouldn't complain about it. I could also feel that I should be grateful to the therapist for seeing me in his own time.

PC: Yes, exactly. The therapist might also have allowed himself to think that he had dealt with the lateness, by making up the time. But has he? The notes continue:

> Therapist: Well, I wonder about that. You see, today you have come an hour early for your session.

PC: Let us take a few moments to consider the sequence here. The therapist might feel quite seriously threatened by the idea that his patient could be experiencing him as failing her, and that she may be thinking of leaving this therapy. In his countertransference he could therefore feel very vulnerable, in the face of this. But here he is able to swing the problem away from himself, and from his failure of yesterday. He has known all along that he is seeing this patient in his time, not in hers, and she seems not to know this. So, how might she feel when he springs this upon her at this moment in the session? Try being the patient here.

GROUP: I feel the rug is pulled from under my feet.

PC: Yes. The patient had been telling him in so many different ways how shocked and disorientated she had been, because of his failure to be there at the proper time. Now, suddenly, the patient is faced with another mistake. This time it is *she* who is not there at the right time.

Incidentally, as another teaching point, this is what I mean by *criticism by mirroring.*[3] The patient unconsciously enacts a version of the

---

3 This example could equally be seen as *unconscious criticism by introjective reference*, in that the patient may have introjected the therapist's error, enacting this in her mistake over the time. However, these two forms of unconscious criticism by the patient are not always so similar.

therapist's failure. It is now she who gets the time wrong but it could be a way of holding up a mirror to him, about the previous day. The notes continue:

Patient: I haven't, have I? (Obviously quite shocked.) What's the time? (Looks at watch.) Is it all right?
Therapist: Yes it is.
Patient: I've never done that before. (She laughs nervously.) Normally I'm so punctual. Why did I do that? I wonder.

PC: We can see that she is completely thrown. She is now the one in the wrong. He has (apparently) been so good to her, even seeing her in his time rather than making her wait. But he could have let her know about the mistake about the session time. She could then have had all of this session to work through more of what she had been experiencing, around his not being there for her the previous day. Instead, she now has to put aside her anger with him, to see him in this new light as the person being wronged *by her*.

Still practising with this, we can also see here that the patient uses the word 'punctual', which the therapist didn't use in his interpretation, even though this notion was around in his earlier comment (in his notes) that she seemed to be unaware of her 'over-punctuality'. To continue:

Therapist: You said earlier that you couldn't wait to get back home tonight but maybe it has also been difficult to wait to see me today, especially if you had the thought that I might have been in a car crash.

PC: The therapist is, by implication, picking up some reference to the patient's anger towards him. But in the context of her now feeling so at fault, because of her mistake over the time of this session being now pointed out to her, I am not sure whether she will be able to stay with her anger towards him.

Patient: I don't know why I thought of that. (Pause.) I was just thinking about my previous counsellor. We never had regular times. She would sometimes phone me up and change sessions or cancel them. I didn't know where I was. I used to feel sometimes with her as if I was oozing out under the door. The chair I used to sit in felt wobbly. I kept feeling I was falling off it. I told her and she said that no-one else had complained. In the end I just got used to it.

PC: This was near to the end of the session. What seems to be happening here is a massive retreat from the patient's earlier criticism of her present therapist. Instead, all of her criticism and anger is now being split off, away from him, and being deflected onto the former counsellor. In effect she seems to be saying to the therapist that he needn't worry about yesterday, as if she were saying: 'It was nothing really. It was only a few minutes, after all. Just see what things were like with the previous counsellor. We never had regular times.' So how could the few minutes of yesterday have seemed like such a problem to her?

We hear that the patient felt like 'oozing out under the door', with the counsellor. But it could be that this is also how she feels with this therapist when he exposes her mistake about the time of her session. She might have 'wished that the floor could swallow her up', as we sometimes say in that kind of situation.

We hear that she felt 'wobbly' with the counsellor, just as I think she has been feeling with this therapist. She also felt she was 'falling off' that chair, alongside her saying she kept feeling that she was 'falling apart' in relation to what had happened the previous day.

I like to believe that this therapy was able to recover from the repeating traumas that we have been hearing about. Not only has there been the trauma of the previous day, but there have also been the traumas in this session, in which the patient has shown that she was not feeling well held. Added to that, there has been the further trauma of being made to feel that she had no right to be so angry with her therapist when it could seem as if he had, in his own eyes, been treating her so well, seeing her in his own time and without complaint.

Whatever else we might say about this session, I want to repeat how deeply grateful I am to this therapist for having had the courage to present this session, and for us to have had the opportunity to be learning from it. I am hopeful that he would be better able to listen to his patient in other sessions than he seems to have been here, while his attention was inevitably being diverted by the knowledge that he would need to remember the details of the session in order to present it. I think we have all had a chance to benefit from this.

That is the kind of way this workshop usually went. Participants often found it useful. I hope it can be of similar use to those who read of it here.

Chapter 9

Developing clinical antennae

Throughout my clinical work and my writing, I have guarded against making any claim to have found 'the way' for doing psychoanalysis. I don't believe there is such a thing. The way that has worked for me is that which has grown out of my immersion in clinical work, trying as best I can to learn from each patient what might be most appropriate in my work with him or her. My work has therefore been, in some ways, different with each patient.

Seeing things from more than one perspective

I have found great value in being able to find a change of perspective that helps me to see things in a fresh way, beyond how I may have been seeing them before. I was first stimulated to explore the potential of such a change of perspective when I was working with the patient I called Teddy (see Casement 1985: 53–55, 1991: 49–51).

Before being brought to me by his mother, Teddy was treated as a catatonic schizophrenic in the local mental hospital. His mother had eventually insisted she be allowed to take care of him at home and brought him to me. I was then still a social worker with the FWA.

When Teddy first came to me he had been almost totally silent for over two years. His responses to anyone had been limited to 'Yes', 'No' or 'Not really.' After seeing him three times and finding no way of being with him except in asking questions, trying to find out something about him, I felt that I could not go on like that. I had therefore changed my approach.

When I next saw Teddy I thought aloud (to myself as much as to him) about how it might feel being *him*, with someone firing questions at him. I said that I would probably want to shut out that person with answers like his – 'Yes' and 'No' and 'Not really' – or perhaps by not saying anything at all. Teddy amazed me then by adding to what I had been saying, giving his own very vivid account of how it had felt. This was the first time he had really spoken to anyone in over two years; and he had only become able to speak with me when I had begun to see things from his point of view. It seemed that no one else had tried doing this.

So, after those years of catatonic silence, Teddy began to open up to me. In the second year of seeing him he felt able to go to work in a toyshop, where he was able to deal with the children and eventually their parents too. This turnaround, by someone who had been so withdrawn, had been extraordinary. It is therefore not surprising that I began to develop the notion of *trial identification with the patient in the session*, to consider the patient's perception and experience of me. This frequently helped me to see more clearly what my own contribution might be to the interactions between a patient and myself, and to become more sensitive to what I was putting into the analytic space.

Because so much gain came from this change of perspective with Teddy, I have since enjoyed telling a story that illustrates this matter of needing to be able to look at things from more than one point of view. I had heard of a British soldier who was serving in Khartoum, a city known to many after General Gordon became a hero in British eyes when he died in its defence during the siege of 1885. A statue in his honour now stands there.

The soldier had become a great admirer of this British hero, going frequently to look at the statue of Gordon sitting on a horse and taking his little boy with him. When the soldier was recalled to England, he told his son that they were about to leave Khartoum. As a treat, his son could choose what he would most like to do before leaving. The boy replied that he would like to be taken to see Gordon just one more time. A few days later, they were both standing before the statue in silent admiration. After a while, the little boy said to his father: 'Dad, who is that man sitting on Gordon?'

During all those previous visits, father and son had been looking at quite different things in what had seemed to have been a shared experience. I therefore find this a useful reminder to look beyond our familiar ways of seeing patients. We can so easily be blinded by accepted theory or by our clinical experience. It is always useful to try looking at things from a fresh perspective.

Developing an affective openness to the patient's state of mind or feeling

The analyst's affective openness, or lack of it, is similar to the resonances in a piano. If we raise some of the dampers in a piano by silently depressing certain notes, let's say the notes of a C major chord, this will leave just those notes free to resonate. If we then make a loud noise nearby, we will hear the key of C major resonating in the piano, but no other key will resonate. So, if we happen to be a *C major kind of person* we may tend to hear our patients in that key, or in a related major key. Likewise, if we are a *C minor kind of person* we may tend to hear our patients in C minor, or in some similar minor key. I believe that an important function of our own analysis is to free us to the point where we can resonate to our patients across as wide an affective and experiential range as possible.

If we are too much attached to our own experience, we are liable to read our patients in ways that *fit in* with this. At the same time we are likely to be missing other ways of understanding, which may go beyond what we have so far experienced. I know that after my first therapy (see Chapter 2) I was largely limited to responding to 'major keys' in others. It took me a long time, and years of further analytic work, to become able to resonate across a wider range of response to my patients.

Object relations in practice

I continue to understand the concept *object relationships* as illustrated in Chapter 2 (pp. 34–5). We all relate to others in terms of how we are seeing them. We have an 'object' in our minds that represents the other and we relate to that other in terms of this *internal object*.

Analysts are used to working with their patients in these terms. They try to help them to see how their relationships are affected, and sometimes dominated, by the way they are seeing the other. Interestingly, what is not so often considered is the way that we analysts are in danger of being in the grip of our own object relationship to the patient, which is often coloured (and may sometimes be dominated) by our assumptions about the patient, usually formed from our use of theory. I therefore believe that we need to be monitoring ourselves constantly for these assumptions preconceptions, which can so readily interfere with our being open to the otherness in our patients.

Preserving the analytic space

Most analysts and psychotherapists are familiar with Bion's dictum that the analyst should start every session 'without memory, desire or understanding' (Bion 1967a, 1967b: 43–45). This is not, however, intended to be a prescription to reassure elderly analysts! He is prompting us not to allow a session to be taken over by any active memory[1] about the patient, or about what we had previously thought we understood. Previous understanding, as from memory or from supervision, should not intrude upon the process of a current session. Also, we are encouraged not to allow ourselves to be led by any wish of our own, whether to provide a particular kind of experience or to pursue a given line of exploration. It is an admirable aim, often honoured more in principle than in practice.

This reminds me of a patient who had often told me that she experienced her mother as trying to run her life. Because I had been hearing so much about that constant interference, I tried to acknowledge the problem for my patient, eventually responding by saying that her mother didn't seem to be familiar with a passage in *The Prophet* where Gibran says:

> Your children are not your children.
> They are the sons and daughters of Life's longing for itself.
> They come through you but not from you,
> And though they are with you, yet they belong not to you.
> You may give them your love but not your thoughts,
> For they have their own thoughts. . . .
>
> You may strive to be like them, but seek not to make them like you.
>
> (Gibran 1965: 20)

---

1 I refer to 'active memory' here, which is different from *memory through passive recall* in response to what emerges from the patient in a current session.

My patient roared with laughter. She then explained that her mother had exactly that quotation written out and stuck with magnets on the door of her refrigerator, but she continued treating her children as if she had never come across it.

I have since thought that there may be many analysts who have Bion's dictum as it were stuck on their refrigerator doors, who nevertheless practise analysis as if they had never heard of it. It is immensely valuable to start each session afresh. For, as Bion used to remind us, we have never met the patient of today. We do not know where the patient is, what may have happened to the patient since last we met, or what may now be preoccupying the patient's conscious or unconscious mind.

In order to help me monitor myself in each session, I have learned to think of the analytic space. I am then asking myself: 'Who is putting what into this space?' It helps to highlight those times when I, or someone in supervision, has brought something into a session that has not been introduced by the patient. Very often we can then see that this intrusive element from the analyst provides a focus that has not been initiated by the patient, who may then say: 'I hadn't thought of that.'

When a patient responds like that, some analysts see this as confirming the value of what they have just said to the patient, on the grounds that this has uncovered something new from the patient's mind. But we could also hear such a response as the patient's unconscious supervision, perhaps indicating that the analyst has introduced something foreign to the patient rather than following what is actually in the patient's mind.

When the analyst introduces something that is not recognisably connected to what the patient is saying, it is likely to deflect the analytic process. It can even hijack the rest of the session, the patient now attending to what the analyst has introduced. Even if this leads to fresh memories, not yet revealed by the patient, I do not think that we should assume this to be evidence that the analyst's intervention has further enabled the analytic process.

This way of monitoring the analytic space has also helped to sharpen my awareness of the nature of the process that is happening between myself and a patient, or in someone else's clinical work. A lot of interpretations have an air of assuming to know what is in a patient's mind, whilst in fact we may be putting our own ideas into the patient.

Exceptional measures when under pressure[2]

The notion of the analytic space also gives me a perspective on what I hear about other kinds of analytic work, such as the exceptional measures that are sometimes used to deal with unbearable experience. In his paper 'The analyst's participation: a new look', Jay Greenberg (2001) gives some examples of occasions when analysts had resorted to unusual demonstrations of caring for the patient in order to deal with intense pressure or difficulty in the analysis.

Inevitably, there are occasions when the tension in an analysis comes to be experienced as unbearable, or almost unbearable, for both participants. Some analysts feel justified in resorting to unusual ways of dealing with such moments in order to break this tension. We all probably know of times when we have been under a similar pressure, with the analysis feeling to be in crisis. So how are we to proceed?

The crux is in the struggle we encounter at times like these, especially when we feel drawn into resorting to some non-analytic way of trying to resolve the tension. We need to remember that we do this for ourselves as well as for the patient. The issue is then whether these exceptional strategies lead to a real resolution of the difficulty, or whether they bypass the central problem.

This kind of pressure from a patient is always important, especially as it may represent something the patient has previously experienced as unbearable. It is often the case that the patient has experienced significant others as also finding his or her most intense feelings to be too much for them.

Any exceptional measure introduced by an analyst, which deflects the patient from the unbearable intensity of feelings, will be noted by the patient for what it could indicate about the analyst. Is the analyst really to be relied on? Is the analyst committed to 'being there' for the patient, even when the going gets tough? Is the analyst more able to cope with pressures from the patient than others have been?

---

2 An earlier version of this section was published in *Clinical Social Work Journal* (Casement 2005: 383–394). I am also referring to my 'Commentary' on a paper by Jay Greenberg (Casement 2001: 381–386).

As an example, an analyst may be tempted to steer the analysis away from a particularly stressful negative transference. This is often designed to lead the patient into seeing the analyst again as a caring person, as distinct from the uncaring figure re-experienced in the transference. This deflection is sometimes justified as being necessary for the patient – perhaps in order to restore a therapeutic alliance.

The apparently more positive state of affairs that may follow such a manoeuvre is often regarded as evidence of the idea that the analyst's handling of the crisis has benefited the analysis. However, I do not believe that the patient's apparently positive responses here can reliably be taken to indicate that the core of the impasse has been resolved. Rather, it may be a sign that the patient is now feeling a need to look after the analyst by avoiding what may have been perceived as too difficult for the analyst to stay with.

A more hopeful patient may later re-present the storm that has been circumvented by the exceptional behaviour of the analyst. I regard this return to the core problem as an expression of unconscious hope that the analyst might yet find the courage to engage more fully with the patient's difficult state of mind – this time without taking flight from it.

Some analysts may recognize the implications in this return to the impasse and proceed to engage with it more directly. Other analysts may again resort to the avoidance or deflection that had seemed successful before. The patient may then have to settle for the apparent gain of being with this new person, the analyst, who seems to be more caring and giving than others have been. But the core of earlier bad experience may remain avoided rather than more fully dealt with.

The use of an object

It took me many years before I really began to understand what Winnicott (1971) meant in his seminal paper 'The Use of an Object', which goes much further than a discussion of the analyst being used to represent some bad object of the patient's past. It means the analyst being there to be 'destroyed' by the patient, in the patient's mind; destroyed by all that the patient associates with the object collapsing or retaliating. It means, ultimately, being destroyed in phantasy but in reality being discovered as surviving.

When I have been most tested in this way, as I was by the burned patient I have described elsewhere,[3] I have had to struggle within myself to remain surviving, in the sense that Winnicott means. Only then could that patient come to realize that I had been truly in touch with what was most terrible in her mind, and yet I had survived it. Only then did she begin to find release from the 'monsters' in her mind, from which she had always felt she had to protect the other. Only then could she begin to find a freedom to be as she felt and to become more truly alive.

That kind of sequence has been central in my work with a number of patients. It is the work I have found most difficult at the time, but which I have most celebrated when the patient and I have found a way *through* rather than *round* the most terrible moments. The analysis in each case would have been entirely different if we had been limited to *talking about* early trauma, rather than directly *re-experiencing it* in the analytic relationship.

Enabling what is more real to emerge in the patient

Another area of work that I have especially valued has been with patients who were trapped into a false-self existence, like Mr D in Chapter 5. The clinical challenge in that kind of work has involved me in a quite different way of being with a patient. Instead of regarding difficult behaviour as acting out, or lateness as resistance, or negativity in a session as an attack on the analysis, I have often come to see these clinical phenomena as indicating the importance of engaging with these tentative expressions of the inner/core self. I then feel clinically hopeful that essential change may begin to be possible.

A false-self patient who begins to dare to be more real with the analyst is likely to bring into the analytic relationship precisely those aspects of himself or herself that seem to have been too much for the parents. The analyst is then likely to be severely tested, the patient needing to check that there is a genuine acceptance of this realness in the patient. The analyst is also likely to be tested for his survival, whether this too is genuine or just a cover for the expected

---

3 I am referring to the patient I call Mrs B (see Casement 1985: chapter 7, 1991: chapter 7, 2002d: chapter 7).

collapse or retaliation that the patient has learned to expect in response to daring to be real.

The notion of analytic space, and who puts what into this space, also helps me to monitor what is being left out by the patient or the analyst. When a patient mentions something important which is then not picked up by the analyst, the patient is likely to perceive this as an indication that the analyst wants to leave this outside the session. Inevitably the patient is going to wonder why. Is it that there wasn't time to deal with that just now? Does the analyst really see what he or she chooses to comment on as more important? Or could it be that the analyst finds the left-out issue too difficult, or perhaps even personally threatening?

Some patients will not return to what has been overlooked by the analyst, but this does not necessarily mean that it is not important to the patient. Quite often it turns out that a patient does not return to what was overlooked because the patient sees the analyst as needing to be protected from it.

Healthier patients will more often come back to what has been overlooked; but not patients who have learned to be compliant, in particular those patients who have developed a false self, like Mr D. We therefore need to be especially alert to those times when we may have chosen the easier thing to comment on or to interpret, leaving out something that may have been more important for the patient.

I am indebted also to another patient for providing me with an image that lends itself well for considering issues related to compliance, in life or in analysis. This patient (Miss J) vividly described that sort of problem in her own way:

> She told me that she felt like a round person in a square world. This was said in the context of her PhD work, where she was with a supervisor who seemed unable to respect the fact that she did not come to her research from the same position as other students. Some years of work in her particular field of experience had inspired her to submit her chosen research project, but she felt that her supervisor wanted her to start from scratch, as if she were a student straight from college. He also seemed to want her to do *his* research rather than to pursue her own.
>
> Miss J felt that her supervisor had been wanting to knock her into *his* kind of shape rather than being able to respect hers, to make her

square rather than to respect her roundness. In the end, so that she could have a chance to pursue her own research, Miss J found another supervisor.

Playing with this image, it occurs to me that we each of us have our own 'shape', whatever that might be. I have come to regard the task of psychoanalysis as that of fostering whatever is true for the individual – not trying to change it. I do not think it is a proper use of analysis to impose things on a patient.

Any of us might be naturally round or naturally square, or any other shape. We should be able to celebrate the roundness of one person or the squareness of another. I do not think that we should treat either as 'out of line'. Of course, analytically, there must be a place also for being concerned about a solipsistic attachment to one's own ways of being. But I think it important to respect individuality when this does not in itself indicate pathology.

When someone in an analysis has allowed their own shape to be knocked into something else, let's say a square, we may then find ourselves confronted by *a convert to squareness*. And if that patient is an analyst in training, this can lead to problems for their patients also. Converts have often given up much in order to fit in with what someone else has expected of them. They may then feel driven to do the same kind of thing to others, likewise depriving them of their natural shape just as they have been deprived of theirs; a common dynamic of any conversion.

This process of knocking a patient into a shape is something that can all too easily happen in an analysis when an analyst too often interprets from a position of authority, especially when the analyst's work has come to be tinged with the sureness (even certainty) of their own training and experience.

Monitoring the effects of our own contributions

Someone who had been blind from birth once told me how he had learned to find his way around. He always had metal bits added to the heels of his shoes, so that he could listen to *the echo of his footsteps*. In this way he created his own kind of radar, learning to recognize the changing sounds as he walked along the street. For a while I tried this out for myself and I was amazed to notice how a gateway or a house set further back from the pavement gave back a quite different sound. I didn't continue this experiment for very long, afraid that I might fall into the road, but I learned to see how valuable that extra sense could be. Incidentally, when it snowed my friend found himself immediately deprived of his radar and he then got easily lost.

In relation to my clinical work, I have tried to develop a similar sensitivity, trying to listen to my own 'footsteps' in a session, listening for how a patient was responding to my own input from moment to moment. In following a session in this way I came to realize how often patients were unconsciously indicating how they were perceiving my input, either from my choice of focus or from the manner in which I was addressing them.

I later came across Langs' notion of a patient's *unconscious supervision* (1978) and his focus on the 'communicative quality' of interpretations, which I found very affirming of my own observations.

Practising with clinical material

In the process of looking for a sense of direction in the encounter with each patient, rather than being guided by an unquestioning application of technique, I developed the process of internal supervision; and, as a part of that, the discipline of trial identification with the patient in the session (as illustrated in the previous chapter). This inner processing of each session has assisted all my clinical work, helping me to find reasons for working in a particular way, moment by moment in a session, rather than by rote. I have also used every opportunity to practise with clinical vignettes (my own and other people's), looking for alternative ways of understanding them and different ways of handling them. This practising has helped to alert me to many things that I might otherwise have not been able to recognize, especially in the heat of the moment of a session in process.

For example, I have frequently noticed the importance of what I call the 'direction' of an interpretation. I first wrote about this in 1990 and I have continued to find it useful.[4] We are often looking for connections, in what a patient brings, that link the past to the

4 Casement (1990: 49–50, 1991: 331–332).

present. I have noticed, however, that there can be big difference in how things go in a session, depending on how we point to this kind of connection.

A therapist or analyst often sees a connection between something in a session and a particular moment in a relationship in the patient's past. However, I have come to see that when the *direction* of the link being made is *from* the session *to* the patient's past, this invites the patient to move away from what is currently alive in the session. This shift of focus to the past is most unfortunate when it results in moving away from something difficult in the session, looking instead at some other difficult time in the easier context of the past; easier for the analyst or therapist, that is. If the connection is subsequently brought back into the session, there is often then an emotional distance from what had first indicated the link with the past. The connection may thereafter be explored with the patient's mind somewhat distanced from the feelings that had been around before that exploration of the past.

I think this loss of immediacy can be avoided if the connection with the past is followed in the opposite direction, from the past back to the present. For instance, I might say: 'I am reminded of that time when you were very angry with your father; so it may be that some of that anger is now here between you and me, about something that feels similar.' The direction of the link, made in this way, is more clearly inviting the patient to stay with the difficulty *in the present*; to explore it there, with the help of whatever light may be thrown on it from the past.

An example of practising

I heard of a patient who had been so upset and angry at work that she was close to handing in her resignation. This had been set off by the sense that her boss seemed to be about to promote a younger male colleague to the post she had believed would be offered to her.

The therapist had made an immediate link between this reported anger and the fact that she had told the patient, some 12 months before, of her intended retirement – a matter which had often been referred to in the therapy. On this occasion, however, the patient didn't see any connection. I suggested that it might have been useful to pick up more specifically what the patient's anger and upset could be about, not just about her work, nor yet so directly about the therapist's retirement. For example, the therapist might have brought in something from the patient's childhood to throw more light upon this. But, in practising with this vignette, I also used it as an opportunity to consider the *direction* of the links, so that the intense feelings could be kept in the session or brought more into the session, rather than kept outside (as with the work) or deflected to the past. I therefore suggested that we could perhaps say something like:

> I am reminded of how angry and upset you have often felt at being displaced by your baby brother [which had been a central feature of this therapy] when he took your place with your mother. Your upset then, and for years since, seems very similar to the rage you have been telling me about when you sensed that your boss might be promoting your junior colleague to the place that you thought would be yours. I think that old anger with your mother is still very present with you now.

What I am also trying to illustrate here is that we sometimes need to take more than one step before making a transference interpretation. Here, I believe, it would be useful to pick up some connection between the patient's childhood experience, and the problem at work with the boss, before taking the later step of relating these parallel situations to the transference. I think that patients more readily follow these connections when they are explored in sequence rather than in a single jump to the transference.

The connections found here might have kept more of the sense of immediacy in the feelings rather than using a rather cliché attempt at making connections. Also, the feelings remembered from the past might have helped the patient to realize a bit more of why she was feeling so upset about a situation that was parallel to that time in her childhood, whether at work or in the therapy. In addition, it could open up a fresh dimension in the patient's feelings about the end of therapy, not just that the therapist is leaving but that there may be a sense of upset around someone else in the therapist's life taking her away from this patient.

Looking beyond dogma

I have come to see all dogma as problematic when we consider things in the concept of the analytic space:

> Analysts and therapists become experts in making connections. *We can connect almost anything with anything!* And we can always use theory in support of this, however wild these connections might be.
>
> (Casement 2002d: 4)

I am frequently worried by the tendency for analytic theory and analytic technique to become self-proving. We can always interpret the course of an analysis in terms of our theory, or as evidence that our chosen technique is fruitful. But it is also possible that we may be seeing things as we want to see them.

During my psychoanalytic training I was questioning every bit of theory, being devil's advocate in my own mind, rather than accepting theory as 'given'. This clinical approach certainly made it more difficult for me to find my way through the clinical maze, and yet I preferred to stay with this more problematic way of working rather than make things simpler for myself at the risk of imposing theory upon a clinical sequence.

I have come to regard the analytic space as belonging to the patient, into which patients may begin to risk putting their innermost thoughts and phantasies; needing us to respect the products of their minds – to understand these if and when we can. I believe that we should never intrude upon a patient's mind, nor should we deflect it. Above all, I believe that we should not impose our own thinking upon a patient's thinking. If we do, we need to be asking: 'Whose thinking is it, and whose mind is it that could then be dominating the patient and beginning to run the patient's life?'

Part 2

Reflections

Chapter 10

Some things difficult to explain

Understanding everything?

During adolescence and for some years later I liked to think that I could understand just about everything. I had built what used to be known as a 'wireless' before I left my prep school and another soon after I went to Winchester, using circuits that I learned to understand and old-fashioned valves, which needed an 'accumulator' battery to run alongside a high tension battery, things unheard of nowadays. I also knew how steam engines worked, and petrol engines. I knew how electricity was made and how the atom bomb worked. So, as the years passed, I began to think that everything lay within my grasp. Perhaps it would only be a matter of time before I understood everything.

When I was at Oxford, for the social studies course, I was grappling with what then seemed to be one of the few remaining mysteries. I was fascinated by what I thought of as 'instant dry-cleaning machines' that were to be found in many toilets. It seemed that it was possible to dry clean and iron a roller towel so quickly that it could go in wet and dirty and come out clean and ironed. I fretted over the way in which this could be possible. What sort of cleaning liquid could be used? What kind of quick-heating rollers would be required to iron the towel? The problem fascinated me.

One day, however, it was all made clear when I went into the gents of the PPE[1] library. There I saw the shocking truth spread out before me. About 30 yards of dirty towel were strewn all around the floor. There was no dry-cleaning system, such as I had almost

---

1 Philosophy, Politics and Economics.

invented. It was all a sleight of hand. There was no magic. There then seemed to be no mystery left in life and I spent the rest of the day feeling depressed, while also laughing at myself and wanting to tell this story to my friends, to have them join in the laughter.

Why was I depressed? Was it that I was faced with the truth that I could not, after all, understand everything? Probably. It was certainly time for me to have my omnipotence challenged. But it may also have been that I had always enjoyed testing my mind against things not yet understood. How would I still do that if there remained no mysteries still to be solved?

This incident left me with two quite different views on life. In one view there was an assumption that, given time, all things would be explainable. Everything could or should be amenable to scientific investigation. There should be a rational explanation to all phenomena. Another view, however, also persisted. Maybe there is a place for those things that cannot be understood. Perhaps there is still a place for mystery in life alongside the systems of explanation that are provided by science, or by philosophy and/or psychology.

A strange coincidence[2]

When our second daughter was still at primary school she was asked to write about a religious experience. 'Dad, have you ever had a religious experience?' she asked when she got home one day. I said I didn't know but I would tell her a true story; maybe it would count at her school as a religious experience. She wrote down what I told her and she got an 'A' for it at school. This is the story.

In the early 1950s, when I was 17, during the Easter holiday time when my parents were abroad and I had remained in England, I had spent part of that time with my grandmother. She was in her last year before she died. She lived about four miles from my parents' home. During that time I heard my grandmother talking a lot about her life. She felt that she'd had a wonderful life. She had only one real regret. She had lost touch with her best ever friend from childhood, explaining that during the war there had been many moves and changes of address. Then, when the war was over, she had not been able to find this friend. All letters to her, sent to

---

2 This example has been retold with my permission in *Extraordinary Knowing* by the late Elizabeth Lloyd Mayer, PhD, New York: Bantam Dell (in process).

any address she might have been at, were returned. She seemed to have lost this friend for ever.

On that Easter Sunday I went to my parents' usual church, knowing that I would meet other people there whom I knew. For my return journey I had three choices. I could wait 40 minutes for the bus, I could hitch a lift, or I could walk. I had about four miles to walk back to my grandmother's house and it struck me that there was an interesting challenge here, to see if I could get there before the bus. It was like those questions in mathematics: 'If I walk at 4 mph and a bus drives at 30 mph, and I start walking 40 minutes before the bus is due, who will get there first if the journey is 4 miles?' I decided to walk, definitely not hitchhiking, and if the bus caught up with me I would take the bus for the remainder of the journey.

Setting off with this challenge very much in mind, I ignored all cars that might have been able to give me a lift. But, for no explicable reason, when one particular car came round a corner, my right hand took over as if by some reflex and thumbed a lift. I was angry with myself, as this threatened to spoil my 'race', seeing who got there first – the bus or myself. Fortunately the car carried on, so I seemed to have the challenge still in place, but then suddenly it stopped. I therefore had to accept the lift I didn't want, but which my involuntary action of thumbing for a lift had requested.

I ran up to the car and got in beside the chauffeur. He had clearly chosen to ignore this hitchhiker until told to stop. When I thanked the lady in the back she amazed me by asking: 'Were you at Winchester?'[3] I said I was still at that school and she replied: 'I used to know someone called Roddie Casement. He went to Winchester, but that must have been a long time ago now. It was before the war.' When I told her that she was speaking of my father, she was delighted and asked: 'Is his mother still alive?' I said we would soon be driving past her door, about two miles down the road. The lady then told me a parallel story to the one I had heard the previous week, that she had been trying to trace my grandmother, with whom she had lost touch during the war. 'She is my best friend. I would love to see her again.'

When we arrived at my grandmother's house I ran in to her, saying: 'You remember that friend you had lost, your best friend.

3 Winchester College.

Well, I have just found her for you. She is in the car outside wishing to see you.' The two friends spent the rest of the day together and my grandmother died not long after that, happy to have met her friend again.

I have no idea what to make of this. Some of it, but not all of it, can be explained. It is possible that this lady may have recognized a family resemblance between myself at 17 and my father at a similar age. Just possibly she might have made the chauffeur stop because of some sense of déjà vu if she had caught a glimpse of me as the car was driving past. But what I cannot explain is my involuntary action of thumbing a lift from this particular car, let alone the strange coincidence of her car driving that way on that particular day. The lady did not normally travel in that direction, living a long way off.

I have treasured this memory because it cannot all be explained, and I still like to find that some areas of mystery remain in life. It can stimulate curiosity, which I enjoy. I also enjoy being reminded that we don't understand everything. Maybe there will be some things that we are never going to understand.

Another coincidence[4]

Mrs F was in her late sixties when she first came to see me. She had been referred by a psychiatrist after she had attempted suicide, and had been hospitalized for some time because she had caused quite serious damage to her nervous system with a massive overdose.

Mrs F tried to explain to me her reason for having attempted to kill herself. She was convinced she would never be able to cope with her husband dying before her. He was ten years older, so it was likely he would die first. As we worked on this fear, Mrs F came to focus her dread most specifically on the moment of her husband's death. She knew she would have to cope with that on her own. She was adamant that there was nobody she could turn to at such a time, having convinced herself she would not be able turn to her children, nor to a neighbour or friends. She would be utterly alone.

I had eventually met the husband whom I will call James. He had come to see me, asking what he could do to help his wife with

4 This example is taken from Casement (2002b).

her continuing dread. We had considered the practical things he might be able to do, to make it easier for her to take over the reins if he did die before her. He had always managed the finances, the pensions, the shares and all matters to do with the house. We went through this and he indicated what he could do towards handing over these things to her or to an adviser, so that she would not be burdened with matters she did not feel competent to manage.

Some three years later, by which time her husband was in hospital, Mrs F was still coming to see me. She would drive up to London each week from the country cottage they had bought. One day, as Mrs F began to sit down for her session, she said: 'I don't think I should be here to-day.' When I asked her why, she replied:

> I am sure James is dying. I went to see him this morning and I just know he is dying, but he said to me I *must* come to see you today. He made me promise I would come as he knows that today is my day for seeing you.

About 20 minutes into the session I was startled to hear my phone ring. I usually make it my business to pull the plug before a session, though I do of course occasionally forget. But one thing I never ever do is to answer the phone during a session – regardless of who might be ringing. If I have forgotten to unplug the phone, I always just pull out the plug immediately and leave the answerphone to take a message. On this occasion, for reasons I could not explain, I found myself saying to Mrs F: 'I have a hunch that I should be answering this call. Would you please excuse me?' I picked up the phone to find that Mrs F's daughter was ringing from the hospital to say her father had just died. She had rung me because she had learned from him that her mother was coming to see me about this time. I said she was with me right then, so she could speak to her herself. I handed the phone to Mrs F.

What followed in this session was remarkable. Mrs F found that the one thing she had most dreaded, the thing which had driven her to attempt suicide and which had brought her to me, had after all been manageable. She had not been alone at the moment when James had died. She was with the one person who might be able to have some sense of how much she had feared this, someone who could be with her at the moment of his dying. She also felt convinced that James had somehow hung on until he knew she would be with me, and that was why he had made her promise she would keep her appointment.

So, by a sequence of unusual happenings, Mrs F could be supported at the very time her husband died. If I had remembered to unplug the phone this would not have happened. If I had observed my absolute rule of never answering the phone during a session, it would not have happened. But, by chance, Mrs F could be helped in a way no one could have planned. She was able to find herself not alone at the moment she had dreaded for so long.

An uncanny awareness

When I was a probation officer I was in court with a female colleague, both of us being duty officers for that day. During the court proceedings there was a young teenage girl in the dock. My colleague was taking notes in preparation for the subsequent enquiries that would be asked for and I was just listening. I turned to my colleague and said: 'That girl is pregnant.' My colleague thought I was talking nonsense and said so, but it turned out that the girl was indeed pregnant. She had learned this just a few weeks before she had committed the offence that brought her to court.

My colleague asked me how I knew. I wasn't quite sure but I thought it was from the way she had held one hand across her stomach. It seemed to me this may have been partly to hide being pregnant, in case it had begun to show, and partly perhaps as a protective gesture. But it also occurred to me it might have been an unconscious communication, drawing attention to a fact which only a part of her wished to hide. Maybe she also wished it to be known. These were my thoughts at the time.

I did not think more about this then, but it came back to mind when (during my analysis) I kept noticing early pregnancy in people. On one particular occasion I had been sitting beside a friend (Peter), driving back from a concert where we had met with other friends. When one of them was talking with Peter during the interval, I noticed something about her face and eyes. She seemed lit up in a way I had not seen in her before. In the car I said to Peter: 'How long has she been pregnant?' He was shocked and replied: 'Did she tell you too?' She had not; in fact I hadn't spoken with her at all, I just knew. Peter said this pregnancy had only been confirmed that day.

As I was in analysis at the time it is not surprising that this turned up in some sessions, which is how my sensitivity to early pregnancy came to be understood in relation to my mother's miscarriage (described in Chapter 2).

Beyond being controlled by a patient

I was seeing a patient (Anne) in psychotherapy when she had surgery on her spine for what turned out to be a prolapsed disk. She was a nurse who had already experienced back problems from lifting, so it was very strange when the surgeon had assumed that he should operate as for cancer on the spine. I gather that the surgical procedures for these two operations are completely different, the muscles being left intact as far as possible if there is any risk of a prolapsed disk. As it happened, the surgeon cut up and down the spine, looking for the cancer that was not there, until a disk slipped right out, paralysing the patient for life.[5] For the next 14 years I visited Anne in hospital, or in a home for the disabled, until she died of medical complications from her paralysed condition.

Anne's problems, before the paralysis, were profound. She was also addicted to bingeing and vomiting and to chain-smoking. She felt unloved by her mother. She hated herself. She often said that she only lived for her eating and for her nursing.

After her paralysis, Anne felt she had nothing left to live for except the next opportunity for binge eating, followed by vomiting. Her smoking was just a way of filling the time until her next binge. Nursing had been the only other distraction that worked for her, and now even that was impossible. Instead, she had to suffer agonies of envy for the nurses around her, who were still free to do the only other thing she had ever enjoyed.

Anne often treated my visits as if they were unwelcome and unwanted, but she telephoned me to make sure I knew where she was and which ward she was on when in hospital. During the session time she would frequently shout at me to go away. (She was on a private ward which gave her that freedom.) I would reply along the lines of: 'I know you are angry. You have a lot to be angry about, which is why I am here. At least you can be angry with me. I am therefore going to stay until the end of your time.'

---

5 The surgeon was found to have been drunk at the time of the surgery. He had proceeded to operate without a definitive diagnosis. Eventually, Anne won a case against him for professional negligence.

Gradually, Anne would relax into allowing me to be there, but she still made it clear that she resented my presence. She would say: 'When you are here I am not free to be thinking about food, which is all I ever want to do. I wish you were not here.' Even though Anne used a lot of her session time being angry with me, expressing much of her resentment, I continued to visit.

In the home where she often was, the nurses were also having a difficult time with her. The GP, who stayed in touch with me in relation to her management, told me the nurses were frequently complaining that whatever they did for Anne it was never right for her. They resented having to take care of her. She was said to be almost impossible to care for.

I thought there was an important communication in her behaviour, so I suggested to the GP that Anne seemed to be behaving in ways that were likely to induce in those around her a similar angry state of paralysis and helplessness to her own, about which nothing could be done. Nothing was right for Anne. The only thing that could have been right would have been for her to be released from her paralysis, which of course was impossible. She probably felt an unconscious need to force others to experience, however briefly, some of what she was experiencing all the time; another example of communicating through projective identification.

I believe that this formulation gradually began to make some sense to the nursing staff in the home. Meanwhile, I continued to visit Anne and she began to adjust to her paralysed state and such life as was still possible for her. One day I went as usual to the place where Anne had been the week before. On this occasion, for the first time ever, Anne had not telephoned to tell me where she was. I arrived at the home to find she had been readmitted to hospital. I went to her usual ward to find she was not there. I went to the reception desk and was told she had been admitted to another ward. There I found her and she was completely amazed to see me. How did I know where to find her? I explained how.

For the very first time Anne was faced with the fact that I must have cared enough to take the trouble to find out where she was. Until that day she had always been able to explain my coming in terms of her having made me come, even though she would so often then attack me for coming. It was not only to tell me where she was that she had always phoned. She had telephoned to make sure that I came, being convinced that if she didn't remind me I would forget her.

I had never imagined how Anne might be affected by this new discovery, that I came of my own volition and not just because (in her mind) she had made me come. From that day she stopped bingeing and she stopped smoking, having always smoked at least 60 cigarettes a day, chain-smoking most of the time.

What then surfaced from beneath the defence of her addictions was her hidden dependence on a person. This fierce dependence had seemed to have been too much for her mother, and therefore was assumed to be too much for anyone. Instead she had come to depend upon substitutes that could never replace what they were meant to substitute. Now, without her dependence being channelled elsewhere, Anne became acutely and extremely dependent upon me. There was no way she could manage a whole week without contact with me, even though I continued to visit her every week. I could not manage visiting her any more frequently as it took the time of two sessions to travel and to see her. Instead, I arranged at least two other times in the week when she could telephone me and I would be there to speak to her. I kept these telephone arrangements as rigorously as I would any session time, and Anne always phoned exactly on the minute that I had set aside for her.

For the remaining years of Anne's life we were gradually able to move on from this first eruption of dependence, needing frequent contact, towards her becoming able to internalize something from these contacts, which she could draw upon between my visits. She remained not smoking and not bingeing. Alas, however, her life was still to end in hospital – in her death. But I learned many useful things from my work with her.

A woman who felt she should have been a boy

I once worked with a woman (Dr G) who came to me with the problem that she could not conceive. She was a medical doctor who knew all the treatments that were available for infertility, but none of these had worked for her. 'Is it possible there might be some emotional block against my fertility?' she asked when she first came to see me.

What emerged in the following months of therapy was the story of her childhood and subsequent life, in which she had come to feel she could not please her parents in any way. They had wanted her to be a boy and she felt burdened with their disappointment in her for being a girl. There were many sessions during which I was given further details that illustrated this theme. But, consciously, she had no wish to be anything other than the woman she was.

Eventually we came to a session in which Dr G made a most revealing slip of the tongue. She was saying that the only thing she had ever done right in her parents' eyes was in becoming a doctor. They could at least think of her as 'my son the doctor'. I asked her if she had heard what she had just said. Strangely, she hadn't. She was utterly surprised when I told her she was speaking of herself as her parents' son. Later in this session I said to Dr G:

> I cannot promise anything. But I do believe that, if you can really bear the possibility you might never be able to please your parents, and if you can bear the thought of becoming unmistakably and irretrievably female, I am beginning to think that you could also bear a child.

Some three months later Dr G conceived and had a chance to grow into her new role as a mother, with a new-found confidence in herself. Gradually too her parents began to accept her for what she was. It is, of course, possible that the timing here was just coincidence. But Dr G remained convinced that she had needed to work through her block about being a woman before she could allow herself to become 'unmistakably and irretrievably female'.

Missed sessions

A supervisee once left me a message saying: 'As my patient has cancelled all three sessions since my last supervision I am ringing to say that I am cancelling my supervision.' I replied:

> In my way of thinking, patients can't cancel sessions. They can choose not to attend but the session still exists. We therefore should not agree with a patient's idea that a session has been 'cancelled' even if that is what they have communicated. So, if your patient has missed three sessions we have a lot to think about at your usual supervision time. It is possible that there is something here we have not yet understood.

The point of the following vignettes is to invite some thought into how we spend time that is freed by patients who announce they are not coming to a session. My own practice is to observe all sessions as still existing, whether or not a patient is going to attend. I also make it my practice to connect my consulting-room telephone during any session time until the patient has arrived, in case patients choose to ring during their time. After all, they are still paying for this. Just occasionally, a patient has telephoned during that time; and when that has happened I have always been glad I had continued to regard the session as still there for the patient.

A very interesting mistake

During a long analysis, I had been working with a patient through a time of prolonged but very fruitful regression. She had then begun to surface from this, resuming her life with a new sense of direction and energy. She was on holiday with her children, wanting them to have the full school holiday period abroad (this time) rather than have it again shortened by her commitment to the analysis. She was therefore not going to be present during my first week back at work.

As usual, I had connected my phone during each of this patient's session times, even though my patient was still on holiday. Then, just after the start of one of her sessions, the phone rang. I gave my number, as I usually do, and heard this patient say: 'Oh. I thought I was telephoning my mother.'

What was extraordinary about this was that the patient had hardly ever telephoned me and, as far as I could recall, not for many years. She had now dialled my number instead of her mother's at a time that happened to be her usual session time, even though she was phoning from abroad and a different time zone, and there she found the person who had often been experienced as her mother in the transference. My number had been remembered all of that time and unconsciously dialled by mistake. Her mother was not even in England at the time, so this mistake also involved a different country code as well as my personal number, instead of her mother's.

A prolonged absence[6]

I had one patient who had been adopted in childhood. Her reading of this had been that her mother hadn't wanted her. In the course

---

6 This example is from my paper 'Between Patients' (Casement 2002c).

of quite a long analysis, five times per week, this patient went abroad during my Easter break. At the end of the break she wrote saying she had got into some special experiences where she was on holiday, and she felt it was important for her to remain there for another month. Would I please keep her times for her? She promised that she would pay for those sessions when she got back. Her fee was only a token fee, so I was not going to be seriously disadvantaged by having to wait to be paid. I wrote back agreeing to keep her times.

At the end of that month I received another letter from this patient saying she had decided to stay away for longer still, so would I please extend the same arrangement? She would let me know when she would be coming back.

Throughout this time I observed this patient's sessions. I used to put my diary on the table that is between our chairs, as she was then not using the couch. I also reconnected the phone. So even though I did not spend all of each session *actively* thinking of this patient, I always had her 'in mind' for each of these times.

After an absence of about two and a half months, and I had as usual just put my diary in place for this patient's session, I heard the patients' doorbell. I opened it with the buzzer and there she was. She hadn't let me know when she was coming back. Instead, she had come unannounced, expecting to find that I was either out or had someone else there in her place. She had not expected to find my consulting room set up ready for me to see her, if she came. In the discussion that followed, she learned that I had in fact kept each of her sessions for her throughout her absence. But, under-standably, she had needed to test me out on this.

As this analysis continued it became apparent that, quite apart from any insight this patient may have gained during it, one of the most telling experiences for her had been that I had truly – and not just in words – kept her in mind during her absence. She could not remember having had this experience with anyone else before.

Diagnostic dreams

One patient telephoned from abroad during her usual session time and found me available as described above. She was ringing to tell me a dream in which she had symbolically diagnosed a serious medical condition that had become physically apparent three days later, and which had then been confirmed in the hospital she had immediately taken herself to. The diagnosis was of a life-threatening condition. She didn't feel she could wait until she got back from her time abroad, which is why she had telephoned – hoping that I would be there. It turned out to be really important to her that I had been.

I have met several patients who have diagnosed their own medical condition in dreams, some many months before the condition would have become evident under normal circumstances. One patient diagnosed her own breast cancer, even which breast, and she had persisted from one doctor to another until someone was prepared to take her seriously. A scan, which would normally not have been agreed to without more definite evidence of the need for it, confirmed her diagnosis. The surgeon found a small, highly invasive tumour that was thereby discovered many months (she was told it might have been two years) earlier than would have happened had she waited until a tangible lump had developed. She has not had any recurrence in the many years that have followed.

Another patient (Mrs H) had two dreams which I later came to realize had also been diagnostic. This was early in my training and I did not then have the confidence in my reading of such dreams to persuade her to have herself checked out. If she had been checked when she first had these dreams, she could have been diagnosed about six months earlier.

In the first dream Mrs H was sitting on a toilet, trying to evacuate something that would not come away. 'It just seemed to go on for ever, as if it was endless.' In the second dream she was in Eastbourne, by the sea, and the sea was full of dead bodies. She was desperately trying to rescue her two boys 'from the deadness in the sea'. Her associations to Eastbourne were to the time when she had first heard she was pregnant. It was the place she had usually associated with birth but, in this dream, it was full of death. Her eventual diagnosis was cancer of the ovaries, from which she later died.

There was an interesting sequence during the time of her medical treatment, which the medical director of the clinic (then Dr Nina Coltart) had wanted me to write up. As part of the early stages of her treatment for cancer, the doctors opened up the patient to see if they could operate. They found too many vital organs had become attached to the cancer so that it was impossible. During the first year after her diagnosis, we had to work hard on her suicidal thinking. She often wished herself dead. She had only managed to remain alive 'for the sake of the children', but never really for herself.

We explored the roots of this wish to be dead, finding much in the patient's relationship to her mother that had fed into her wish to punish her. She had felt that her mother had never really wanted her. She added: 'If I die, she would have her wish granted. She could have a dead daughter rather than one she had not wanted.' There was much to be done in our working through of this insight, and gradually Mrs H began to come alive in a new way. It seemed that she had begun to value being alive, and had been fighting to remain alive, faced with the reality that she might die of this cancer.

After a year the doctors opened up the patient again to see what progress had been made and they were amazed to find the cancer had retreated from all vital organs to such an extent that they were able to operate. They had removed the cancer in its entirety. They said they could not explain how the cancer had retreated so much. It was not at all what they had expected. Mrs H said to me: 'They don't know what made it retreat, but we do.' She seemed to have a deep belief that it had been the analysis, quite as much as the chemotherapy, that had saved her life.

Mrs H felt she had been reprieved from her death sentence, but she then retreated into magical thinking. She persuaded herself she had been cured and made plans to live her life more fully in celebration of her new freedom. Against my judgement, however, she also chose to reduce her analysis – so that she would have 'more time for living'. I was very concerned at this but could not persuade her otherwise.

For three years, with her analysis reducing to three times a week and then eventually to once a week, Mrs H remained well. But the death wish that had gripped her had not been entirely dealt with. Nor would she countenance giving herself more time in analysis to allow us to deal with it more thoroughly. Alas, the cancer returned and this time she died of it. Dr Coltart thought that I had colluded with her death wish, in allowing this patient to withdraw from her analysis. She felt the evidence supported the possibility that it had been the analysis that had enabled her to respond so well to the chemotherapy first time. She felt it had been the loss of the analysis that had contributed to the patient ultimately co-operating with her wish to die, still active in her unconscious. We shall never know.

Another strange coincidence

While working with the FWA I had a dream, out of the blue, about my first girlfriend,[7] who had left me for a friend of mine (David). I had last seen her in hospital, some year or so before. I don't now remember the dream, but what was strange was that I had dreamed of her on that particular night. Soon after I got to my office she telephoned me, her first contact for over a year. She wanted to see me that day.

My diary was usually completely full and it would normally have taken me about a week to arrange an absence. But on that day I found, for the only time ever, my diary was almost empty. Anything entered was easy to cancel or postpone. I took a day's leave and spent the day with this girl and her two-and-a-half-year-old daughter. She used the time to make her peace with me, and at the end of the day I met up with David, who had by then been ordained. From this meeting we arranged that they would meet with me and the person I was then soon to marry. David's wife died quite soon after that. But it had been possible for peace to be made between her and me and for me to meet David again. It had also led to my future wife meeting the person who, until then, had remained an upsetting but unknown presence in our relationship. It was a very fruitful and helpful sequence.

Telepathy?

Many of us have had experiences of strange timing, as with telephone calls that happen just when we had decided to ring the other person. Quite recently I had been concerned about my former patient (Mrs Y),[8] wondering how she was doing, especially as she was the person I had stopped seeing about five years before when it seemed I could no longer help her.

While I was still seeing Mrs Y, I had given her the name of an analyst I could recommend for her husband. It was tempting to ring this analyst, to ask news of my former patient but I knew I must resist that temptation. I needed to respect the boundaries of that analysis. I also stayed firm, as I always do, in my respect for a

7 See also Chapter 2.
8 See Chapter 3.

former patient's privacy. So I did not telephone the patient or write to her. Instead, I looked her up on Google. There I found a reference to her taking part in some public occasion. It looked as if she was doing well, but I could not tell more from this.

A few days later I received a letter from Mrs Y, a very generous letter in which she thanked me for the time I had spent with her in analysis and saying how much she had gained from that experience. She also said it had been right that I had ended the analysis when I did. It was reassuring and affirming to receive this letter. She told me that she had thought of writing several times, but on this occasion it had suddenly felt the right moment. I replied, appreciating what she had written. I also mentioned the timing of her letter, which was interesting as I had 'googled' her just a few days before getting it. When she and I compared these dates it seemed that she had either written the same day as I had looked her up on Google, or the day after. Had there been some telepathic resonance here? We will never know.

Chapter 11

Certainty and non-certainty

In 1962 I was asked to preach a sermon in the north of England town of Oldham, where I had been doing a placement as a student social worker. My sermon was to be in a series of four, on the traditional themes for Advent, the 'Four Last Things' (death, judgement, hell and heaven). I was asked to preach on hell.

I no longer have the sermon I gave on that day, but I remember that I was giving a view of hell as self-made. I suggested that we are offered God's love, an unconditional love, to which we may respond or not. We are left free to make whichever response we choose. Often we may turn our backs, feeling unable to respond to it or refusing to accept the love that is offered. We may refuse this love out of arrogance, believing that we can do without it. Or we may claim to know better than God, in seeing ourselves as being beyond the reach of that love through being unworthy of it. How could we receive the Grace of God? Should we not first become deserving of it through our own good works? Yet another kind of arrogance.

The hell we may experience does not have to be a hell that we are condemned to by a vengeful God. The vengeful god we hear about may simply be the invention of our own imagination, being often so much nearer to how we are than the all-loving God that we are invited to turn to. Therefore, when we feel we are 'in hell' this may be hell of our own making, beyond which there may yet be a loving and grieving God who waits for the return of those who turn their backs upon His love.

The seeds of that view of hell were sown during my time at Cambridge. For instance, while I was still there, I heard Mervyn Stockwood preach on Dostoyevsky's 'The Grand Inquisitor'. I don't remember the sermon but I have never forgotten being introduced to that visionary chapter in *The Brothers Karamazov*. It has remained an inspiration for me ever since. Dostoyevsky highlights there some of the things that have gone wrong with institutionalized Christianity. He also shows a prophetic insight into some of the dynamics in Communist Russia.

Dostoyevsky describes an imaginary sequence that takes place in Spain, in Seville, during the Inquisition. It is set 'at the moment when, a day before, nearly a hundred heretics had been burnt all at once by the cardinal, the Grand Inquisitor, *ad majoram gloriam Dei*' (p. 291).[1] Into this scene the risen Christus (the living Christ) appears: 'He appeared quietly, inconspicuously, but everyone – and that is why it is so strange – recognized him' (p. 291).

People are gathered in great numbers around the cathedral to do homage to the Grand Inquisitor, for having (yet again) saved the Church from heresy. But then they see the Christus amongst them:

> The people are drawn to him by an irresistible force, they surround him, they throng him, they follow him. He walks among them in silence. . . . He stretches forth his hands to them, blesses them, and a healing virtue comes from contact with him, even with his garments.
>
> (p. 291)

Further scenes repeat moments from the life of Jesus, as recorded in the Gospels. A blind man receives his sight again. They bring him a child who is being carried in an open coffin. He speaks to the child, once again saying the words 'Talitha cumi', and she is raised from the dead. At this moment the Grand Inquisitor passes by and sees what is happening. He recognizes the Christus and orders that he be arrested.

For the rest of this extraordinary chapter the Grand Inquisitor is with this figure, in the prison where he has been sent, questioning and challenging him. The prisoner remains silent. What the Grand Inquisitor is saying throughout this monologue is that Jesus had got things wrong:

---

1 All the page numbers in this chapter refer to the Penguin Classics edition of *The Brothers Karamazov*, translated by David Magarshack (1958).

Everything . . . has been handed over by you to the Pope and, therefore, everything is now in the Pope's hands, and there's no need for you to come at all now – at any rate do not interfere.

(p. 294)

The Grand Inquisitor explains that, though Jesus had offered to make people free, they do not want to be free. They cannot bear being unsure. They want certainty in belief, and instructions for life that are beyond question:

For fifteen centuries we've been troubled by this freedom, but now it's over and done with for good. . . . I want you to know that now – yes, to-day – these men are more than ever convinced that they are absolutely free, and yet they themselves have brought their freedom to us and humbly laid it at our feet. But it was we who did it.

(p. 294)

The Grand Inquisitor goes on. Jesus had refused the only ways that could have worked with the masses when he had rejected the temptations presented to him in the wilderness. He could have turned stones into bread. People who are free do not share their bread. Instead, the Grand Inquisitor says that the Church now takes people's freedom and their bread. It is now the Church that distributes the bread. He continues:

Man, so long as he remains free, has no more constant and agonizing anxiety than to find as quickly as possible someone to worship. But man seeks to worship only what is incontestable, so incontestable, indeed, that all men at once agree to worship it all together.

(pp. 297–298)

It is this need for *universal* worship that is the chief torment of every man individually and of mankind as a whole from the beginning of time. For the sake of that universal worship they have put each other to the sword. They have set up gods and called upon each other, 'Give up your gods and come and worship ours, or else death to you and to your gods!'

(p. 298)

Only he can gain possession of men's freedom who is able to set their conscience at ease. With the bread you were given an incontestable banner: give them bread and man will worship you, for there is nothing more incontestable than bread; but if at the same time someone besides yourself should gain possession of his conscience – oh, then he will even throw away your bread and follow him who has ensnared his conscience.

(p. 298)

You wanted man's free love so that he should follow you freely, fascinated and captivated by you. Instead of the strict ancient law, man had in future to decide for himself with a free heart what is good and what is evil, having only your image before him for guidance. But did it never occur to you that he would at last reject and call in question even your image and your truth, if he were weighed down by so fearful a burden as freedom of choice?

(p. 299)

There are three forces, the only three forces that are able to conquer and hold captive for ever the conscience of these weak rebels for their own happiness – these forces are: miracle, mystery, and authority. You rejected all three.

(p. 299)

We have corrected your great work and have based it on *miracle, mystery, and authority*. And men rejoiced that they were once more led like sheep and that the terrible gift [of freedom] which had brought them so much suffering had at last been lifted from their hearts.

(p. 301)

The Grand Inquisitor reminds the Christus that, if he had accepted the temptations set him by the devil in the wilderness:

you would have accomplished all that man seeks on earth, that is to say, whom to worship, to whom to entrust his conscience and how at last to unite all in a common, harmonious, and incontestible ant-hill, for the need of universal unity is the third and last torment of men.

(p. 302)

The Grand Inquisitor's monologue ends. The story continues:

> He waited for some time for the Prisoner's reply. His silence
> distressed him. He saw that the Prisoner had been listening
> intently to him all the time, looking gently into his face and
> evidently not wishing to say anything in reply. The old man
> would have liked him to say something, however bitter and
> terrible. But he suddenly approached the old man and kissed
> him gently on his bloodless, aged lips. That was all his answer.
>
> (p. 308)

> The old man showed him to the door: 'Go, and come no more
> – don't come at all – never, never!'
>
> (p. 308)

I have quoted from this chapter because I think it spells out so
much that is true about organized religion and, in time, also about
any totalitarian state. It is remarkable how similar the dynamics
between them can be, but I think the chapter points to much else
that is also true.

Throughout the history of the Christian Church we see signs of
people improving on the message given them by Jesus. Men prefer
to have their god made in their own image. In the service of
controlling the masses in the name of religion, it might well be
more effective to have a vengeful god, with the fear of damnation
and the fires of hell, to bind men to a fearful observation of the
rules set out by the Church, than to risk losing control over the
masses. Never mind, perhaps, that this reduces much of religious
observation to a superstitious fear of the consequences of failure.
The masses are more readily brought to heel by fear than by any
vision of a different way of life that is not governed by laws, but is
a matter of individual freedom. Where superstition reigns there will
more often be full churches. Just look at the few numbers of those
who still respond to that invitation to freedom, so scorned by the
Grand Inquisitor, for which he criticizes the Christus. That freedom is more than most people can bear.

In the Grand Inquisitor chapter, nevertheless, we still get a sense
of the untainted message presented to the disciples in the life and
death of Jesus. He seemed to have been pointing them beyond the
limitations of the ancient law, as passed on to them from the Old
Testament. Jesus had been presenting people with a sense of a life

that could be self-giving for others, a vision to inspire them and to show them a different way. Those that could respond to this vision would not need to be told how to live their lives. Instead, people were invited to find their own way to respond to it. So it would only be those who could not see it, or who could not respond to it, who might need to be told how to live the 'good life', though all might need help in dealing with the obstacles in themselves that get in the way of a fuller response to that vision.

I believe that Dostoyevsky points out the damage that has been done by the institutionalizing of Christianity, with its accumulation of new laws and the listing of sins committed in breaking them, with the related system of confession and absolution – all under the authority of the Church.

I believe this passage also shows the effect of the divisions that have grown up from the attempts, by many, to define their own versions of how the Church should be, each saying to others: 'Give up your gods and come and worship ours.' Throughout the history of the Church we find this splitting over differences, each schism being man-made but each claiming to know the mind of God better than others do. Wars have been fought, and terrible atrocities committed, in the name of these rival claims.

Much, if not everything, of what is claimed to be in the name of God is what men have created. This is what Dostoyevsky is pointing to, in saying that the authorities have corrected Jesus' errors, building a system more suited to the masses so that they might at last be united 'in a common, harmonious, and incontestible ant-hill'.

A brief experience of fundamentalism

I wrote in Chapter 2 that for a while I allowed myself to feel that I was in safe hands when I was being persuaded to join an evangelical group that claimed me as a convert. Behind them, I was being assured, was the ultimate guide – God. I was being promised much. I was promised forgiveness. I was promised that I would always be safe in 'the everlasting arms of the Father'. How very appealing it was for an adolescent looking for certainty. I did not care that my mind was being taken over by others. I thought I was being brought to the Truth. I should therefore welcome giving up the error of my ways, or my wrong thinking. Also, when I doubted, I could pray to be helped 'in my unbelief'.

In addition, I now realize, I was able to disown my own doubts by addressing doubts that I could find in others. The evangelicals saw themselves as the holders of ultimate truth: truth for all the world. We were therefore encouraged to seek out those who needed to be given 'the truth' as we had been given it. The world was seen in black and white terms. But the dynamics of certainty were still unknown to me. I did not recognize that I was being brainwashed.

The appeal of certainty

We are readily attracted to a notion of being certain. We like to believe that we are right. This can make life seem simple, as anyone who disagrees can be assumed to be in the wrong. Also, when a group forms around a shared belief, the group dynamic that develops will often reinforce a sense of rightness. Especially as regards religion, people claim to be on the side of the right and the good. Then, in the name of truth, they proselytize amongst those who think differently, and it is easy to feel specially blessed when one is on a crusade for one's own idea of 'the truth'. Like the Grand Inquisitor, people have fought wars and burned heretics for the greater glory of God. But what is missing is a proper realisation that what is right for one person is not necessarily right for all. What feels true to me does not have to be true for you.

Not long after the last war, I had a salutary lesson with regard to this idea of fighting on the side of right. I was staying briefly with an Austrian family in Salzburg, and was shown the funeral card of a son who had died as a pilot during the war. He had been shot down by the Russians. On this card were written the familiar lines: 'I have fought the good fight and I have kept the faith.' But, what an irony! Those same lines were used for many of our own war dead. In Ireland also, the two warring sides have felt passionately that they have each been 'fighting the good fight,' with terrible acts being done in the name of their separate ideas of truth, and we find a similar dynamic throughout the world.

Some dynamics of certainty

The appeal of certainty has roots that go very deep. We should not be surprised at this, for we are born into the uncertainty of a world so different from that in which we were conceived. In this uncertain world we have to find such security as we can. So, from the start, we have had to believe that we were being taken care of by the 'best mother in the world', regardless of anything that might bring that belief into question.

Also, in the service of that illusion we soon learned to split off whatever experience challenged that idea of security, thus inventing a 'good' mother from whom only good could come, and a 'bad' mother to whom all bad experience could be attributed. One version of that is to be found in the concepts of a 'good breast' and a 'bad breast'; and other versions abound in tales of the 'good fairy' and the 'wicked witch'. Adult versions of these illusions can be found in the notion of idealized parents, which may also be projected onto God the Father and the Blessed Virgin Mary, over against the Devil – that ultimate 'not me' wicked one.

It was part of our earliest system of defence, to protect us from conflict, that we built up a split view of the world. This included a split between 'me' and 'not me'. Thus the outside world, insofar as we were then aware of it, could seem to be a tidy enough affair with good and bad each in its place. Similarly, our own 'inside' could be thought of as the place where good should be, and some bits of 'the outside' as the places into which all bad could be expelled. So, in the service of security we developed these splits.

With systems of certainty in place, we might seem to be protected from some of the unavoidable conflicts of living – in particular the conflicts of ambivalence, uncertainty and indecision. For within a system of unquestioned belief, as children or as adults, we may feel that we are able to know where we are and how we stand in the world.

The defence systems of childhood frequently persist in other apparently more adult worlds. Religion naturally becomes a playground for primitive defences, in particular those of idealization, splitting, projection and denial. People in politics also make much of these, our own party being regarded as the fount of all that is good and the other party being blamed for whatever is wrong in the world. The field of psychoanalysis is also not free from this.

Most of us who work in the psychoanalytic world would wish to believe that we have been well enough analysed not to resort to such primitive defences. It is to be hoped that, as individuals, we may become less prone to do so. But when we identify ourselves with a particular group that has developed around a given theory, we often revert to splitting and projection. We find here too a tendency to believe that the views of our own group are right and the views of others mistaken. Or we see some old theoretical position as now superseded by another, sometimes presented as the new way. Inevitably, schisms develop in psychoanalytic societies too.

In belonging to a group of like-minded colleagues, we may find some respite from the aloneness of the consulting room. Those of us who work long hours, without much contact with anyone other than our patients, may not want to question too much the basis of such harmony as we find in a like-minded group. There we can find a sense of cohesion around a common belief system.

Hardly a single psychoanalytic society has been able to remain coherent and undivided. It has been said that it is only here in Britain, maybe because of our national readiness to compromise, that the London Psychoanalytic Society has not split. We have somehow held together three groups under one roof. But within this nominally single society, fundamental differences remain unresolved.

So where do we each stand in relation to our own belief system in psychoanalysis? Do we believe that we know, or that we belong to the group that has it most right? And if we do not believe that, where are we? Are we merely doubters, sceptics or muddled thinkers? How do the more sure relate to those who do not claim to be so sure? Are they respectful of that difference, or are they contemptuous of it? What then is the dynamic that exists between these different positions? With regard to this, are we analysts really so different from people in the field of politics and religion.

Religion and superstition

It is tempting for psychoanalysts to believe they have been able to analyse religion away, and they can quote Freud in support of their preference for seeing it in terms of projection. There is a serious point being made by these critics of religion, and it is partly for this reason that I considered myself an agnostic for most of my time as a practising psychoanalyst. However, I did not altogether divorce myself from my roots, having once thought that I might become a priest and having graduated in theology. I therefore chose to think of myself as a 'Christian agnostic'.[2] At least I could never assume

2 By 'Christian agnostic' I was acknowledging that I continued to be influenced by my familiarity with Christian thinking and practice, but without the same conviction in believing as those calling themselves Christians.

the position of an atheist who claims to know that there is no god. I cannot know that there is or that there is not a god, a creator and/or an intelligent mind behind the infinity of the cosmos, and the amazing beauty and diversity that we find in nature. Can it all be put down to chance? Can it all be put down to evolution?

I recall, with some discomfort, a time when I was present at a training committee that was deliberating a candidate's readiness to qualify. All the reports were in favour. The only dissenting voice came from one person who knew the candidate continued to practise his religion and said: 'He obviously needs more analysis as he is still caught up in superstition.' Despite this reservation, the candidate was allowed to qualify, but it continued to trouble me that Freud's prejudice against religion was still so active. Much later I was prompted to rethink my own prejudices against religion.

Still beyond our ken

A few years ago, one of our daughters was getting married and I asked our local vicar if his church could be used for the wedding ceremony. He agreed, but added that he thought at least one member of the family should begin to attend some of the services at the church. I chose to be the one to attend.

A particularly important experience for me, in my wife's planning for this wedding, was the fact that she had the inspired idea of asking my old friend (and former enemy) David[3] to conduct the service. This was a most healing choice. It gave him a role in relation to all of us. He had long since lost his first wife, who had died as had been expected. I was fortunate still to have my wife. Soon he was to be in our local church, conducting the marriage service for our daughter's wedding. He, whom I had once hated with a passionate jealousy, was to be with us as (once again) a friend to me and now a friend to all my family.

In attending this church, in place of the seemingly unthinking recital of liturgy I remembered in many other churches, I was surprised to find thoughtful and thought-provoking sermons. I also found a sense of relief at being back in a religious setting I had scorned for many years. I was glad to be once again confronted by

3 David, referred to in the previous chapter and in Chapter 2.

mystery and a sense of transcendence, both of which seem to have little place in psychoanalysis.

I had then to be asking myself whether psychoanalysis can really claim to have the last word on matters of religion. That would mean standing in judgement over many great minds, and I could no longer assume them all to be mistaken. It would also go against much of my own thinking about people in my clinical work, through whom I have come to an increasing sense of the otherness of the other. In church there can also be a sense of otherness, an awareness that the god (or God) being worshipped is not necessarily all man-made. Maybe, after all, there is something 'other' that draws people to bow before transcendence, before mystery. Maybe we need to acknowledge that there really could be more in life than we can know or understand, recognizing that the ineffable will always lie beyond our ken. Maybe there is also something to celebrate in this.

I am not suggesting that I have returned to where I was when I turned my back upon the Church and all it seemed to stand for. I am beginning to find a different place in a larger scale of things, no longer feeling that I can be an analyst who claims to be above it all. Once again I too can bow before what we do not understand.

Our other daughter's interest in Buddhism has also led me to think further about the unknowable and the meaning of life. And I have noticed a much greater sense of reverence in a Buddhist temple than I usually find in a western church. Do we need to be divided by our different loyalties?

Looking at the history of religion, we repeatedly find that divisions are set up in the name of different creeds, the different views on what lies beyond our understanding. But people naturally prefer to find agreement with their own kind, seeking a 'universal unity' such as Dostoyevsky wrote about. So, when people agree upon definitions, of what this group or that group holds to be 'the truth', inevitable divisions then develop and wars are still fought to put down those who dare to believe differently.

I have therefore found myself thinking that unity does not necessarily have to be found in the unity of rational thinking, where logic holds sway and definitions determine whether others hold to our own view of the truth, or are against it. Perhaps, unknown to ourselves, we are joined in a different way, as the spokes of a wheel are joined at the centre. Maybe, without knowing it, the long-established faiths are drawn towards a centre that remains beyond our ken, even though each faith lies in a different position in relation to that centre. Maybe each has a sense of some aspect of a greater truth that we all reach after, over which no single group has a monopoly.

It is, after all, the human dimension that divides each faith from the others, each claiming its own version of the truth to be the only one for the world. It is this human determination to grasp at a particular idea of the divine, and to claim ownership, that creates the definitions that divide us. Just possibly there is something that lies entirely beyond us that will always defy definition, that cannot be grasped or owned. I have therefore come to believe that there is still a place for bowing before mystery.

A few years ago I was telephoned by a fellow training analyst, inviting my wife and me to a Christmas Midnight Mass in a well-known church. We agreed to go together. Before entering, I asked my colleague if it would be embarrassing to find me going up to the altar to receive communion. I was surprised and delighted to discover that my colleague would also be receiving communion. I don't know that either of us believe all that those around us might claim to believe, but it seemed entirely appropriate that some analysts could be looking outside the usual realm of their profession, to share a sense of something 'beyond', before which they too could bend a knee.

Some readers might think I am revealing here that I need more analysis, like the candidate whose qualification could have been held up. Or might it be that there really is a place, even in our consulting rooms, for a sense of something that could be bigger than either of the two people who are engaged in the analytic process? We know that this process develops between the patient and the analyst, but who or what brings about this process? Is it the analyst? Is it the patient? Or is it something that develops between the two, which sometimes shows a wisdom that seems to come from elsewhere?

Non-certainty

I return to something I learned from a patient and included in my most recent book:

> It is very interesting to find that, in Sanskrit, the word for 'certainty' is the same as the word for 'imprisonment'. And the word for 'non-certainty' is the same as the word for 'freedom'.
>
> (Casement 2002d: 16)

I see *non-certainty*, as very different from *uncertainty*. Non-certainty is not about indecision, nor is it about ignorance. Rather, we can make a positive choice to remain, for the time being, *non-certain*. This can help to keep us open to meaning that we have not yet arrived at. I also try to return to a position of non-certainty when I notice that I am beginning to claim too much sureness in relation to others, because anyone who is too sure can quickly become someone who is sure that those who disagree must be in the wrong.

Psychoanalysts sometimes inhibit the discovery of fresh understanding by being too sure about the understanding they already have. When we are too sure, we are in danger of becoming slaves to our own thinking and to our own preferred theories. We may then become trapped by preconception, which can blind us to what else may lie beyond the limits of our current thinking.

Of course patients need to find that the analyst can sometimes be sure. I believe that a particular occasion for such firmness is when the analysis, or the patient, is felt to be at risk. The patient then needs to know that the analyst has a clear sense of this. There will also be occasions when confrontation is called for, and there too the analyst has to be able to stand firm. But, in the process of trying to understand what is not yet understood, I believe that the analytic process is often better served by our maintaining a sense of non-certainty until we are better able to understand. What is then understood may not always fit into what could be expected on the basis of established theory or other clinical experience.

With this discipline, of returning to non-certainty when necessary, psychoanalysis can continue to be the liberating process that it has the potential to be. It can be the very opposite to brainwashing. It is also entirely different from the bullying or pressurizing that one person might put upon another to bring the victim of that treatment into line with the bully's own ways of thinking. I believe that it is towards this freedom, in thinking and in being, that psychoanalysis offers a way. And it is within this freedom, I believe, that the future of psychoanalysis lies.

Paradoxically, non-certainty does not have to be a defence against ignorance, or lack of experience. It takes the confidence of experience for an analyst to be able to maintain non-certainty as the creative mindset it can be. This is the challenge we are constantly having to face in this 'impossible profession'.

Chapter 12

Looking back

Patrick Casement's book. . . . seemed to come from nowhere, to be met with critical acclaim and the status of a modern classic.
(Review in *Changes*, July 1986)

Challenged by that review of my first book, I have tried to describe something of where my books have come from. They grew out of a journey that could not have been planned but which proved to be fruitful. It also continued to be complicated but interesting.

Even when I got round to exploring the possibility of doing the psychoanalytic training it was by no means straightforward. My first application was turned down without interview, but I was allowed to meet one of the admissions committee to consider what my options might be. I met with Adam Limentani who explained that, even though I had started in a promising way with my 2 : 1 in Anthropology Part I, my final degree in Theology had not been good. I had a poor degree in an irrelevant subject. He added: 'You have three possible courses open to you. You can qualify in something like Psychology. You can aim to get a better degree. Or you can go off and become an exceptional person. Then you can reapply.' Fortunately, the requirements for admission changed a few years later and I didn't have to do any of those things.

After my training I attended the 1979 IPA[1] Conference in New York, where I was introduced to the analyst and publisher Jason Aronson. For reasons I didn't understand, as he had never met me before, he invited me to submit a book for publication. I had no

1 International Psychoanalytic Association.

intention of writing a book, nor did I have any subject I wished to write on and therefore no title, but the idea of eventually writing a book was sown in that brief encounter.

There the matter rested for several years until one night I found myself not getting to sleep. My mind was over-active, thinking about nothing in particular. Then, out of the blue a phrase came to my mind: 'Learning from the patient'. I was suddenly wide awake, my mind racing around this idea, finding that all of my past 20 years had been about exactly this, without having previously put it into words. Here, I realized, was a title that was not going to let me go.

My book title

When I was working on that first book a colleague commented scornfully on the title, saying, '*My* patients learn from *me*.' When it was eventually published I looked forward to getting feedback from my British colleagues. For a long time none came except from one who asked me whether it was true I had written a book *On Learning from the Patient*? I proudly replied that I had, to which he said: 'You must be mad.'

My chosen title also gave some problems in translation. The translator for the French edition took about three months before he was satisfied that he had adequately translated this. He explained that in France (apparently) no one learns from anyone. He said: 'Here you either teach or you are taught.' In the end he settled for *A l'écoute du patient*,[2] which imaginatively conveys the sense of my title.

In the Netherlands there seems to have been a similar problem. Unfortunately, I gather that they chose the Dutch equivalent of 'Being taught by the patient', which the publishers told me might have contributed to the initial lack of interest in the Dutch edition. I don't suppose that many people relish the idea of being taught by their patients, whereas learning from them, as a mother learns from her baby how to become a mother, is something very different.

I am told that there have been other translation difficulties, one of which I find particularly amusing. It has been drawn to my attention that in Hebrew there are three quite different words for

2 Published by Presses Universitaires de France.

the word analyst. That chosen for the Hebrew edition of my first book is apparently the word for 'financial analyst', the translation having been given to someone outside the field of psychoanalysis. I assume that it now reads as if all transactions referred to in that edition appear to be between the patient and his accountant! This mistake reminds me of an early version of the Bible which came to be known as 'the naughty Bible'. Someone had omitted 'not' from one of the Ten Commandments, leaving it to read: 'Thou *shalt* commit adultery.' Not quite what was intended.

I did eventually begin to get some comments from fellow training analysts, several of them asking me: 'What is this book that my patients are saying I should read?' So, my book gradually came to be noticed in my own society as well as elsewhere.

Reviewing some themes

In the process of writing this present book, I have been constantly reminded that most of analysis is concerned with the phenomenon of the patient's past being found to be dynamically alive in the present. For all of us, our present is at least informed by our past. For many of us, patients and analysts, our present can be dominated by our past. So, in this book I have been following the interweaving of past and present, in my own life just as much as that of my patients.

What have I learned in this time? Certainly my view of myself has greatly changed since I began the personal journey I have been describing. From being an adolescent who wavered between a faltering inner directedness, which often showed up in being difficult and rebellious, and at the same time being caught in a contrary search for external direction, I have developed a passion for clinical work in analysis and psychotherapy, discovering what makes other people tick. I now enjoy not having to be an expert who 'knows', but being someone who has specialized in learning how to find what makes most sense in clinical work with each patient.

All kinds of early experiences have helped to shape me in my clinical work, some of which I have sketched in this book. From thinking that I knew what patients needed, for instance, a better experience than they have had before, I have come to be increasingly convinced of the importance of learning to follow patients, and so to recognize and respect their unconscious prompts and cues, whereby they indicate what they need and the ways in which we may be failing them in their search for that.

I have also been asking myself what it is in analysis and therapy that brings about change in patients. I have become increasingly convinced that it is by no means just from the content of interpretations. As well as needing the interpretive work that they cannot do alone, patients also benefit from the close attention being paid to them over time. This may in itself be unique in the patient's experience.

I have also wondered about how a patient benefits from the long and complicated interpretations that we hear or read about in the work of some analysts. Such interpretations can be works of art in themselves, bringing together, in a way that can be amazing in its craftsmanship, the diverse details of a whole session. All manner of detail may be brought into the service of such an interpretation, and the skill of crafting an all-embracing interpretation can readily be admired, even envied. But I am not sure that every patient can appreciate such complex structures.

It was after a presentation at a scientific meeting of my society, many years ago, that I was pondering upon this question of benefit from such interpretations. I had been hearing an example of this, which had been the keystone of a session presented. I had noted 14 elements in one interpretation. How had that benefited the patient? I also wondered, what if the patient had replied to this by agreeing? What might the patient have been agreeing with?

Driving home after that meeting, and still thinking about the artistry of that interpretation, I found my mind wandering into free association. Where my mind went was perhaps not just a change of subject, as I first thought. Maybe it was an unconscious comment on the question I had been asking myself about that long interpretation.

Some years before, I had hired (as I thought) a carpenter, to make a toy-cupboard for our children's bedroom. We had wanted this to be simple and plain; I would then paint it. But when we received the finished article, I came to realize that I had not hired a carpenter; I had hired a cabinet-maker. So, until this day we have not been able to paint the cupboard. It would have seemed like doing violence to it. Instead, we have varnished it so that the craftsmanship could still be seen; every edge lined with hardwood, every corner mitred. We ended up with something quite other than we had wanted, but it has remained an object to admire.

With this image in mind, I returned to the tapestry of that long interpretation. Whatever else might be conveyed to the patient by the content, when an analyst gives such clear evidence of having attended to the detail of a session, with that degree of concentration, any patient is likely to feel special. When else might a patient have the experience of being followed so closely, with the evidence of such care and attention? Some of the benefit from that kind of interpreting might well be from the specialness it conveys to the patient as much as from its content.

The late Dr Clifford Scott told us at a conference in London commemorating the life of Melanie Klein that she once made such a long interpretation she had written it down and wanted to read it to him. 'It took three sessions to read,' he told us, but he didn't say whether he had agreed with it or not.

In following my patients, in whatever way belongs to their own individuality, I have often discovered the central importance of allowing patients to use me as if I were really the bad object(s) of their past. When this has been triggered by some failure by me, patients have felt justified in their anger, seeing me as just like a key figure from their past. At such times I have come to see the importance of allowing patients to be as angry as they feel, not treating this as if it were transference until the patient is able to see that there may be more in the situation than just the anger with me. The transference frequently develops around such triggers, but I believe we still have to accept that it is not only transference.

A major part of my clinical work has been with traumatised patients, with whom I have repeatedly come to find a value in seeing trauma as 'that which cannot be managed alone', with echoes of my own experience of being alone in a state of trauma.

However little I may at first be able to offer a traumatised patient, however impotent I may feel in the face of their trauma, I have learned that I can at least offer the one thing that has perhaps not been available before. I can continue to be 'there' for the patient and the patient's most difficult feelings, which have often been avoided by others in the past. Over time this has helped to make sense of the patient's need to bring to me precisely those feelings that others have not been able to bear, or have not been there for.

Throughout my clinical journey I have looked for ways to make sense of what I find myself trying to do with patients. I have never been content with any theory until it has begun to make sense with a patient. I have also not been prepared to reuse meaning found in my work with other patients. As far as possible, I have looked for meaning afresh with each patient.

I have also not been content merely to follow rules of technique. These too I have preferred to work out afresh with each patient, trying to find what seems best in how to work with him or her. This has meant closely monitoring each clinical sequence for what I may have least wanted to recognize in it, because it may indicate ways in which I have been getting it wrong, or failing a patient in how I have handled the clinical situation.

After years of resisting any use of *projective identification* in my clinical work, because I was seriously sceptical of its reality or usefulness, I came eventually to see it as clinically indispensable – as a way of understanding this particular form of communication. Since then I have also come to value the more general notion of *communication by impact*,[3] trying to get a sense of what a patient may be communicating through difficult behaviour. This often opens up different ways of thinking about such things as missed sessions or lateness, and other behaviour that is often regarded simply as acting out.

Some of my clinical work that seems to have been most productive has been with traumatized patients, with whom I have often had to be there for what they could not yet manage in themselves. To that end I have also aimed to become as open as possible in myself to what a patient may be prompting me to sense in them.

Throughout my work I have been concerned to be learning from my patients, following their unconscious cues, trying to sense how they may be experiencing me in how I am being with them, as well as in terms of any transference that may also be developing. I have

3 Casement (1985: 72–73, 1991: 64–65).

enjoyed rediscovering theory from my clinical work. I have enjoyed finding connections, along with the patient, rather than simply making connections that can so easily become self-proving. And I have tried to keep all of my clinical work under the constant scrutiny of my internal supervision, trying to see where the process leads rather than trying to lead the process along more familiar lines.

From this open-minded testing of my clinical work I have been led to work with patients in ways that have felt genuine, arrived at clinically rather than by prescription. I now find myself faced with the interesting task of looking around me to see those ways in which my clinical work has developed similarities to the work of others, as in the work of interpersonal and relational analysts in the United States. I have deliberately not been reading these other theorists, while continuing my clinical work, as I have not wanted to be tempted to impose new dogma in the place of old. Maybe, now that I am retired, I will be reading more of those related fields, to enjoy the ways in which others have come to work similarly, and wondering also about the differences.

Bibliography

Alexander, F. (1954) 'Some quantitative aspects of psychoanalytic technique', *Journal of the American Psychoanalytic Association* 2: 685–701.

Alexander, F., French, T. M. *et al.* (1946) *Psychoanalytic Therapy: Principles and Application*, New York: Ronald Press.

Alvarez, A. (1973) *Beckett*, London: Collins/Fontana.

Bair, D. (1978) *Samuel Beckett: A Biography*, London: Jonathan Cape.

Beckett, S. (1934) *More Pricks than Kicks*, London: Pan.

Beckett, S. (1969) *Murphy*, London: Calder Publications.

Beckett, S. (1970) *First Love*, Harmondsworth: Penguin.

Beckett, S. (1976) *Watt*, London: Calder Publications.

Beckett, S. (1976) *Molloy; Malone Dies; The Unnamable*, London: Calder Publications.

Beckett, S. (1977) *Four Novellas*, London: Calder Publications.

Bion, W. R (1962) 'A theory of thinking', in W. R. Bion *Second Thoughts*, New York: Jason Aronson.

Bion, W. R. (1967a) 'Notes on memory and desire', *Psychoanalytic Forum* 2: 271–280.

Bion, W. R. (1967b) *Second Thoughts*, New York: Jason Aronson.

Casement, P. J. (1969) 'The setting of limits: a belief in growth', *Case Conference*, 16, 7: 267–271. Republished (1992) in *The Journal of Social Work Practice* 6, 1: 25–30.

Casement, P. J. (1982a) 'Samuel Beckett's relationship to his mother tongue', *International Review of Psycho-Analysis* 9: 35–44. Republished in P, Rudnytsky (ed.) (1993) *Transitional Objects and Potential Spaces: Literary Uses of D. W. Winnicott*, New York: Columbia University Press.

Casement, P. J. (1985) *On Learning from the Patient*, London: Tavistock.

Casement, P. J. (1990) *Further Learning – The Patient: The Analytic Space and Process*, London: Routledge.

Casement, P. J. (1991) *Learning from the Patient*, New York: Guilford Press.[1]

Casement, P. J. (2000) 'Mourning and failure to mourn', *Fort Da* 6, 2: 20–32.

Casement, P. J. (2001) 'Commentary on Jay Greenberg's paper "The analyst's participation: a new look"', *Journal of the American Psychoanalytic Association* 49, 2: 381–386.

Casement, P. J. (2002a) 'Learning from life', *Psychoanalytic Inquiry* 22, 4: 519–533.

Casement, P. J. (2002b) 'Between patients', in J. Raphael-Leff (ed.) *Between Sessions & Behind/Beyond the Couch*, London: Karnac.

Casement, P. J. (2002c) 'Foreword', in B. Kahr (ed.) *The Legacy of Winnicott: Essays on Infant and Child Mental Health*, London: Karnac.

Casement, P. J. (2002d) *Learning from our Mistakes: Beyond Dogma in Psychoanalysis and Psychotherapy*, London: Brunner-Routledge/New York: Guilford Press.

Casement, P. J. (2005) 'Using analytic space: a challenge to contemporary psychoanalysis', *Clinical Social Work Journal* 33, 4: 383–394.

Casement, P. J. and Lewis, E. (1986) 'The inhibition of mourning in pregnancy', *Psychoanalytic Psychotherapy* 2, 1: 45–52.

Charles-Edwards, A. (1983) *The Nursing Care of the Dying Patient*, Beaconsfield: Beaconsfield Publications.

Dostoyevsky, F. (1958) *The Brothers Karamazov*, trans. D. Magarshack, Harmondsworth: Penguin.

Freud, S. (1917) 'Mourning and melancholia', *Standard Edition* 14.

Frost, R. (2001) *The Poetry of Robert Frost*. E. C. Lathem (ed.), New York: Vintage.

Gibran, K. (1965) *The Prophet*, London: Heinemann.

Giovacchini, P. L. (ed.) (1975) *Tactics and Techniques in Psychoanalytic Therapy, Vol. II*, New York: Jason Aronson.

Greenberg, J. (2001) 'The analyst's participation: a new look', *Journal of the American Psychoanalytic Association* 49, 2: 359–381.

Isaacs, S. (1948) 'The nature and function of phantasy', *International Journal of Psycho-Analysis* 29: 73–97.

Klein, M. (1946) 'Notes on some schizoid mechanisms', in J. Riviere (ed.) (1952) *Developments in Psycho-Analysis*, London: Hogarth Press.

Langs, R. J. (1978) *The Listening Process*, New York: Jason Aronson.

Matte Blanco, I. (1975) *The Unconscious as Infinite Sets*, London: Duckworth.

Racker, H. (1957) 'The meanings and uses of countertransference', *Psy-*

---

1 This American edition is a combined volume that contains both *On Learning from the Patient* (1985) and *Further Learning from the Patient* (1990).

choanalytic. Quarterly 26: 303–357. Reprinted in H. Racker (1968) *Transference and Counter-Transference*, London: Hogarth Press.

Rosenfeld, H. (1987) *Impasse and Interpretation*, London: Tavistock.

Rudnytsky, P. (ed.) (1993) *Transitional Objects and Potential Spaces: Literary Uses of D. W. Winnicott*, New York: Columbia University Press.

Sandler, J. (1976) 'Countertransference and role-responsiveness', *International Journal of Psycho-Analysis* 3: 43–47.

Searles, H. (1965) *Collected Papers on Schizophrenia and Related Subjects*, London: Hogarth Press.

Searles, H. (1975) 'The patient as therapist to his analyst', in P. L. Giovacchini (ed.) *Tactics and Techniques in Psychoanalytic Therapy, Vol. II*, New York: Jason Aronson.

Willoughby, R. (2004) *Masud Khan: The Myth and the Reality*, London: Free Association Books.

Winnicott, D. W. (1947) 'Hate in the countertransference', in D. W. Winnicott (1958) *Collected Papers: Through Pediatrics to Psycho-Analysis*, London: Tavistock.

Winnicott, D. W. (1956) 'The antisocial tendency', in D. W. Winnicott (1958) *Collected Papers: Through Pediatrics to Psycho-Analysis*, London: Tavistock.

Winnicott, D. W. (1958) *Collected Papers: Through Pediatrics to Psycho-Analysis*, London: Tavistock.

Winnicott, D. W. (1963) 'The development of the capacity for concern', in D. W. Winnicott (1965) *The Maturational Processes and the Facilitating Environment*, London: Hogarth Press.

Winnicott, D. W. (1967) 'Delinquency as a sign of hope', in C. Winnicott, R. Shepherd and M. Davies (eds) (1986) *Home is Where We Start From: Essays by a Psychoanalyst*, New York: Norton.

Winnicott, D. W. (1971) *Playing and Reality*, London: Tavistock.

Winnicott, D. W. (1974) 'Fear of breakdown', *International Review of Psycho-Analysis* 1: 103–107.

Index

Absence of patient 63–4
addiction 173, 175
adoption 177–8
affective openness 153
aggression 56–8, 75–6, 77–8, 83–4
agnosticism 191–2
Alexander, F. 11, 18, 19
Alvarez, Al 117
ambivalence 87–8, 190; maternal 62; and mourning 127; towards mothers 104–5, 111
analogy 98
analytic curiosity 69–70
analytic space 3; as belonging to the patient 164; monitoring 155; 'realness' of patient 159; preservation 154–5
anger 107; expression in therapy 15–17, 92–3, 97–8, 173–4, 200
antisocial tendency 8–9, 89
anxiety 135, 137, 139–41, 143–4
Aronson, Jason 196–7
art therapy 42–3
atheism 192
attachment: disrupted 14, 28–9; pathological 104–5
attentiveness, of the therapist 199, 200; divided 142
authority 186

badness 190
Bair, Deirdre 101
Beckett, Frank 103–4
Beckett, Samuel 2, 46, 100–19; adoption of the French language 100–2, 106–7, 110–17; break with his mother 106–7, 115, 117; childhood 103; circularity 111–12, 117; creativity 107–9, 115–16, 117; and his mother's death

112; *Malone Dies* 109, 116; *Molloy* 102, 104, 105, 106–7, 109, 111–12, 113, 114–15, 117–18; *More Pricks than Kicks* 109–10; *Murphy* 105, 110; need for psychological space 107–9; night terrors 104; preoccupation with death 108–9; psychoanalysis 104; psychosomatic ailments 103, 114, 115; relationship with his mother 101, 102–7, 108–9, 111–12, 115, 117; *The End* 113; 'The Expelled' 102, 110; *The Unnameable* 103, 107–8, 111, 112, 113; translation of his French writings into English 112–17; war experience 110–11; *Watt* 105, 106, 109, 110, 111, 116–17; word play 114–15, 116
'behaviour as communication' 50–1, 55–6, 201
bereavement counselling 120
'better parent', wish to be 72, 85
Bible 198
bingeing 173, 175
Bion, W. R. 89, 91, 104, 154, 155
Blanco, Matte 146
Blau, Herbert 102
body types 41
Bowles, Patrick 113
brainwashing 189, 195
breakdown 1, 36–42, 45, 125–6; as breakthrough 34
breast, good/bad 190
breast cancer 179
British Broadcasting Corporation (BBC) 101
British Psychoanalytic Society 118
Buddhism 193
Bulletin of the British Psychoanalytic Society 118

cancer 179–80
caring: insecure 81–5; secure 81, 85
Casement, Patrick:
  breakdown 36–42
    admitted to hospital 36–41, 45;
      insomnia 36; psychotherapy
      41–2; suicidal 39, 42
    career choice 7, 14–16
    childhood 8–11, 13–14, 22–30
      absent father 24, 25; childcare/
        governess 25–6; childhood
        colitis 23–4; 'crimes' 8–9;
        disrupted attachment 14, 28–9;
        perceived as 'difficult' child 23,
        25–6, 27; saying 'sorry' 9–10
    children 17–18, 168, 192; on coming
      to terms with his aggression 56–7;
      depression 14;
    education
      at boarding school 11, 26–9, 167;
        exams 27–8; Home Office
        diploma in social studies at
        Barnet House, Oxford 36, 38, 39,
        40, 42, 167–8; studies
        anthropology and theology at
        Trinity College, Cambridge
        33–5, 183–4, 196
    on the expression of anger 15–17;
      factory work in Sheffield 35–6;
      family tradition 22–33; flirtation
      with evangelical Christianity
      29–30, 188–9; gender identity 23,
      24, 25;
  hypersensitivity to pregnancy 23–4,
    172–3; illness, departure and death of
    his girl friend 36, 181; marriage 43;
    national service in the Royal Navy
    31–3; On Learning from the Patient
    197–8; personal analysis 13–17, 23–4,
    41–2, 44; psychoanalytic training 44,
    164, 196; and public speaking 45; and
    the 'rebel within' 45; Royal Naval
    family 22, 27, 31, 33; on self-exposure/
    disclosure 1–2, 7–8; on strange
    coincidences 168–70; thinking about
    becoming a priest 30, 34, 35–6; on the
    unconscious 12
  work as probation officer 2, 9, 43
    on applying theory 46–9, 51–6;
      learning to say 'no' 73–9; 'on
      going the extra mile' 73– 5;
      student experiences 46–9;
      insomnia 78–9; violent
      behaviour 55–6, 75–6

  work as social worker (family
    caseworker) 2, 43–4
    on applying theory 49–50, 58–62,
      66–9, 70–1; on changing
      perspective 151–2; on
    collusion 64–5; on demanding
      patients 58–61; family therapy
      work 66–9; learning to set limits/
      saying 'no' 79–80, 82–4; marital
      therapy 70–1, 79–80, 128–9;
      supervision 61–2 64–5; on
      writing 196–8
Casement, Roddie (Patrick's father) 169
Casement, Sir Roger 47
catatonic schizophrenia 151–2
certainty 3, 183–95; appeal of 188–9;
  dynamics of 189–91; flirtation with
  29-30; and non-certainty 183-195
change, therapeutic 199
'child within' 139
child work 81–2
childcare 13–14, 25–6
childhood, defence systems of 190
childhood experience 163; delayed
  processing of trauma 50
children: and containment 82, 87–93,
  96–8, 99; death of 49–50, 122–5,
  129–31; fear of being too much for the
  parent 87, 89, 91–2, 95–9, 175; and
  hate 87–8, 92–3; and love 87–8;
  'replacement' 123
Christianity: evangelical 29–30, 188–9;
  institutionalized 184–8, 193, 194
circularity 111–12, 117
clinical antennae 3, 151–64
clinical fluency 133, 145
coincidence, strange 168–72, 181
collusion 64–5, 180
Coltart, Dr Nina 180
communication: behaviour as 50–1,
  55–6, 201; by impact 201
communion 194
compliance 45; of the false self 87;
  superficial 27, 92, 97
concern, capacity for 9–10
confidentiality 3–4
conflict 190
containment 82, 87–88; Bion on 91;
  clinical example 91–9; definition 87;
  failure 87, 89–90, 91; and hate 87–9,
  92–3; Winnicott on 89–91
control: resistance to 26; social 187
corrective emotional experience 2,
  11–12, 16–17, 72–3

countertransference 19, 90–1, 95, 147; indirect 134
creative play 108–9, 116
creativity 107–9, 115–16, 117
criminality 90
crisis, therapy in 143–4, 147–9, 195
crying 98

Dante 110
death 120–31; attempts at replacements and substitutes 122–3; of children 49–50, 122–5, 129–31; and identity 121–2; parental 50, 58, 91, 120–2, 125–6, 131; of partner 122, 131, 170–2; preoccupation with 108–9; sibling 121, 122, 123
death wish 180
debt 83–4
decision-making, snap 136–7
defence systems: childhood 190; religion as 190; self sufficiency as 27
demanding patients 58–61
denial 138, 190
dependency 95, 175; 'spread' 58–9
depression 62, 128
destructiveness 96; children's 90, 96; creative aspects of 90
Devil 190
diabetes 58
difference, hatred of 86
discontinuity 12–14
dogma, looking beyond 163–4
Dostoyevsky, Fyodor 183–8, 193
drama 59–60
dread 170–2; nameless 91
dream work 100, 117, 141–2, 144–5, 181; diagnostic dreams 178–9; latent content 100; manifest content 100, 142

early patients (over-punctuality) 135–7, 147–8
ectomorphs 41
emotional experience, corrective 2, 11–12, 16–17, 72–3
emotional space 101
endomorphs 41

'falling to pieces', feelings of 142, 149
family therapy 66–9
Family Welfare Association (FWA), London 43–4, 54, 61, 69, 82–4, 128, 151, 181
fathers: absent 24, 25, 66–9, 103; alcoholic 91; death of 91; hostile 67–9

fear, superstitious 187
free floating responsiveness 19
freedom 195; unbearable nature of 185–6, 187
Freud, Anna 138–9, 141–2, 144
Freud, Sigmund 127, 191, 192
Frost, Robert 22
fundamentalism 188–9

gender identity 175–6
gestalt therapy 15
Gibran, Kahlil 154
God 188, 189, 190, 193; human knowledge of 194; love of 183; vengeful 183, 187
good life 188
'good' person, therapist as 2, 15, 16, 60–1, 72–3
goodness 190
Gordon, General 152
Greenberg, Jay 156
guilt 8–9, 127–9
Gurkhas 55–7

hate 86–88; and containment 87–9, 92–3; in the countertransference 90–1; definition 86
hell 187; as self-made 183, 185
Herbert, George 31
HMS Aisne (ship) 32
HMS Glasgow (battle cruiser) 31
holding 37; physical 82; self-holding 138, 141, 142–3
hope: delinquency as sign of 51; unconscious 8–9, 51, 87, 89, 107, 157
hospitalization, frequent 134–5, 146
hostility, engaging with 75–6

idealization 3, 184–90
identification: projective 49–50, 174, 201; trial 3, 133, 152, 181
identity 121–2
illness: life-threatening 178–9; psychosomatic 128–9
impotence, of the therapist 79
indecision 190
infantilization 61–2
infertility 121, 175–6
insanity 110
insight 20
institutions 90
internal supervision 132–50, 202; abstracting themes from detail 132–3, 142; and clinical fluency 133, 145;

criticism by mirroring 147–8, 149;
indirect countertransference 134;
listening with both hands 133; needing
two heads in 133; practising with
clinical material 133, 134–50, 161–3;
session example 134–50; trial
identification with the patient 133,
161; unconscious criticism by the
patient 133–4; unconscious
supervision 133
interpretation 143–5, 161–3;
complicated 199–200; direction
161–2; ruining 139, 144–5; tentative
143
introversion 27
IPA Conference, New York, 1979 196–7

Janvier, L. 111, 113
jealousy 94–5
Jesus 184–8
juvenile delinquency 50–6, 89–90; as
sign of hope 51

key points, missing 61–2
Khan, Masud 2, 118–19
Khartoum 152
Klein, Melanie 200
Klein, Dr Josephine xi
Kleinian theory 49
knives 55–8; in the consulting room
57–8

La Nouvelle Revue 118–19
Langs, R. J. 161
language 100, 101; Samuel Beckett and
100–2, 106–7, 110–17
lateness, patient 63–4
latent content 100
learning from patients 21
leaving home 52–3
life-threatening illness 178–9
Limentani, Adam 196
limits, setting 60–1, 73, 79–85
listening, with both hands 133
London Institute of Psychoanalysis 44
London Psychoanalytic Society 191
loneliness 139
loss 121
love 87–8; God's 183

magical thinking 180
manifest content 100, 142
marital therapy 64–5, 70–1, 79–80,
128–9; taking sides in 65

masses, control of 187
maternal ambivalence 62
Matthew, St 72
maturity, false 90
McGelligott, Mr 48
McGreevy, Thomas 104
medication: allergies to 38–9; overuse of
38–9, 45
memory, active/passive 154
Menzies, Isobel 44
metaphor 26
mind, state of, openness to the patient's
153
miracles 186
mirroring, criticism by 147–8, 149
miscarriage 23–4, 121, 123, 173
missing sessions 176–9
mothers 17–18; ambivalence felt by 62;
ambivalence towards 104–5, 111;
being alone in the presence of the
108–9; and child deaths 49–50; and
containment 88, 91; death of 50, 58,
125–6; dominating/interfering 154–5;
'good' 190; insecure 81–5; nursing
triad 18; overprotective 61–2;
rejecting 81–2, 91–2, 180; Samuel
Beckett on 101, 102–7, 108–9,
111–12, 115, 117; unavailable 68–9
Mountbatten, Lord Louis 31, 32
mourning 3, 120–31; and ambivalence
127; attempts at replacements and
substitutes 122–3; and bereavement
121–2; failure of/pathological 121,
125–7, 129–31; as letting go 123, 125,
131; listening to the bereaved 123–5;
melancholic 127; and unconscious
guilt 127–9
murderous feelings 57–8
mystery 168, 170, 186, 193, 194

negation 137–8
night terrors 104
'no': failure to say 94–6, 98–9; learning
to say 72–85, 88
non-certainty 3, 183–95; unbearable
nature of 185
nurses 122
nursing triad 18

object: bad 19, 157–8, 200; child's need
to destroy 90, 96; external 90; internal
90, 96, 153; patient's need to destroy
157–8; persecutory 110; use of the
157–8

object relations 35, 153–4
occupational therapy 40–1
Old Testament 187
open-mindedness 34, 45, 153, 195, 202
orgasm 131
other: God as 193; hatred of 86; as
    internal object 90; otherness of 34,
    42–4, 153–4
ovarian cancer 179–80
over-punctuality 135–7, 147–8
overdose 62, 63–4, 170
overlooked material 61–2, 159

pain, gynaecological 129–31; psychic
    49–50, 124–5, 130–1, 138
pain of contrast 19-20
paralysis 173–4
parents: confrontations with their
    children 90; and containment 87–9;
    controlling 51–5; death 50, 58, 91,
    120–2, 125–6, 131; idealized 190;
    insecure 81–5; overprotective 53–4,
    61–2; rivalry 17–18; setting limits 88;
    wishing to please 175–6; see also
    'better parent'; fathers; mothers
partner, death of 122, 131, 170–2
past experience: relevance of 198;
    traumatic 20; see also childhood
    experience
Pentonville Prison 47
persecution, internal 110
perspectives, multiple 151–3
phantasies: of being overwhelming 98,
    99; destructive 90, 98, 99; murderous
    57–8
potential space 101
practising with clinical material 161-3
pre-delinquency 50–1, 89
pregnancy, hypersensitivity to 23–4,
    172–3
present, the, and the past 198
Prince, Stewart 42, 44
probation officers see Casement, Patrick,
    work as probation officer
projection 190, 191
projective identification 49–50, 174, 201
psychoanalysis 200–2; applying
    exceptional measures under pressure
    156–7; and certainty 190–1, 193; and
    clinical antennae 151–64; enabling
    realness in the patient 158–60;
    liberating process of 195; monitoring
    the effects of the contributions of
    therapists 160–1; using multiple

perspectives 151–3; and non-certainty
    195; use of an object 157–8; object
    relations in practice 153–4; and
    openness to the patient's state of mind
    153; practising with clinical material
    161–3; preserving the analytic space
    154–5; and primitive defence
    mechanisms 190–1; and religion
    190–1, 192, 193; self-proving nature
    of 164
psychological profiles 48
psychological space 107–9
psychosis 125–6
psychosomatic illnesses 128–9
punctuality: lateness 63–4; over-
    punctuality 135–7, 147–8

Racker, H. 134
realness, enabling in the patient 158–60
regression 177
religion 3, 184–95; fundamentalism
    188–9; man-made elements 188, 194;
    organized 184–8, 193, 194; as
    primitive defence 190; and social
    control 187; splitting of faiths 188,
    193; and superstition 187, 191–2; and
    ultimate truth 188–9; see also
    Christianity
responsibility 11
Ricks, Professor Christopher 100–1
rightness 189
Rome 32
Royal Naval Voluntary Reserve
    (RNVR) 31
Royal Navy 22, 27, 31–3

sadism 61
Sandler, J. 19
sarcasm 26
schizophrenia, catatonic 151–2
Schneider, Pierre 113
scoliosis 58
Scott, Clifford 200
Seaver, Richard 113
self: authentic/true 2, 10, 158–60;
    discovery through creativity 108; false
    2, 15, 87, 93, 158–60
self sufficiency, defensive 27
self-attacking behaviour 14, 15
self-destruction 127, 129
self-esteem, by association 73–5
self-exposure/disclosure 1–2, 7–8
self-holding 138, 141, 142–3
self-interest 72

sex, painful 129–31
shock, state of 38
siblings, death of 121, 122, 123
similarity, hatred of 86
social control 187
social withdrawal 151–2
social workers *see* Casement, Patrick,
    work as social worker (family
    caseworker)
somatization 138
space: emotional 101; potential 101;
    psychological 107–9; *see also* analytic
    space
Spanish Inquisition 184–7
splitting 149, 190
spouse, death of 122, 131, 170–2
stealing 51–4
Stewart, Dr Harold, xi
Stockwood, Mervyn 34–5, 183–4
suicide: attempted 60, 63–4, 170, 171;
    completed 62; thoughts 179–80
sun dancing 98
superstition 187, 191–2
supervision: unconscious 133, 161; *see
    also* internal supervision
supervisory triad 18

tantrums 88
Tavistock Clinic 104
telepathy 181–2
Ten Commandments 198
terminating therapy 61
theoretical orientation 7
theory 46–71; application straight from
    training 46–9; cautions regarding the
    application of 46–50, 61–2, 71
therapeutic change 199
therapists: anonymity 1; attentiveness
    199, 200; career choice 7; coping with
    the expression of anger 15–16; coping
    with unbearable experience 156–7;
    defensiveness 139; failure 147–8; as
    'good' person 2, 15, 16, 60–1, 72–3;
    impotence of 79; insight 20; intrusive
    elements 155, 164; knocking patients
    into false shapes 160; learning from
    patients 21; missing key points 61–2;
    monitoring the effects of their
    contributions 160–1; and non-
    certainty 195; object relations 153–4;
    patient testing 99; personal analysis
    13–17, 23–4, 41–2, 44, 153; pregnant
    57–8; saying 'no' 2; self-exposure 1–2,

7–8; self-interest 72; terminating
    therapy 61; theoretical orientation 7;
    unconscious responsiveness 18–21;
    being used as object 157–8
Thompson, Dr Geoffrey 104
totalitarianism 187
transcendence 193
transference 163, 200, 201; negative 2,
    15, 157; and self-disclosure of the
    therapist 7–8
traumatic experience 20, 38, 200–1;
    delayed processing of childhood 50;
    re-experiencing through therapy 158;
    unconscious preparation for repeat
    occurrences 146; when mental health
    services add to 37
trial identification, with the patient in the
    session 3, 133, 152, 181
truth, ultimate 188–9
tyrants 90

unbearable experience 49–50, 124–5,
    130–1; exceptional measures for
    dealing with 156–7; freedom as
    185–6, 187; non-certainty as 185;
    supporting patients through 200–1
uncertainty 195
unconscious 12–14; guilt 127–9; hope
    8–9, 51, 87, 89, 107, 157; patient cues
    198–9
unconscious responsiveness 18–21
understanding 167–8; limits to 69–71,
    170
unsafe, feeling in therapy 142–4
use of an object, the 157–8

violent behaviour, communication
    through 55–6
Virgin Mary 190
vomiting 173, 175

Walls, Canon Roland 36
war 189
Williams, Revd Harry 34, 39, 45
Williams, Professor Paul x
Winnicott, D. W. 8, 9–10, 18, 50–1, 87,
    89–91, 96, 101, 108, 116–17, 142,
    157–8
words, therapist's choice of 145
worship 185–6; sear for universal 185,
    186, 193

York, Clifford 44